# FOR MY EYES ONLY

JOHN GLEN

WITH MARCUS HEARN

BRASSEY'S · INC · WASHINGTON · D.C.

**To my children, Andrew, Matthew and Samantha**

Text © John Glen 2001

All rights reserved. No part of this book may be reproduced, stored in a retrieval system or transmitted in any form or by any means, electronic, mechanical, photocopying, recording or otherwise, without the prior permission in writing of the copyright owners.

The James Bond films are made by Eon Productions Ltd, and the views expressed by the authors and contributors are not necessarily shared by the producers.

007 gun symbol logo TM Danjaq LLC and © 1962 Danjaq, LLC and United Artists Corporation. All rights reserved.

James Bond film images reproduced in this book are © 1962-1999 Danjaq, LLC and United Artists Corporation. All rights reserved.

First published in the USA in 2001 by

Brassey's, Inc.
22841 Quicksilver Drive
Dulles, Virginia 20166

Printed in spain by Bookprint, S.L. Barcelona

ISBN 1-57488-369-0

# Contents

# Acknowledgements

My sincere thanks to Anne Bennett, Gill Burrows, The Joel Finler Collection, Alan Hume, Roger Moore, Adam Newell, Andrew Pixley, Adrian Rigelsford, Tony Rudlin, Meg Simmonds, Michael G Wilson and the staff at San Remo's.

Special thanks to Marcus Hearn, who put up with me droning on for hours, and my wife, Janine, who just puts up with me.

# 007™

# FOREWORD

…or should I say a Forewarning, because John Glen is the man I like to call 'the actor-killer'.

In 1975, I was appearing in the film *Shout at the Devil* and John was the second-unit director. The film was set just before the First World War and the Germans were moving giant plates of steel across Africa to repair one of their battleships. My co-star Lee Marvin and the director Peter Hunt were at the top of a hill, and I was at the bottom with John and his camera crew. The idea was that Lee would fire at the poor wretches pulling the enormous wheels that were transporting these plates. They would throw themselves to the ground to dodge the bullets and the enormous wheels would roll down the valley to where John and I were supposed to be. I say supposed, because when these wheels started hurtling downhill I, the young hero, was standing in front of the camera like a lemon while John and his crew were halfway up the hill on the other side of the valley. Thank you, John.

My memory often plays havoc with me – too many Bonds and too many bangs (of the noisy variety of course). One thing I do remember of my time as James Bond is that John had more than one way of killing an actor. John was the editor of *The Spy Who Loved Me* and *Moonraker*, and editors see more of an actor's bad habits than anyone else. The editor rolls film backwards and forwards, day in, day out. In the end, he assembles all of the good takes and hopefully discards the bad ones. On the Bond films, however, the bad ones were never discarded – John would keep them and use them to assemble an end-of-shooting reel. This comprised all the very worst takes, including me scratching my crotch or blinking whenever I fired a gun. All in good fun, and incredibly bad taste, and most definitely for our eyes only.

John directed my final three Bond films, and I certainly had a good time working with him. He is a marvellous technician. My only regret is that he's never given me another job since then.

After this forewarning, I don't suppose he ever will.

October 2000

# 007

## CHAPTER 1

## NOBODY DOES IT BETTER

Mount Asgard is a frozen slab of rock in the middle of Canada's Baffin Island. Baffin is the largest island in the Canadian Arctic and not the sort of place most people would choose for a holiday. In June 1976, however, I elected to spend three weeks on one of Asgard's flat-topped peaks patiently waiting for the right time to push someone off. We were making a James Bond movie called *The Spy Who Loved Me* and after an uncertain period in the history of this particular film series, the producer wanted to open the new film in style. He asked us for something breathtaking – we gave him something more.

Since the second Bond film, *From Russia With Love*, there had been a tradition of beginning each new movie with a short adventure, placing our hero in some outlandish peril. Bond's miraculous escape would seamlessly lead into the elegant title sequence, which would in turn herald the beginning of the film proper. For the pre-titles sequence of *The Spy Who Loved Me*, James Bond is seen returning from a mission in the Austrian Alps when he was intercepted by a squad of Russian hit-men. Bond evades the Russians through some deft skiing, killing their leader in the process. The three remaining Russians relentlessly pursue Bond until there seems to be no escape. With the Russians behind him and a sheer drop ahead, Bond does the unthinkable – he skis over the edge. Time stands still as Bond plunges into the abyss. He seems certain to plummet to his death when he releases his skis and pulls his parachute cord. A Union flag parachute billows open above his head and the memorable theme song 'Nobody Does It Better' begins.

The stunt was the idea of a self-professed 'ski bum' called Rick Sylvester. Rick had written to Eon Productions, makers of the Bond films, suggesting the idea after he had done something similar in a magazine advert for Canada Dry. He showed us a copy of the advert, which appeared to show him skiing off a mountain. When we cross-examined Rick about the stunt, he admitted that trick photography had been used to make it look he was skiing off the mountain – the helicopter they had used couldn't reach the necessary altitude and the weather had been atrocious. Before we could explain that we didn't like using such trick photography on Bond films, Rick told us that he felt the stunt could be filmed for real, and showed us some pretty awful footage of him skiing off El Capitan in the Yosemite National Park. He didn't look terribly dignified. In fact he flew off that mountain like a sack of potatoes. 'This is all very well, Rick,' I said, 'but if we're going to include this in a James Bond film,

Seal-spotting with
two of the local
hunters.

it must be done with some style and grace. We couldn't use something which looked that untidy.' He agreed and said he could perform the stunt to our satisfaction if we could find him a helicopter powerful enough to get him on top of Mount Asgard, provide him with his own hand-picked team of mountaineers, and give him a specially packed parachute. I pondered the potential problems and the undoubted risk, while wondering how the man before me could double for James Bond star Roger Moore. Rick would be saddled with not one but two parachutes – his pack would have to contain a reserve in case of an emergency – and he was a bespectacled chap who stood no more than five foot six inches tall. Appearances can be deceptive: I would soon discover that Rick Sylvester was made of steel.

Rick told us all about Mount Asgard on the Cumberland Peninsula of Baffin Island. The nearest civilisation of any significance was an Eskimo village called Pangnirtung, which was accessible by plane from Frobisher Bay, the most northerly scheduled airfield. James Bond producer Cubby Broccoli put me in charge of a small scouting team and sent me to Asgard to make a feasibility study. I was charged with costing the sequence and shooting some footage that Cubby could then show to the executives from United Artists, the distributor fronting the budget. I set about recruiting a team from some of the most reliable and experienced people I'd worked with before. These included line producer René Dupont and cinematographer Alan

The lodge at
Pangnirtung.

Hume, both of whom joined Rick and me for the journey to Canada.

We landed our tiny Otter plane on a gravel beach and emerged to find the desolate outpost that was Pangnirtung. The local Eskimos had permission to shoot any wildlife they wanted. I saw them perched on rocks, training the telescopic sights of their rifles onto holes in the ice. As soon as a seal reared its head to come up for air, they'd shoot it and quickly dash across the ice to grab its body before it sank into the water. They would skin the unfortunate creatures they managed to catch, throw the meat away and take the skins to the local store, which was operated by the Hudson Bay company. The store would exchange the skins for TV dinners, which the Eskimos kept in a communal deep freeze. This was a government-subsidised community; every year, the Eskimos received new skidoos to help them get around. Looking into the gin-clear water, I could see last year's abandoned models piled high in the depths. There were plenty more where they came from.

The Eskimos lived in huts with steel cables stretched over the roofs to keep them secure in the 150 mph gales. Often they put huge rocks on their roofs as well, just to make sure. A satellite dish received TV pictures and was pointed not at the sky but level with the ground, such was the latitude. As I wandered around this freezing outpost, I was amused to notice that one enterprising soul had a greenhouse.

We were billeted at a lodge that was dominated by a fearsome German cook

The fearless stuntman Rick Sylvester during a helicopter journey to Mount Asgard.

called Fritz. We were served Arctic char for breakfast, lunch and dinner, and as if the monotony of this type of salmon wasn't bad enough, Fritz would appear in his nightshirt and admonish us for making too much noise. Alan stood to attention and received the dressing down manfully, considering he was in the process of washing up Fritz's pots and pans. At that point Alan nicknamed him 'Achtung Spitfire', which stuck for the duration of our stay.

Our helicopter was flown from Montreal by a pilot called Bill Henderson. He had to land on an ice floe in Hudson Bay and hand-pump some extra fuel into the tank in order to complete the final leg of the journey to Pangnirtung. He was a day late and when he arrived, he landed his helicopter onto some oil drums so we could replace the floats with skids. The local engineer lent us a hand – he was a man from Putney, who during the winter would fashion 'genuine' Eskimo art from soapstone. We had to wait another few days before the weather on Mount Asgard was good enough for us to make the journey.

Mount Asgard is 6598 feet above sea level and the flat-topped peak we were aiming to land on was no bigger than a football pitch. As we approached the peak, the lights on Bill's control panel started flashing furiously and alarms began ringing. 'What the hell have you got back there?' he yelled, indicating the hold of the helicopter. We had brought our camera equipment, which was extremely heavy. 'You've overloaded us!'. There is the danger in these situations that the main rotor blades can flex and sever the tail. We made an awkward landing, the helicopter whipping up the light dusting of snow around us. As soon as I got out, I could see that the peak wasn't very level. There was a sharp incline on the north face and the ice was compacted where it opposed the prevailing wind. One problem became apparent very quickly – anyone parachuting off the north face would run the risk of being blown back into the side of the mountain; there wasn't a rope long enough to rescue Rick if that should happen.

Rick drove an iron pole into the ice at the top of the north face and attached

some climbing ropes to it. He handed Alan and me a rope each and we tied them securely around our waists. We took it in turns to lower ourselves down a precipice to the edge of the mountain, looking for camera positions. I walked the perimeter and found a horseshoe-shaped outcrop that afforded a good view of the entire mountainside from top to bottom. Alan was not content to stand on the edge looking down and decided to undo his rope and clamber over the edge. He climbed down about 10 feet and soon reappeared saying he'd found another good camera position. I was happy to take his word for it.

Atop Mount Asgard with stuntman Rick during the meticulous preparations for the jump.

I was starting to go snow-blind and getting more than a little giddy when Bill suggested we take advantage of the beautiful weather and fly around the mountains. We shot about ten minutes of footage in total, including a number of shots of Rick throwing toilet rolls off the north face so we could see the effect of the wind. We calculated that the jump would have to be made when there was no more than a five mph wind speed. On the way back to England, René was feverishly making notes in preparation for our presentation at Eon Productions. René told me the budget for the shoot would have to be $250,000, plus Rick's fee of $25,000 for two jumps. In 1976 this represented a serious investment – and this was only for one shot in a pre-titles sequence.

I presented the budget to Cubby. When he read the bottom line, he didn't blink. He took my report and went inside the viewing theatre to join Lewis Gilbert, the director of *The Spy Who Loved Me*, and Danny Reisner, the vice-president of United Artists. They ran our footage and I nervously waited outside. When Cubby emerged 15 minutes later he looked me in the eye and simply said, 'Do it.'

We needed to select a fit, independently minded crew. Alan suggested we hire a camera operator called Brian Elvy, and Rick nominated two mountaineers to assist him. We were obliged to keep the numbers small because we were limited by the number of people we could fit inside two helicopters. Another important member of the team didn't come with us: my next-door neighbour, a clever mathematician called Walter Latusek. I asked him to calculate Rick's flight speed if he skied off the mountain at 30 mph, and if he skied off at 45 mph. From the graphs he prepared for me we calculated Rick's trajectory, and how long he should wait before opening his parachute without fear of being blown back into the mountainside. We soon realised that Rick would have to jettison his skis shortly after taking flight because they would begin to act like a parachute themselves and flip him upside down. We fixed a couple of quick-release mechanisms that could be activated by toggles placed at knee height, and Rick was briefed to release the skis five seconds after he left the edge of the mountain. There were no medical facilities at Pangnirtung, so the final member of the team was a doctor, who we asked to join us from Montreal. There was every possibility that Rick could be injured and we needed someone on hand in case of emergencies.

When I returned to Pangnirtung, Bill Henderson, who had been working in Alaska, was waiting for me. For this trip, we were accompanied by a second helicopter, which made the journey from Montreal. For the first day on Asgard, the weather was ideal, but we had to wait for the mountaineers to fit the pitons that would hold the camera crew in position. Rick and I were the last two people deposited on the mountain, and while everyone else was ferried back to base, dark clouds started to gather overhead. The weather prevented Bill from picking us up, and Rick and I were stranded. I was suddenly filled with dread at the thought of spending a night on the mountain without as much as a bar of chocolate to keep me going. Rick remained cheerful throughout. 'Don't worry John,' he said. 'If the worst comes to the worst, we can always walk down!' There was apparently an extremely hazardous route, but I didn't fancy taking it. After about an hour, I was relieved that the sun finally came out. It was cloudy below us, and it felt like we were sitting on cotton wool. I heard the helicopter, and looked down towards the sound. Bill had stuck what looked like a big fishing rod, longer than the length of his rotor blades, to the front of his air-speed indicator. He was inching his way up the side of the mountain with this rod scraping the side as he went. When he cleared the mist, he landed the helicopter and took us back.

Rick and I had worked out that it would take us two hours to set up and actually film the jump. The sun was off the mountain by 2pm, which meant our deadline to begin on any given day would be noon. We spent a week waiting for the mist shrouding the mountain to clear. There were no telephones at Pangnirtung, so I wasn't getting any pressure from London, but on the tenth day an anxious message arrived from Montreal. René asked if there was any way I could cut down on our preparation time and be ready to move a bit quicker when the weather cleared, so we decided to camp out at the bottom of the mountain. René had some tents flown in from Montreal, and when they arrived we camped beneath a huge lake which had been created by a glacier pushing in all the gravel like a natural reservoir. During the night, the persistent noise of what sounded like rattling tin cans reminded me that the glacier was constantly on the move. Our three tents proved completely inadequate and we all ended up huddling together in one just to keep warm. The cold had the unfortunate effect of shrinking our bladders, so there were numerous trips outside. The doctor was in the sleeping bag nearest the doorway, and he had to put up with people stepping over him every half an hour. I fell asleep with the noise of the glacier above me, and had a nightmare that the gravel would suddenly collapse and we'd all drown. I was later reassured that the glacier had been there for over a million years and was unlikely to go anywhere.

After two weeks, our doctor had to return to his hospital in Montreal, but he sent a replacement. Our new doctor brought a bodyboard with him, which he explained we could use in case Rick injured his spine. We continued huddling at the base of the mountain as the weather got worse and worse, and we were surprised to be joined by a lone Alsatian. He wore a badge around his neck proclaiming that he was rabies-free, so we fed him and kept him warm. When we decided to head back to Pangnirtung, Bill refused to take the dog in the helicopter, so we reluctantly left him behind with the rest of our food. We returned three days later when the weather improved and the dog was still there, desperately trying to get into the remaining cans with his teeth. I decided that it was too uncomfortable to camp out every night, so we returned to Pangnirtung every day thereafter. Bill relented, and allowed the dog in the cockpit. 'At the first sign of trouble, he goes straight out the window!' he warned me, but luckily the dog behaved himself. On the way back we saw some hikers, so I asked Bill to hover above them. I stuck the dog's head out of the window. 'Is this your dog?' I shouted. They shook their heads and we continued back to base. The poor dog found few friends back at Pangnirtung. The owner of the lodge where we were staying was horrified at the new addition to our party. 'I'm not having any dog in here,' he said. 'He can stay outside, and if no one claims him after two days I'll shoot him!' I believed him. Fortunately, on the second day, the dog's owners finally turned up.

After weeks of inactivity, I didn't want Rick's first skiing trip to be the actual jump, so during our daily visits to Asgard I filmed Rick skiing on a neighbouring mountain. These filmed dress rehearsals helped raise morale, and later came in very useful when I cut them into the film. During one of our daily visits, the weather seemed to improve slightly. Bill looked up through the clouds and turned to me. 'I think we're going to get a break.' He started his engine, which was the signal for everyone to come down from wherever they were climbing and get aboard the two helicopters. When we landed on top of the mountain, the last-minute preparations were made, which included the crew wearing white oversuits so they'd be invisible to the helicopter camera. I walked over to Rick and checked his wardrobe. 'If you don't want to do this, I won't make you,' I told him. 'I won't throw you off the mountain if you refuse.' Rick shook his head – he didn't look too happy, but he was ready to go.

When I briefed him for the approach to the precipice, I told him not to trust the radio he was carrying. 'Try to keep your eye on where I'm standing. Don't go until you see me bury a red flag in the snow – no matter what you may hear on the radio, don't start the run while the red flag is visible.' The camera crews were all in position, the focus-puller (who had practised keeping focused on various objects that had been thrown off the mountain) knew exactly what he was doing and everyone was ready to go. Our Canadian cameraman was immediately below the precipice, ready to shoot at 36 frames per second, and I was ready to shoot at 72 frames per second – three times faster than the usual speed. The helicopter carrying Alan and his camera took off and hovered in position. Alan had a 400-foot magazine attached to his camera – barely three minutes' worth of film – so I knew he couldn't turn over until we were absolutely ready. I looked at my watch – we were about 10 minutes late and

were losing the light rapidly. We had to go now.

All the camera crews reported back to me on the radio, and I gave the order to turn over. Crews number one, two and three all gave confirmation. 'Don't forget, Rick – *you are James Bond*,' I called through on his radio. 'Go!' I buried the red flag in the snow and ducked out of sight. The last thing I saw was Rick gathering speed as he skied towards the precipice.

Rick shot off the side of the mountain, disengaged his skis, went into free-fall and deployed his parachute. Alan got a good shot of Rick skiing towards the edge of the mountain from the helicopter camera. Then his pilot went into autogyration to keep up with Rick – the rotors freewheeled and they dropped like a stone. Rick disappeared from view, but miraculously Alan managed to pick him up again, and the footage he shot was used in the opening seconds of the title sequence. Brian's camera followed Rick down, with the focus-puller adjusting the zoom on the way. While Rick was sailing through the air, Brian became worried that he seemed too distant and adjusted his camera, even though the focus-puller was taking care of that for him. The result was a slight bump in the smooth progress of the downward shot, but the fact we were shooting at such high speed helped iron things out a little and it didn't spoil anything. The Canadian cameraman under the ledge missed Rick altogether, and got a great shot of his own feet.

And then it was over. My first concern was for Rick's well-being. The helicopter descended to the glacier beneath the mountain and found him with one of his skis snapped in two and lying beside him. The footage later revealed that when Rick opened his parachute he had slowed down, and his free-falling skis had caught up with him. One of them had hit the canopy, but luckily Rick had survived the fall unscathed. Bill brought Rick back up to the summit, where we gathered round to congratulate him. As soon as Rick got out of the cockpit, I could see he was green. Without a word he rushed to the edge of the mountain, pulled his trousers down and dumped in the snow. His stomach had turned to jelly.

René took the film to Montreal to be processed and we nervously waited to see whether we'd have to film another jump. News came back that it looked wonderful, except for the moment when Brian adjusted his camera position and the focus went slightly soft. There was much debate over whether those few seconds spoiled things, and I decided that this was a minor imperfection. As far as I was concerned, we had our shot in the can, and I wouldn't wait to see the rushes. I didn't want to put Rick through all that again and run the risk of killing him. The rushes revealed that God was smiling on us with the weather – the only thing illuminated by the sun was Rick, who seemed to have a natural spotlight on him as he raced towards the edge of the mountain and flew off.

Back at the lodge, Fritz hugged and kissed me as soon as I walked through the door. He seemed just as pleased as we were. 'Could I have the doctor's bodyboard?' he asked me. 'I'd like to roll my pastry on it!' The doctor let him have it, and that night we had a big party. As we celebrated, a prolonged period of bad weather set in and we had to abandon some of our equipment on the mountain. Another jump would have been impossible anyway.

We received a heroes' welcome at Pinewood, where I cut the footage together with the shots I had previously filmed of Rick skiing on the neighbouring mountain. I began planning the rest of the pre-titles sequence,

Stunt man Rick stares into the abyss.

James Bond-
producer Cubby
Broccoli (left) and
Lewis Gilbert,
director of *The Spy
Who Loved Me.*

and hired expert cameramen Willy Bogner and Alex Barbey to join me shortly after Christmas. Over the next few weeks, word began to spread that there was a very special stunt sequence in the new James Bond film. Numerous visitors to the studio requested to see the footage, including the ex-King of Romania. Prince Charles also asked to see it, and once it had finished, he asked to see it again. We ended up running it for him three times. Cubby Broccoli, Lewis Gilbert, Roger Moore and Danny Reisner all loved it. The atmosphere on *The Spy Who Loved Me* was electric, and we knew we had the makings of a fantastic movie.

The ski-parachute jump has long since been considered one of the most daring and spectacular stunts ever committed to film. In 1982 Cubby Broccoli received the coveted Irving G Thalberg Memorial Award for 'a consistently high quality of motion picture production'. A sequence of highlights from his movies played on the big screen behind him, culminating with his favourite – the shot of Bond skiing off the mountain and parachuting to safety. The audience at the Motion Picture Academy rose to their feet in appreciation. Credit is due to all the members of the small team responsible, but especially to Rick Sylvester who risked his life, and to Cubby and Danny, who placed their trust in me to deliver.

When I look back over 50 years in the film industry, it's easy to pinpoint the moment that represented my transition to the big time. When I launched Rick off that mountain, my career went with him.

# CHAPTER 2

## A TASTE FOR ADVENTURE

I felt the hairs bristle on the back of my neck and the next thing I knew, I was covered in tadpoles.

As one of the tallest children in my class, I had been seated at the back of the room. There was a window ledge above me and a bowl of tadpoles precipitously placed on the shelf behind. Following a rush of wind outside, the window flew open and hit the bowl. I barely had time to register that I been showered in baby frogs before a terrific explosion alerted me to the fact that something more serious was happening outside. Only after this terrific noise did I hear a teeth-grinding shriek, which I would later come to recognise as the sound of a V2 rocket homing in on its target.

The V2 that struck Ashford, Middlesex, in 1944, was the first to hit British soil. That evening, I visited the bombsite with some school-friends. We were only 13 years old and so found it relatively easy to sneak past the policemen ushering the crowds away. The devastation we saw was in the process of being hushed up, but I will never forget what I witnessed: as far back as I could see, every building on each side of the street had been flattened.

As I embarked on the five-mile journey from Ashford back to my home in Sunbury-on-Thames, I wrestled with the images of devastation. I was seven years old in 1939, and I remember my family gathering around the wireless to hear Neville Chamberlain's grim declaration of war. Every now and then my mother would hold a finger to her lips and say 'Ssshh' as the radio's fading battery muffled our Prime Minister's solemn message.

From that point on, my life was turned upside down. The very next day, I joined my family in the garden to prepare our defence for the forthcoming onslaught. We dug a deep hole and went to the local pit to grab any corrugated iron we could find to improvise an air raid shelter.

It may be a strange thing to admit, but despite the near misses while we huddled in our shelter, and the subsequent V2 attacks, I don't think I experienced any fear during the war. The buzz of other people's behaviour made me acutely aware of the enormity of events, and I only remember excitement. The First World War veterans who lived down our street recounted tales of the trenches, and Mr Crow, our next-door neighbour, even produced his old Lee Enfield rifle from his attic. I watched him clean the barrel as if he were about to go into action the next day.

My father was an engineer and he used to fire watch at his factory during the night. Sometimes I would accompany him with buckets of sand while he did the rounds checking for firebombs. During air raids, my mother and three sisters would sleep downstairs, where my mother insisted they would be safer. My father slept upstairs ('No bloody German's going to get me out of my bed!') and, as the only boy in the family, I stayed upstairs with him. It was only when the air raids got close enough for me actually to see bombs falling from aeroplanes that my father finally relented. 'Follow me,' he ordered, and we clambered downstairs to join my mother and sisters in the cellar.

My sisters, Margaret and Joyce, both volunteered for the WRAF. Joyce was eventually posted to Biggin Hill, where she did very good work as a teleprinter operator and plotter. I received an exciting letter from her in which she described her team's efforts in trying to down the V2 flying bombs before they reached London.

Sunbury-on-Thames is a quiet suburb, but we nevertheless experienced several raids. The railway station booking office was blown up, but fortunately the booking clerk happened to be in the toilet at the time and escaped. Tragically, the Running Horse pub received a direct hit during a packed night and almost everyone inside was killed. A local story had it that someone was about to walk into the pub when the bomb hit, and he died with the detached doorknob in his hand. Sounds dubious to me.

A family was killed when a bomb hit a house in Greenleas, which was nearby, and two of my school-friends died when another hit the house opposite us. I was asleep in our coal cellar at the time and our house apparently jumped two feet in the air when the bomb hit. I must have been a very heavy sleeper.

Then our school was firebombed. I joined a group of mates to witness Kennington Manor Elementary literally go up in smoke. As if that wasn't enough excitement for one evening, someone shouted 'Phosphorous bomb!' and we all rushed to the scene of the crime. We were greeted with the bizarre sight of the chief air raid warden on his hands and knees cautiously approaching a cylindrical object lying in his very own garden. After careful consideration, he soon revealed that the object was not in fact an incendiary device, but a discarded lawn roller.

The next morning, we turned up for school to discover that the top storey wasn't there any more. The consequence was a blissful summer – actually six whole months – without being made to learn a single thing. We would go into Sunbury-on-Thames, swim into the middle of the river and muck about for hours on end, terrorising people in boats. The daring ones among us dived off Walton Bridge as the ultimate test of our prowess.

I was 14 years old when the war ended in 1945 and for half my life I had known nothing but action. My experiences in the war gave me a taste for adventure and stoked the fires of a vivid imagination. Both would serve me well in the years to come.

# 007™

# CHAPTER 3

## CUTTING IT FINE

I was introduced to cinema during the war when we were packed off to the Roxy in Feltham for the Saturday morning film clubs. Audience participation was the 'in' thing – kids would fire arrows at the screen when it was exciting and urinate between the seats when they were bored. All manner of objects could roll down the sloping floor towards you and you had to watch your feet.

The Saturday morning cliff-hangers would depict the adventures of Flash Gordon and Buck Rogers, and they certainly cultivated my interest in the world of film production.

In 1945 I joined the Sea Cadets, mainly because I fancied the uniform. One of my fellow novice sailors was a Sea Scout called Eric 'Wacker' Williams. At that time, Wacker was the messenger boy at Nettlefold Studios in Walton-on-Thames, but he was ready to hang up his bicycle clips and enter the camera department. He told me there was about to be a vacancy, so the next day I headed for Nettlefolds. I was greeted by a uniformed commissionaire who dealt my career aspirations a terrible blow. 'I'm sorry, laddie,' he told me, 'but we've only got one messenger boy's uniform and you're too tall for it.' My heart sank. 'Mind you,' he added, 'I've got a friend at Shepperton. That's a much bigger studio.' I perked up – if Shepperton was bigger, they might have more than one uniform. Maybe one of them would fit me. 'Why don't you go over there? I'll give them a call.'

I cycled over to Shepperton Studios and left my name at the gate. Two weeks later, I was invited over for an interview and was duly appointed studio messenger boy. I was on the bottom rung of the ladder, but I knew next to nothing about any of the rungs above me. The idea of working in a real-life film studio was enormously appealing, but I had no burning ambition to be an editor, director or producer. I did suss, however, that as a messenger boy I would be able to work for a couple of years without any pressure and get to know every department that contributed to the production of a movie. Maybe that would help me decide what I wanted to do. One of my favourite places was the master carpenter's office, which was where I developed a love of woodwork that remains to this day. Percy Rawlinson, the master carpenter, was a wonderful man in charge of around 100 carpenters, some of whom I had known from school. One carpenter, Bill Broom, would let me use his tools and his bench when he was called away. Over a six-month period of using Bill's tools, I learned how to be a carpenter.

Shepperton Studios was run by the charismatic producer Sir Alexander Korda. There were whispers about Korda's chequered wheelings and dealings in the film industry, but he was much loved by his workforce and he made some high-quality films. Korda brought with him a number of people from his previous base at Denham Studios. These included Papa Denier, who together with his wife ran the magnificent galleried restaurant, and the wonderful matte artist Percy Day. The restaurant was subsequently turned into a stage, which I thought was a great shame.

To my teenage eyes, Shepperton was a wonderland. During the production of such films as Korda's *An Ideal Husband,* I would wander around and gaze in awe at the huge Technicolor cameras. I later realised that the early colour processes required an enormous amount of light. The heat that the lamps generated would be so colossal that it was not unusual to see overpowered technicians slumped asleep. One electrician had a habit of falling asleep during filming, and scenes would sometimes be interrupted by the sound of loud snoring from the gantry.

As the messenger boy, I got to know everyone and spent time in each part of the studio learning about film production. The editing department was the one that fascinated me the most, and when I got a foot in that door, my days as a messenger boy were numbered.

My promotion to the editing department meant a pay rise from 25 shillings (£1.25) to four guineas (£4.20) a week. This was the first piece of good news. The next piece of news was also encouraging – we were about to work on an adaptation of the Graham Greene novel *The Third Man.*

*The Third Man* was produced by Korda's London Films and directed by Carol Reed. Both Reed and his assistant director Guy Hamilton, who later directed four James Bond films, appeared on set wearing collar and tie and trilby hats. Nowadays, it's virtually unheard of for a director to be so formal on set, but in the late 1940s this was nothing unusual. The only exception I can remember was Anthony 'Puffin' Asquith. 'Puffin' considered himself one of the workers and always wore a boiler suit, so of course I didn't recognise him, even after I collided with him on my bicycle. He got up and apologised to me, which was typical of his kindness.

Despite the formal dress code, I soon learned the film industry didn't really have a class structure. I was a working class lad, and I was mingling with public school boys. We were all learning the business together. The great thing about the film industry was that there was every kind of person you could imagine: homosexuals, heterosexuals, relatively uneducated people and very highly educated people. People attracted to the film industry seemed to have a very broad outlook on life.

I started my training in the cutting rooms, where my first job was to empty the bins of extremely flammable nitrate film. The film was then sent to a factory where it was washed and the silver reclaimed from the emulsion. It was not economical to salvage the smaller reels of film so we used to take the scraps out on to the back lot and burn them on a big heap. One day I was on the back lot with my friend John Lee when a high wind caused a bit of a mishap. The weather made it difficult to light the match we needed to start the bonfire, so we edged nearer and nearer to the pile of film. When we

finally succeeded in lighting a match, the film exploded. After I picked myself up, I realised that my eyebrows had been singed clean off and the neighbouring field was half alight. We scrambled back towards the fire and attempted to beat it out with old sacks. For a few nervous minutes, I imagined myself responsible for burning down Shepperton Studios and putting myself out of a job I had barely begun.

Despite this mishap, I eventually progressed from the worst job in the cutting rooms. I was taught how to number film, and thereafter spent days up to my neck in thousands of feet of the stuff. I numbered the sound and the action in synchronisation so the editor could put the two together and know they were correctly matched.

I happened to be a similar build to *Third Man* star Joseph Cotten, which came in handy during the post-production dubbing. In those days, we didn't have the technical ability to flip a switch and create an echoing sound. Echoing footsteps often had to be recorded in a special chamber and carefully synchronised. Jack Drake, the sound editor, found a stairwell with a promisingly hard surface outside the Westrex theatre in Shepperton. I went into the theatre and watched a continuous loop of film of Cotten's footsteps, memorised their exact speed, then dashed outside to the stairwell and walked along the hard surface. The echoing footsteps that Jack Drake recorded are the ones accompanying Joseph Cotten in the film.

The famous *Third Man* theme was performed by zither player Anton Karas, who came to London to record the music. Anton initially worked in

Joseph Cotten and Orson Welles in Carol Reed's classic thriller *The Third Man*.

Carol Reed's house on the King's Road, Chelsea, and I was dispatched to run a copy of the film for his benefit. I lugged the gear over to Reed's house, met Mr Karas and plugged everything in. As soon as I touched the pedal to begin running the first reel, all the lights fused and we were plunged into darkness. Next thing I knew, Reed's butler and I were on our hands and knees in the pantry, trying to find the fuse box. We ended up knocking a nail into it to stop the fuse from blowing. Nowadays, when I pass that house I wonder if the nail's still there.

Back upstairs, I ran the film for Anton and he strummed away, working through his ideas and planning how to fit his music to the film in advance of the recording sessions. He didn't speak any English and I didn't speak any German, so we got on very well.

Later on, Carol Reed invited me into his lounge for some refreshment. He offered me a sherry, which to a 17-year-old seemed very sophisticated, and I declined. Before I sat down, I noticed he shared his settee with a rabbit which was busily munching a cabbage.

The editor on *The Third Man* was Oswald Hafenrichter, an Austrian who had escaped the Nazis during the war. One night, Oswald went to have a bite to eat with Edith, his assistant. Unfortunately some film had been left draped over the sound head, which used to get very hot. The film heated up and eventually exploded, causing a huge fire in the cutting rooms. Ossie rushed back and tried to get back into the room. We did our best to restrain him, but he broke free and waded in through the thick smoke. He emerged, not with any of the precious film, but with his smouldering jacket. It had been hand-woven in Austria and was very dear to him.

A lot of film was lost in the fire and this caused something of a crisis. Almost eight reels – virtually the whole movie – had to be reprinted from the negative, which was thankfully intact. Virtually every editor that was free was drafted to re-cut the film from scratch. Geoff Bottril, one of the assistant editors, was very meticulous, and he had written down the film's code numbers in a book. The key numbers were a code on the negative and were printed through on to the positive prints. This enabled the negative cutters to match exactly the film editor's work print, containing hundreds of cuts. The soundtrack and picture were separate, and editors required key numbers to be printed on the side of the film to enable them to synchronise and identify the shots. We were able to reassemble the reels by following the numbers Geoff had written in his book. Geoff's approach had previously been criticised as bureaucracy gone mad, but in this instance it paid dividends. Carol Reed was a regular visitor to the numbering room, and would sometimes bring me a beer.

We worked all hours God sent to get back on schedule. One Saturday evening, I was in the bath getting ready for a night out, when I heard a knock on the front door. It was the associate producer. I rapidly got dressed and met him on the doorstep. 'We need you at the studio,' he said. 'Can you number some film for us? It's urgent.' Half-an-hour later, a Rolls-Royce pulled up and took me to Shepperton, where I worked until about 2am. I numbered reprints almost every night from thereon and earned a lot of overtime, which supplemented my still meagre salary. After I paid my mother for my keep, I was left with a little more than usual at the end of each week. Not that post-war Britain offered a teenager very much to spend his money on.

Once I settled into the cutting rooms at Shepperton, I got to know all the assistant editors and would occasionally meet an editor. One always had to ask permission to enter an editor's room, and assistant editors would always do their best to make sure that their bosses weren't disturbed during the creative process.

I minded my Ps and Qs, and in between numbering jobs learned how to splice film together. Through trial and error, I became something of an expert at splicing film and discovered I could do it very quickly. Editors would cut film with a pair of scissors and join the two pieces together with paper clips. I would receive a big roll of film studded with paper clips. The roll would be loaded on to a re-winder and I would then splice the paper-clipped film together using acetate cement.

One of the junior assistants I met at this time was Peter Hunt, who would later play a large part in my career. He went on to become an editor and then director, and in both respects made important contributions to the Bond films. Peter had some amusing stories of his experiences in Monte Cassino during the war ('I was in a dugout for two weeks,' he told me. 'I stuck my head in a hole and kept it there for as long as I could!') and was always helpful and encouraging. If Guy Hamilton remembers me from *The Third Man*, I'm sure it's only because he had to throw me off the set.

*The Wooden Horse*, directed by Jack Lee, was the next movie I worked on, and I can think of no better example to illustrate the mixture of people I encountered in the film industry. Humphrey Fisher, the first assistant editor, was the son of the Archbishop of Canterbury, and the trainee editor was the young Lord Brabourne. The editor was John Seabourne and his son Peter was the assembly editor. Both father and son had some interesting wartime experiences: John had been a bugle boy and had deserted, only later to enlist in the First World War. To avoid a court martial, he changed his surname from Diss to Seabourne and the name had stuck ever since. John wasn't much of an editor, but he was a great storyteller. John's son Peter had been an RAF instructor during the Second World War and he told me he had been teaching a trainee pilot night-flying over Reading when the first V1 flying bomb went whistling past their cockpit. I don't think either of them could believe what they were seeing.

After three years of apprenticeship, I was promoted to second assistant editor, the most junior-ranking editor in the cutting hierarchy. One particularly memorable disaster brought me perilously close to demotion. I was charged with assembling a reel of film for an important private screening being hosted by Korda in London. I was splicing furiously, desperate to make the deadline, when paper clips started flying everywhere and I was left amidst a confused jumble of film. I cut the reel together and delivered it on time. I watched from the back of the theatre as the lights were lowered and the film began. All went well until the picture suddenly flipped upside down – in my haste, I had spliced a section the wrong way round. As the film continued, I looked out to gauge the great man's reaction. Before long, Korda beckoned with what looked liked an upward movement of his hand. 'He wants the sound raised,' someone whispered to me. I looked behind me and saw two buttons marked 'raise' and 'lower'. I hit 'raise' as hard as I could. Nothing happened. I hit it again, and suddenly the tabs drew and the lights went up in the theatre. Everyone scrambled over me in an attempt to try to

Off-duty with two
friends during my
National Service
days in the RAF.

undo what I had done. I was relieved to notice that Sir Alexander remained so calm he didn't even look round.

After *The Wooden Horse*, which was released in 1950, I was second assistant editor on *The Long Dark Hall*, directed by Anthony Bushell and Reginald Beck, and starring Rex Harrison. I was now approaching 18 years of age and my compulsory National Service loomed. Before production of *The Long Dark Hall* wrapped, I joined the RAF.

If I was upset at being dragged away from the studio for 18 months, then I was gutted when the onset of the Korean War prompted the government to increase National Service to two years. I had already started counting the days and an extra six months didn't appeal very much.

A national serviceman in the RAF, however, was not required to do as much as I anticipated. The Air Force seemed to be more interested in people who wanted to become pilots and who had signed on for five years. I was quite happy to be a driver and mechanic. The time away from my parents helped me to grow up a bit and I had a few adventures along the way. One of my responsibilities was driving the commanding officer in his Humber Supersnipe, which was a wonderful car. I dropped him off at an airfield and as his plane was taxiing along the runway, I saw him wave at me through one of the windows. 'What a nice man,' I thought, and waved back. When he returned, I got a right talking to: 'You bloody fool!' he yelled. 'I left my briefcase in the car and I was trying to attract your attention!'

While I was away between 1950 and 1952, the British film industry suffered one of the worst downturns in its history. A lot of people I had known left the business during those years because there was such little work. My release from the RAF coincided with a mini-boom, however. My mother had forwarded me a number of telegrams with job offers, and I showed the most promising one to my commanding officer at Manby Royal

Michael Denison and Dulcie Gray, the husband-and-wife stars of *There Was A Young Lady*.

Air College. He was kind enough to release me two weeks early, so I didn't lose the opportunity. I immediately took a position as a second assistant editor at Nettlefold Studios, working for production manager E.S. Laurie. He was tough, but he had a heart of gold.

*There Was a Young Lady*, which featured husband-and-wife stars Michael Denison and Dulcie Gray, was shot at Nettlefolds and gave me some valuable experience. The editor was Joseph Sterling, who I later worked with on a John Guillermin movie. When Joseph fell sick during post-production, he allowed me to carry on cutting the film in his absence. John Guillermin, who employed a lot of avant-garde techniques in his work, proved quite influential to me, and I recall that he introduced me to hand-held filming. John later fell out with the producers and was banned from the studio – I would smuggle him into the cutting room via the fire escape.

It was around this time that I started to think seriously about the mechanics and technique of effective film-editing. The French film *The Wages of Fear* directed by Henri-Georges Clouzot was released in 1953 and had a profound effect on me. Clouzot took around 20 minutes to establish the atmosphere in a remote African village. I noticed how much time he took to paint the scenery, and I was deeply impressed by a sequence in which the power of even a tiny drop of nitroglycerine was demonstrated. Later in the film, a truck carrying a vast amount of this nitroglycerine is negotiating a tight corner on a twisting mountain road. The guy in the front of the truck is rolling a cigarette when suddenly the tobacco is blown out of the paper. A huge explosion follows soon after. The scene took me right back to my experience in the classroom when the V2 rocket exploded five miles away. I analysed how the scene was constructed and marvelled that such a potent demonstration of power had been executed in such a simple way.

When I look back on how I learned my craft, I think it's safe to conclude that Oswald Hafenrichter was the greatest influence on my editing. In fact, he was possibly the only editor who had any influence on me at all. That's not to say that his influence was necessarily beneficial: he was extremely untidy in the cutting rooms, and although he was very creative, I don't think he could handle being around all that film. He was ahead of his time in a way – I think he would have been much happier pressing buttons on today's electronic equipment.

Ossie probably had more influence on me than any other editor because I was closer to him than I had been to other editors. He was very approachable, whereas some other editors of the time, such as Bert Bates and Ralph Kemplen, were terrifically qualified and talented but very difficult to see; their assistants would never let you near them. When I eventually became a fully fledged editor, I was careful to delegate as much as I could and tried to be as open as possible.

In a sense, an editor's life was relatively easy because in the early 1950s not a huge amount of material went into the average British studio picture. I could tell by looking at a roll of rushes how many takes there had been in a day's filming, sometimes as few as four or five shots in a day. Some of the faster directors might do eight or nine set-ups in a day. Today's average lies somewhere between 20 and 30, largely thanks to the benefit of technical advances in lighting, film speeds and the huge penalties incurred by slipping behind schedule.

Many of the films I worked on at Nettlefold Studios are now forgotten. They were produced for the domestic market and would never have translated for an American audience, let alone other international territories. Ealing Studios had been successful with such films as *Kind Hearts and Coronets*, but even they were regarded as small potatoes by American distributors, who restricted their Stateside screenings to art house cinemas.

The people I met were often more memorable than the films. I met Lewis Gilbert for the first time while I was at Nettlefolds and he was directing a much under-rated picture called *Emergency Call*. Lewis is a very bright man with a light-hearted attitude towards film-making. Our paths would cross again. Lawrence Huntington, who directed *There Was a Young Lady*, was someone else with a light approach, and he was a pleasure to work with. Carol Reed's films had a richness and special texture, and I still believe they have a unique look to them. Above all, these directors impressed on me that film-making should be fun.

*Make Me an Offer*, released in 1954, was the first film I worked on for Group 3, a partially Government-backed concern that was based in Beaconsfield. I spent several years with Group 3 as an assistant editor, beginning with *Make Me an Offer,* which was directed by Cyril Frankel and starred Peter Finch. The film was edited by Bernie Gribble, who nearly 40 years later would edit *Aces: Iron Eagle III* for me in the US. Other Group 3 pictures included *John and Julie*, which was directed by Bill Fairchild. Bill had earned a good reputation as the screenwriter of the acclaimed submarine drama *Morning Departure. John and Julie* featured a young Peter Sellers in a tiny role as a village policeman. None of us had any idea that he would go on to such great things.

Bill Fairchild was also the director of *The Extra Day*, my next Group 3 film, released in 1956. At this time, the assistant editor was generally responsible for the soundtrack of the film as well. The designation

changed during this period, so *John and Julie* and *The Extra Day* really count as my first official productions as a sound editor. There were a lot of songs in *The Extra Day* and I remember we tested Frankie Vaughan and Dennis Lotis for one of the leading roles. Dennis was the more laid-back of the two so he got the job, but with hindsight I think Frankie would probably have been a better choice.

The energetic Dennis Lotis beat Frankie Vaughan to a role in *The Extra Day*.

In 1956, I returned to Shepperton Studios where I hadn't been for some years. *The Green Man*, produced by Frank Launder and Sidney Gilliat, was the first film on which I received an on-screen credit as sound editor. It was fun working with those guys and Alastair Sim, the star of the show, was a hoot. I recall that Sim originally intended to direct the film himself but handed over to Robert Day shortly before production began. Sidney Gilliat used to write a lot of his scripts on the backs of cigarette packets – ideas would be jotted down in all sorts of odd places. A friend of theirs called Val Valentine would be invited to all the screenings. Valentine would sit there, laughing away at the gags. Launder and Gilliat would judge the comedic quality of their films by listening to how much Val Valentine laughed, but it struck me that he'd laugh at just about anything.

After post-production on *The Green Man* wrapped, I planned to marry my fiancée Gina. I was almost immediately offered a job on *Three Men in a*

*Boat*, however, so almost everything except the wedding itself – including the honeymoon – had to go. The local paper found out about it and we were the subject of the intriguing headline 'Film-making Stops Honeymoon'.

*Three Men in a Boat* starred David Tomlinson, Jimmy Edwards and Laurence Harvey. One of my more unusual responsibilities as a sound editor was to take care of dog noises. I brought in the renowned animal impersonator Percy Edwards, and I'll never forget watching him recreate yelps and barks for our benefit.

Compared with the two other sound editors on the film, Gerry Hamlin and Stan Hawkes, I was a new kid on the block and they both had a bit of fun at my expense. I used a relatively portable viewing machine called a Moviola for editing. It was a noisy and unreliable belt-driven device that was prone to overheating. Smoke would billow from the back of the machine and time and again I would call the maintenance man. Each time he could find nothing wrong with it and I would return to work baffled. Only later did I discover that Gerry and Stan had rigged the machine with a special line that looked like an electrical cable. While I suspected the Moviola was about to burst into flames, they were blowing cigarette smoke through the cable in between bouts of uncontrollable laughter.

One day, we were denied access to Shepperton's sound recording studio, so I had to give gorgeous co-star Shirley Eaton (later immortalised on film in *Goldfinger*) a lift to Twickenham Studios. My car was a 1935 Austin Lichfield Saloon and I had serious trepidations about letting a highly prized actress into this boneshaker without proper insurance. She was fine, however, and I was very proud to have given her a lift.

*Three Men in a Boat* was continually being re-cut and I adopted a special procedure to cope. A film's soundtrack must, of course, be synchronised with the picture. This was done by spacing out the sound sections with sections of blank film until they could be aligned with the appropriate picture. If someone shortened the picture or added to it, the sound effects went out of sync. If the editor of the film altered the picture (and editors such as Ossie Hafenrichter were prone to working late into the night doing just that), this could make the sound editor's job very difficult. I devised a system that synchronised the sound effects without actually integrating them into the reels of film. I would wait until the last possible moment to lay the sound effects into the finished picture by carefully following the positional notes I had made – and until that point I would tell bemused editors to chop away to their hearts' content.

Ralph Kemplen, the editor on *Three Men in a Boat*, was amazed when he walked into my room and couldn't find any cans of film anywhere. With the delivery deadline a mere week away, Ralph's concern was understandable, but we hit the date. Ralph was able to keep cutting almost up until the last minute without affecting the synchronisation of the soundtrack. Sometimes unorthodox situations call for unorthodox solutions.

*Three Men in a Boat* was directed by Ken Annakin, whose nickname at the studio was 'Pannakin Annakin'. I don't know why – I certainly never saw him panic. I think Ken had fallen out with the producers (not an unusual occurrence for directors), and I found myself in the position of being the only person he felt he could talk to. We worked well together, especially during the unusual post-syncing sessions as animal impersonator Percy Edwards

yapped away as Montmorency the dog.

I went from *Three Men in a Boat* to *The Four Just Men*, a television series filmed at Nettlefold Studios in 1956. The four gents in question were Dan Dailey, Jack Hawkins, Richard Conte and Vittorio De Sica. Signor De Sica could speak very little English and I had to post-sync virtually all of his dialogue. In his native Italy, De Sica was known as 'The King of Naples', and such was his fame that Italians would apparently fall on their knees before him. He smoked his own brand of hand-made cigarettes, but I don't recall ever being offered one.

Dan Dailey was a huge, tough-looking guy, who was actually a surprisingly good dancer. After viewing the rushes one day, co-producer Sidney Cole told me that Dailey had delivered a line with the wrong inflection. He asked me to supervise the re-recording. I introduced myself to Mr Dailey as the sound editor, and asked him if he'd mind giving up five minutes of his lunch break to re-record the offending line. He agreed and at 1pm we began. Dailey read the line in exactly the same way he had delivered it during filming. 'I'm sorry, Mr Dailey,' I said, 'but Mr Cole would like you to give the line a slightly different inflection.' Dailey glared at me. 'I'm no f***ing radio actor!' he scowled, and walked off. I politely suggested to Sidney that next time he might like to ask Mr Dailey himself.

The supervising editor on *The Four Just Men* was Thelma Connell. When the plug was pulled, Thelma had to wrap the editing up as soon as possible. I was sharing the sound-editing duties with another colleague and Thelma knew there wasn't enough money to keep both of us on until the production closed. She called me into her office and asked me if I'd mind leaving a

Dan Dailey – an American star who was light on his feet but sharp with his tongue.

month early. I asked her why. 'Because,' she replied, 'I know that when you walk out this door, you'll get another job straightaway, and I think we both know that when Freddie leaves, he probably won't be as lucky.' I wasn't sure I could see her point, but I went without a fuss.

*The Admirable Crichton*, the classic satire starring Kenneth More in the title role, was being directed by Lewis Gilbert and edited by Peter Hunt. Peter invited me to become sound editor on the film shortly before Christmas and we worked in adjoining cutting rooms. We saw each other every day and became good friends. Kenneth More had already given everyone on the production a bottle of Haig whisky and when he found out I'd joined the crew, he generously made sure I wasn't left out.

In 1957, I worked on *The Scamp*, directed by Wolf Rilla, at Elstree's National Studios (which is now the home of the BBC's *EastEnders*). The Elstree and Borehamwood area was the British Hollywood in the late 1950s: there was also the ABPC studio (most of which has now been demolished) and the MGM British studios (now a housing estate), to name just two of the facilities in the area. The Imperial, Gate and Danziger Studios were also in the neighbourhood, but they have all long since closed.

I continued my tour of British studios at Twickenham, where I was sound editor on *A Cry from the Streets*. The film reunited me with Lewis Gilbert and Peter Hunt, who had respectively directed and cut *The Admirable Crichton*. The director of photography was Harry Gillam, who was definitely a gent of the trilby and tie generation. The film starred Max Bygraves and Barbara Murray. I remember Max quickly writing a song for a rain-soaked scene he shared with some children. Lewis was great with the kids and they loved working with him.

Later in 1958, I returned to Shepperton to become the sound editor on *Life Is a Circus*, a Crazy Gang comedy directed by Val Guest. The Crazy Gang had been reunited for the first time since the war and they didn't seem best pleased about it. Teddy Knox, Jimmy Nervo, Jimmy Gold, Charlie Naughton and 'Monsewer' Eddie Gray were archetypal grumpy old men who forever seemed to be knocking each other. The film was a nightmare because it was shot entirely on a silent stage, and with the noise of the wind machines, I could barely interpret what anyone was supposed to be saying. This made the task of adding the dialogue in post-production even harder. During the dubbing sessions, things got so difficult that I decided to bring the Crazy Gang into the recording studio in pairs. I even devised a Crazy Gang chart – every day I would have to shuffle the pack and call in the various actors and give them their lines before we tried to dub them. Val probably knew the lines because he had collaborated on the script with Len Heath and John Warren, but I don't think anyone else on the crew did. We managed to get through it and avoid a confrontation, but I'm not sure how.

Val Guest was an interesting character. He certainly looked the part, wearing ski pants and a yellow scarf. On occasions he even carried a megaphone. At the beginning of the day, he would show everybody exactly what they were going to shoot by writing everything down on a big blackboard. There were consolations amid the madness – it was wonderful to witness Bud Flanagan and Chesney Allen singing 'Underneath the Arches'.

My next sound editing job was on *Dentist in the Chair*, which was scripted by Val Guest and directed by Don Chaffey, with whom I would

later work alongside on the television series *Danger Man*. The very talented Bob Monkhouse was the star, with capable support from such greats as Eric Barker and Kenneth Connor. Kenny Connor's laughing gas sequence had me in stitches.

The Crazy Gang, featuring Bud Flanagan (centre) and Chesney Allen (top right).

As the 1950s drew to a close, I found myself out of work. By this time I had a wife and two children to support, so this was no joke. I spoke to Ossie Hafenrichter, who told me he was about to edit a film called *Foxhole in Cairo*, which had been directed by John Moxey and starred James Robertson Justice. If I remember rightly, it had been filmed on location in Egypt before production was interrupted. The movie was now being resumed and Ossie promised me the job of sound editor. Soon afterwards, rumours got back to me that someone else had been given the job, so I rushed down to Shepperton and buttonholed Ossie. I told him I was desperate for work and really needed the job. An apologetic Ossie duly went back to the other fellow and explained that he had offered me the job first. Ossie was quite a character, undeniably talented but frustratingly disorganised.

By the end of the 1950s, I had gone from being little more than a messenger boy to a sound editor, but I yearned for greater things. With the film industry in the doldrums once more, my chances of becoming a fully fledged film editor seemed slim. The opportunity I had been waiting for was, however, just around the corner.

# 007s

## CHAPTER 4

### SMALL SCREEN SECRET AGENTS

In 1960, it was very difficult to make the transition from assistant editor to editor. If you were lucky enough to be offered an opportunity, you got only one chance. If you screwed up your first editing job, you would probably never be asked again. It was just the same with directing, as I would later discover to my cost – I knew many top editors who were given the chance to direct, only to return to editing when it didn't work out.

I think it gets harder the older you get. You need to be a certain age to make the move, and if you're too old, there is a risk that you can be set in your ways. Fortunately, I started editing when I was still a teenager, so I was still at a relatively tender age when I was presented with the opportunity to climb the next rung of the ladder.

I took a sideways step in order to bag my promotion. I joined the production team of a television documentary series called *Chemistry for Sixth Forms,* produced and directed by Phil Wrestler, who I had known vaguely. It was shot in the humble confines of Merton Park Studios in Kingston Road, London. Merton Park was a three-stage studio famous as the home of the Edgar Lustgarten thrillers, and was perfect for the modest demands of a low-budget educational series for children.

Merton Park's supervising editor was a legendary Polish gentleman called Sago – his real name was Vladimir, but we all used his nickname. Sago initially approached me to see if I would be interested in the assignment. I was very happy to get a credit as an editor on a documentary.

Phil Wrestler had been an editor himself and had done a lot of documentary work. The show not only gave me the opportunity to hone my editing skills, but also taught me a lot about science. One of the various guest professors taught me how to build an atomic bomb, another explained that peas would grow better if the soil they were planted in was regularly urinated on (the little green fellers like the nitrogen apparently). From a technical point of view, I learned how to produce home-made animation sequences with high-contrast stock and all kinds of stuff that one would normally send to a sub-contractor. All such sequences on *Chemistry for Sixth Forms* were done in-house because on a weekly schedule there was simply no time to get anyone else to do them.

The most valuable thing I learned during my six months on the programme, however, was not film-related at all. Phil convinced me that smoking was bad for your health, so I kicked the habit. Well, switched to cigars anyway.

On location for *Blaze of Glory*, a 1962 episode of the television series *Man of the World*. Racing driver Tony Brooks (left) featured in the episode and Harry Fine (right) was the producer.

By 1961, I had an on-screen credit as an editor under my belt and I had built up my confidence a great deal, but my next job still represented a major step forward. Harry Fine was a former actor who was cutting his teeth as a producer. He invited me to become one of two editors on his television series *Man of the World*, which starred Craig Stevens. Harry encouraged me a great deal during production of the series and before long, he was asking me to leave the cutting rooms and go on to the floor at Shepperton to film material that the main unit didn't have time to complete. I filmed a lot of insert shots, such as close-ups of fingers on triggers or hands knocking on doors. Little shots like these are very important elements in the storytelling process, but often go unnoticed by audiences. These shots didn't involve the main unit, who were often too busy to complete them, and rarely involved any members of the cast, who were generally busy with the main unit. Instead, we would hire 'hand doubles', or simply film a close-up of someone's feet as they walked across a room. Sometimes I would even do it myself.

I began doing more and more second-unit work in whatever time I spent away from the cutting room. I soon progressed to minor action scenes and would pride myself on making my shots dynamic and imaginative. I tried to place the camera at ground level so cars loomed into the lens. In fact, I became something of an expert at car run-bys. These were required during chase sequences, where you would need four or five different shots of cars zooming after each other. I was able to get all the shots I needed without moving the camera more than 180 degrees. I would find a crossroads somewhere, so I could shoot cars driving in different directions and the cameramen taught me how to change a shot quickly without moving. There was no magic involved: we would stick a leafy branch or similar dingleberry in the foreground, move the camera a couple of feet and simply shoot the car again. The foreground object fostered the illusion that the second shot was taking place on a different piece of road. I had to adapt to the economics of television film-making or I would have been fired.

I think Harry was impressed by the imaginative way I would film these generally straightforward shots and he asked me to do the same job on his next series, *The Sentimental Agent*. The series starred Carlos Thompson, who went AWOL towards the end of filming. We had to shoot the last episode without him. Harry and I later got talking about making a feature film together, but two weeks before shooting was due to begin, the money fell through and my ambitions had to be temporarily shelved. It was nice to know, however, that he had faith in me. We all need encouragement.

The turnaround in television was obviously much quicker than it had been for feature films, so I worked very long hours and learned to cut quickly. Despite the pressure, I would always try to keep a particularly good sequence in reserve and show it to a producer only when the time was right. I guess you could call this a presentation ploy, but I had my reasons. Producers were always anxious to see some edited extract from that week's episode as soon as possible. I would frequently receive phone calls, asking whether I had any sequences ready to screen. You could stall a producer for a while, but there came a time when you had to deliver at least something to keep them happy while you carried on working. I believe the worst thing an editor can do is show a producer a sequence that is rough to the point where it doesn't actually work. This doesn't do the director any favours either because more often than not he will then be unfairly criticised by the disappointed producer. A good editor will always make sure that the sequence screened for the producer is presentable, so I always tried to cut something impressive and keep it in reserve for just such an eventuality. Sometimes I'd employ a few tricks to improve it, like shoving on a piece of music from *Gone With The Wind*. Temporary measures such as these can subconsciously lend a sequence a whole new dimension. Music can influence our perception of film like nothing else, elevating the viewer to a new emotional plane.

When I started working in television, I would save what little spare time I had to spend with my family. My cinema-going habits suffered, but in late 1962 a film came along that we all made time to see. *Dr No* was a thriller based on a best-selling novel by Ian Fleming. It was a violent film, undeniably, but more importantly it possessed a style and humour that was all its own, and leading man Sean Connery, who played secret agent James Bond 007, wasn't bad at all.

*Dr No* was directed by Terence Young and edited by my old friend Peter Hunt. I'd bumped into Peter only intermittently in the previous few years, but I was delighted to see he'd done so well and absolutely fascinated by the new technique he'd employed on the James Bond film. Peter was quite an outrageous editor and I'm sure Terence was of the same mind. *Dr No* was clearly the work of people whose philosophy was 'If it's boring, cut it out'. The style of editing was consequently executed in broad strokes and had an almost comic strip feel to it. It didn't seem to matter that an actor had to go from A to B in order to reach C – *Dr No* did without B altogether and eliminated a lot of the pedestrian movement that bogged down so many films of the era. Sean Connery would be seen looking towards a door and it would cut to the corridor outside and him emerge from the doorway. It was an abbreviated style, almost impressionistic. Terence's set-ups and Peter's stylised editing did no less than usher in a new era of film-making with techniques that we now take for granted. As a young editor, I watched carefully and I was impressed.

There are some absolutely extraordinary shots in *Dr No*. Everyone's jaws opened when the Ursula Andress stepped out of the sea with unparalleled beauty and sophistication. The violence in *Dr No* was also unprecedented, at least in an 'A' certificate picture, but I think Terence got away with it because it was laced with a laconic humour. Much of the credit for this innovation must go to Sean Connery, who delivered so many of the tongue-in-cheek lines straight and allowed the humour to speak for itself.

I didn't meet Terence Young until many years after *Dr No*. He was a well-educated man and a real gentleman. I'm not sure he ever received the recognition he deserved for his pioneering work on the James Bond series, although I understand that *Thunderball*, his third and final Bond, at least brought him some significant financial rewards.

Peter Hunt told me that he attended a press screening of *Dr No* with Terence Young, and Terence was so offended by the peals of laughter ringing out from the stalls that he walked out. What he didn't understand was that the press were laughing with the film, not at it. The glowing reviews in the evening newspapers spoke for themselves. The James Bond films quickly became a phenomenon and, for the time being at least, Terence Young and Peter Hunt stayed with them.

The 1960s was the decade of the filmed television series, shot to something approaching movie quality for the benefit of American audiences. I think it's fair to say that *Dr No* kick-started a wave of spy-themed shows. In the spring of 1964, I joined the team of editors on one of the very best: *Danger Man*.

*Danger Man* was one of a number of filmed series produced by the Incorporated Television Company (ITC), the organisation headed by the enigmatic mogul Lew Grade. Lew was great at giving the public what they wanted, anticipating new trends and, crucially, striking American distribution deals. *Danger Man* actually made its debut in 1960, transmitted in 30-minute episodes. After *Dr No*, it was re-launched with a higher budget and a new series of lavish 50-minute episodes. The programme proved very popular in the States, where it was screened under the title *Secret Agent*.

The star of the show was the Irish actor Patrick McGoohan, who played special security agent John Drake. The big difference between *Danger Man* and the earlier *The Sentimental Agent* was that in Patrick McGoohan we had a superb leading actor, a very good-looking man with an assurance that you didn't often find in actors outside the US. He was a star, and I remember that many years later the James Bond producer Albert Broccoli told me that he had considered McGoohan as a potential 007, but McGoohan told him he wasn't interested. Pat had certain rules – as far as I could see, he didn't like kissing women on screen, held deep religious convictions and was devoted to his wife and family. It's probably also significant that his character, John Drake, didn't like using a gun. In short, James Bond represented a lot of things that opposed Pat's personal philosophy, so I can see why it wouldn't have appealed to him.

Pat was a compelling and inventive actor who was very good at developing scenes. You could photograph him at any angle and he was a good mover with excellent voice quality. Just like Roger Moore, who at that time was starring in the television series *The Saint*, Pat never fluffed a line. He became quite a good director as well, so he certainly knew the business.

I joined *Danger Man* as a replacement editor early in the second season while Aida Young, one of only a handful of women producers at that time, was in charge. Aida had a word with Harry Fine about the work I'd done on his series and in no time at all, I was on the floor filming inserts and second-unit shots. I was paid a little extra, but I still had to give priority to my editing responsibilities and I had to make up the time afterwards. At least I was able to delegate work to my assistants while I was away.

Shows such as *Danger Man* afforded me the chance to work with some of the great directors of the British film industry, many of whom had made the transition to television because there was such little feature film work about. On *Danger Man* I was reunited with Don Chaffey and Robert Day, and had the privilege of cutting a few episodes directed by Charles Crichton. Charlie had directed some of the best Ealing comedies, such as *Hue and Cry* and *The Titfield Thunderbolt*, and much later would close his career in fine style with *A Fish Called Wanda*. By all accounts, the decent-sized pay cheque was long overdue – he told me he was paid £50 a week

to direct *The Lavender Hill Mob*, a film that must have earned millions.

I remember editing one of Charlie's *Danger Man* episodes. He would sit by the Moviola and I would feed the film through the machine. On this particular occasion, he stopped the Moviola and sat in silence for what seemed like an eternity. I was worried he might have died (he was getting pretty old even then) so I coughed and said, 'Er…Charlie?' 'Shut up!' he growled. 'I'm thinking.'

He was very instructive and very modest. One day he said to me, 'I'm not sure I'm as good an editor as you are,' which was quite a compliment because Charles Crichton was a much better editor than I will ever be.

Halfway through the series, Aida Young left to work on a film and Sidney Cole stepped in as producer. It was a seamless transition in the head office, but the whole production was shifted from the MGM British Studios in Borehamwood to Shepperton. The final day at MGM was incredible: we had to be out by Friday night, but still had three episodes simultaneously shooting. We didn't want to carry the sets over to Shepperton, so I was on the floor shooting one unit and Pat was changing costumes and rushing from one stage to another. I had to shoot one scene in which John Drake scaled a drainpipe, but because of the time constraints it was still covered in wet paint when the cameras started rolling. I had already rehearsed the scene with Pat, and such was his enthusiasm that he shinned up this thing and got covered in black paint before I could stop him. At the end of the day, all the inserts were completed and we started shooting new episodes at Shepperton the following Monday morning. It was quite an achievement.

Cameraman/ producer John Mackie (standing, left) gave me some valuable experience behind the camera on this shoe commercial.

On location in
Black Park, near
Pinewood, for a
television
commercial in the
early 1960s.

Lee Doig and myself were the principal editors on the series and occasionally other editors were brought in to cut the odd episode. Having watched me direct inserts on the floor, Lee started to do a few inserts himself. Unlike me, however, he didn't go on to make a career out of it.

One second-season episode, a 'mistaken identity' mystery entitled *The Ubiquitous Mr Lovegrove*, was an unusual piece that I think may have anticipated Pat's masterpiece, *The Prisoner*. The episode was difficult to understand and it was left on the shelf until Sid Cole called me into his office. 'I want you to take that episode over and shoot whatever you need to make it work.' This was a great opportunity and I seized it. I devised and shot a number of new sequences and got Pat in for a few new scenes. I cut the new material into the existing film and completed the episode. Although we had a tight schedule and had to get each episode out on time, Sid was clever enough to keep a troublesome episode back and put the next one in its place. This bought us time to lick problematic episodes into shape. I didn't know it at the time, but Sid was preparing me for my next role.

While Sid set up a new series, Pat developed *The Prisoner*. The show now has a cult following all over the world and I must admit I was disappointed not to be asked to work on it. In defending one of my assistants over a financial matter, I had got into a row with the accountant on *Danger Man*; I don't know whether that counted against me when the time came to crew the new series. It's possible I wasn't asked because Sid told Pat he wanted me to carry on working with him.

Sid's new series was called *Man in a Suitcase* and was another filmed show from the ITC stable. The star was an American Method actor called

Richard Bradford who had prematurely grey hair. Richard didn't seem to believe that acting was essentially about pretending and wanted to do everything for real.

I was appointed supervising editor (another promotion!) and ran the whole post-production show. The other editors and sound editors were my responsibility. Every evening, Sid would invite me to join him and the directors in his office to discuss the day's progress and any problems we might have encountered. The drinks cabinet would be open and Sid would start pouring the whisky. When he got to Charlie Crichton, who used to like a drop, they used to wrestle with the bottle as a joke, which we all enjoyed. 'Who supplies all this drink?' I asked Sid one evening. 'Well,' he replied, 'the studio owns the cabinet and Lew Grade owns the Scotch.'

Aside from the free drink at ITC's expense, the evening get-togethers were a good idea because I got to know the directors very well and came to understand their problems. At the end of one of these evenings, I plucked up my courage and asked, 'Sidney, what about giving me a chance to direct one of these episodes?' He chuckled and replied, 'Do you really want to join the other 360 out-of-work directors on my books?' I said I was prepared to take the risk and he said, 'We'll see.'

The last episode of our run was a particularly troublesome script entitled *Somebody Loses, Somebody...Wins?* Sidney offered me the chance to direct it and I eagerly accepted. The director of photography on the episode was a man called Lionel Banes, who had previously been a stills cameraman at Ealing. Lionel had been a highly respected stills man, but he didn't seem to like moving a film camera, which caused me a lot of problems. It seemed that every time I devised a shot my efforts would be met with a discouraging 'You can't put the camera there, sonny.' I found that very frustrating, as this was my first assignment and I needed all the help I could get. He wasn't the fastest cameraman in the world either, and I started getting behind schedule on what was an action-packed episode. One sequence, a car chase filmed in Black Park near Pinewood Studios, proved particularly problematic when our contemporary cars got mixed up with a horse chase being filmed for a nearby production of *Robin Hood.*

Philip Madoc and Jacqueline Pearce both appeared in that episode, and they were good actors who did a good job for me, but I felt I had been allocated a director of photography who seemed preoccupied with doing *The Times* crossword while I was getting behind. We were just not on the same wavelength. I learned a particularly difficult lesson on that show.

I cut the episode myself and tried to make the best of it, but there was no escaping the fact that I'd taken a couple of days too long and this would seriously jeopardise my chances of being asked to direct another show.

I walked away from *Man in a Suitcase* in a depressed state. For the first time in my career, I felt I had been inadequate. I had been fine supervising small units, but the problems I'd encountered running the circus of a whole episode had proved that I wasn't quite ready. Looking back on that time in my life, I can see that things like this probably happen to us all and the experience probably did me some good in the long run.

By 1968, I had dragged myself up by my boot laces and still hoped to get another directing assignment. But I had no agent and was still being nagged by feelings of self-doubt. I took some time off and was then offered

Avco Embassy
a company
on its way to
the moon

# "BABY LOVE" IS COMING!

a fill-in job, re-recording the dialogue for the film *Buono Sera, Mrs Campbell*. Melvin Frank was the director, and the editor was Bill Butler, whom funnily enough I had just employed on *Man in a Suitcase*. He was my boss now, but that's the way it goes. I did a good job with the dialogue and they were happy. It was interesting to watch how Melvin experimented with humour on the screen and to study his timing.

After eight years working in television, I was back in movies, but unfortunately right back to doing sound editing. Salvation came from the producer Michael Klinger, whom I had known for some time. Michael was doing a film called *Baby Love* at Twickenham Studios and he was keen for me to edit it for him. The film was directed and co-written by Alastair Reid, who was a laid-back Scot. We became good friends. The star of the film was a girl called Linda Hayden. She was playing a Liverpudlian Lolita-type called Luci, and I remember we took a publicity photograph of her birth certificate to prove she was 15. Keith Barron played the doctor who adopted Luci after her mother committed suicide. Luci's mother was played by the irrepressible Diana Dors, whom I hadn't seen since the filming of *Passport to Shame* at Nettlefolds over 10 years before. I loved Diana and we had a happy reunion.

On the second day of location shooting in Southall, I felt so ill I couldn't get out of bed. I managed to drag myself to see a doctor, who informed me I had German measles and then insisted I left by the back door to avoid contact with any of the pregnant women waiting in the front of the surgery. I had to spend two weeks lying in bed in a darkened room, isolated from everyone else. I called Michael and explained the situation. 'I can quite understand it if you want to replace me,' I said, 'because I'm sure your schedule can't afford me to be away for the first two weeks.' Michael was lovely about it and said, 'You get better, John. We'll wait for you.'

I turned up for work two weeks later to be confronted by a mountain of film and an assistant on the verge of a nervous breakdown. I started cutting the film and within a week I was back up-to-date again. Michael was a shrewd guy: the film was a reasonable success and it made money.

At the end of 1968, I was still looking for a way to kick-start my career, and was still open to offers of sound editing in order to keep going. I got a call from a sound editor called Bill Creed, who was working with director Peter Collinson on a film called *The Italian Job*. I knew Peter socially through Michael Klinger and had greatly admired a little-seen horror film he'd directed called *The Penthouse*. Some people considered it a little difficult to stomach and it was certainly a disturbing piece of work, but I could tell that Peter had real talent. *The Italian Job*'s editor John Trumper – with whom I had worked at Group 3 in Beaconsfield – asked me if I would cut the riotous traffic jam sequence, which is one of the most memorable sequences in a film that is now regarded as one of the classic caper movies. Funnily enough, the sequence had been directed by none other than Phil Wrestler. John didn't have the time to deal with that section, which I remember was shot on 16mm. Later on, John had to supervise some dialogue replacement with the Italian artists, but he wasn't free to make the trip, so the producer, Michael Deeley, asked me if I was interested in doing it. Three days before Christmas, I flew out to Rome and was met by a driver who handed me a packet of money and took me to the

Linda Hayden played the provocative teenager Luci in *Baby Love*.

best hotel in town. I lived the life of Riley in this luxurious suite, did the job and came back to England on Christmas Eve.

At the beginning of 1969, I started dubbing the film and I could tell even then that *The Italian Job* was going to be terrific. Two days before the end of the session, the phone rang in the dubbing theatre. 'Hello John, it's Peter Hunt,' came a voice I hadn't heard for three or four years. 'I'm calling from the Bond set at Pinewood. I'm on 'A' Stage – can you come over?'

Peter Collinson picked up on what was happening straightaway. 'Great!' he enthused. 'You've got a job on the new Bond movie!' Peter gave me permission to go to Pinewood and then, to my horror, picked up the phone and rang the Bond producer Harry Saltzman and gave him a glowing recommendation of my talents.

I knew that having edited *Dr No*, *From Russia With Love*, *Goldfinger*, *Thunderball* and *You Only Live Twice*, Peter Hunt had been promoted. Producers Harry Saltzman and Albert Broccoli had given him the chance to direct the next production – *On Her Majesty's Secret Service*.

*Dr No* had impressed me enormously and I had seen all the subsequent films in the series. I felt that *From Russia With Love* was a big improvement on the first film. Red Grant, the Russian assassin played by Robert Shaw, was bloody good and brought out the best in Sean Connery as well.

The next film, *Goldfinger*, remains a classic. The novel it was based on was always my favourite Bond book – every page seems to come alive with fresh ideas. *Goldfinger* was directed by Guy Hamilton, who had struck me as a bit of cold fish during my limited experience of him. He seemed shy and a little reserved, but he brought something special out of *Goldfinger*. He shot it beautifully and got everything right. It's a wonderful picture. I first saw *Goldfinger* when it was released in 1964 and I remember being astonished that they had managed to top *From Russia With Love*, which was superb. The series was getting better and better.

Terence Young returned to direct the fourth film, *Thunderball*, and I felt he came a bit of cropper with the extensive underwater scenes that form the climax of the movie. They were breaking new ground by setting so much of the important action underwater, and I don't think Terence realised until too late that everything would slow down to such a degree. The film would have run the risk of grinding to a virtual standstill had it not been for some damage limitation in the cutting rooms. Peter Hunt speeded up a lot of the underwater action by editing a lot of the sequences at double speed, removing alternate frames. The technique works as long as you restrict yourself to cutting footage depicting objects that travel without any reciprocal movement. For example, if you wanted a car to appear to move at double speed then you would simply cut out every other frame. You have to be careful with people: if you frame-cut footage of someone running, you end up making them look like Charlie Chaplin. You also have to be careful when attempting to frame-cut footage that has been undercranked (filmed with fewer than the usual frames per second to give the illusion of greater speed) to begin with. Hindsight is a wonderful thing and I can see that Peter did what he could to keep *Thunderball* moving. Whenever I shoot underwater sequences, I'm very conscious of the potential pitfalls and I try to keep them brief.

The next film, *You Only Live Twice*, was directed by my old chum Lewis Gilbert. Before shooting, Peter Hunt discussed his ongoing commitment to the Bond films with Harry and Albert, and decided that he wouldn't edit the new picture. Editing on *You Only Live Twice* began under the supervision of Thelma Connell, Lewis's regular collaborator. Harry and Albert sent Peter on a round-the-world trip as a thank you for all his hard work over the years, and he wound up in Tokyo, where *You Only Live Twice* was being shot. It soon transpired that Peter was back on board as editor and Thelma left the picture. Peter also directed the second unit. With Lewis directing and Peter editing, the film had to be good. They were a great combination because I think they both understood that the film had to be presented in the Bond style, which was already well developed by that time. Bond films are unorthodox because you're selling things all the time: they're not like other films where you can sometimes afford to use a cut which might not really grab you. The golden rule with Bond films is never to show anything unless it's going to hit the audience right between the eyes. Don't ever show anything you have to apologise for. In short, I think they needed Peter, and I think Lewis had no choice but to admit it. Thelma went on to cut other films for Lewis and her talent is undisputed. It's just that Bond films require something highly specialised.

When I arrived at Pinewood, Peter was in the middle of shooting a scene. He came over to me with the shooting script, opened it up at a particular point and handed it to me. 'Read that,' he said, and went back to filming the scene. I scanned the pages, which described a knife-edge bobsleigh-run pursuit between James Bond and his arch-rival Ernst Blofeld. When Peter finished the scene, he came back to where I was standing and asked me what I thought. 'I love it,' I replied, still slightly mystified. 'Good,' said Peter. 'It's the most important action sequence in the film. I've been watching your career over the years and I want to make you a director.'

At no point over the previous six years had I dreamed that any of the James Bond films would come my way and I felt honoured to have been approached to join the crew of *On Her Majesty's Secret Service*. This was a crucial film for Harry and Albert: Sean Connery had resigned after *You Only Live Twice* and an Australian model called George Lazenby was stepping into the role. Peter Hunt was a first-time director, charged with the responsibility of bringing in a picture starring a first-time actor. There was a lot at stake.

Peter offered me a job on the second unit there and then, but explained that my appointment would be subject to the approval of Albert, who everyone affectionately referred to as 'Cubby', and Harry.

This was Thursday. On Monday I was flying first class to Switzerland, on my way to a new life.

# 007™

# CHAPTER 5

## AN AVALANCHE OF ACTION

The Bond crew had been shooting *On Her Majesty's Secret Service* in Switzerland since October 1968, but the mildest winter in over 40 years had caused enormous problems. By the time I arrived in the last week of February 1969, Peter told me that the second unit had got only 10 seconds of workable footage in the can. Luckily, it had finally started snowing and we had to make the most of it as soon as possible.

After a day-long journey, I arrived at the Palace Hotel in Mürren, an out-of-season resort in the shadow of the 10,000-foot-high Schilthorn in the Bernese Oberland. The meagre population seemed to share only six surnames and I don't think they knew what hit them when 120 film-makers descended on the place.

The Palace Hotel was the home of the Katmandu Ski Club, who had originated downhill skiing, and there was an array of silver cups in glass cases. The place had been used as a prison for captured British airmen who had parachuted into Switzerland or crashed there during the war. Gazing at the luxurious surroundings, I concluded that these POWs must have had the time of their lives.

I arrived at about 10pm and I was checking in when an electrician from Pinewood recognised me. 'Where are you going now?' he asked. 'Bed,' I replied. 'I'm pooped.' He instead suggested I accompany him to The Inferno, a nightclub in the basement. I somewhat reluctantly allowed myself to be persuaded and said I'd go for five minutes. The scene that greeted me downstairs was amazing, but in retrospect maybe I should have had an early night. My chum from Pinewood introduced me to his local girlfriend. 'This is Blacky,' he told me. 'I'm teaching her English,' he added with a wink. I turned to shake her hand. 'How-do-you-f**king-do?' she said.

In the morning, it was time to start work. Peter Hunt was under a lot of pressure: the second unit's schedule was slipping and I was initially employed purely to claw back some of the lost time by shooting the bobsleigh-run sequence. A new two-mile track had been specially constructed by Franz Capose, a lively septuagenarian who trained the Swiss bobsleigh team. Franz built the new track near Mürren on the site of an old track that had closed in 1937 after a series of fatal accidents. Franz's team retained some of the existing elements of the old track and reinforced

Heinz Lau is at the controls as James Bond (George Lazenby) pursues Blofeld in the bob-run.

Director Peter
Hunt and actress
Ilse Steppat (who
played Irma Bunt)
on location in
Switzerland for *On
Her Majesty's
Secret Service.*

it with specially imported blocks of ice. I was keen to map out the track so that I could begin planning camera positions for the complicated sequence we were about to shoot. To get a feel for it, we were sliding our way along the track when suddenly a kid on a wooden sledge came out of nowhere and collided with us. We were sent flying. The kid landed in a heap and we made sure he was OK, but I had already learned lesson number one. I insisted on very strict security from thereon – the last thing I wanted was a four-man bob colliding with an errant child at high speed.

As the day progressed, I could see another problem looming: by midday the sun was beating down and Franz pointed out that the ice on the corners of the track was beginning to melt. We had to cover those corners up, so Franz and his Italian team made provision for sun sails to be placed at strategic points to prevent any structural weakness that could cause an accident. G-force can multiply the weight of a bob by three or four times when it's travelling at high speed and we didn't want any of the corners giving way under the pressure.

I was working with an almost entirely foreign crew largely comprised of Swiss, Germans and Italians. One thing they had in common was that they were all skiers and their familiarity with the mountain was a real advantage. Among the team were Alex Barbey, a cameraman from Basel

who was worth his weight in gold, and a fantastic semi-professional cameraman/director called Willy Bogner. Willy's father (Willy senior) owned a hugely successful textile business and was famous for manufacturing Bogner Ski Clothes. Willy junior had been an Olympic skier and had made his own films in Germany. I could tell he operated at the level of a talented amateur, but I was nevertheless impressed with his rig: he used an Arri camera mounted in a lightweight frame with large hand grips and an adapted Hasselblad viewfinder. I was convinced that Willy would be as useful with his camera as he was with a pair of skis. He spoke perfect English too, so there was no communication problem.

I suspected that some of the British cameramen held Willy's film-making abilities in low regard; this was later confirmed to me one day in the makeshift theatre at the railway station in Mürren. One of the crew-members turned to me and whispered in my ear that he thought Willy's footage was an amateurish load of rubbish and I wouldn't be able to use a single foot of it. What this guy didn't know was that I thought Willy's footage was some of the most exciting stuff I'd ever seen, but it just goes to show how some people can become entrenched in a narrow outlook. I recognised Willy as someone who was brilliantly talented, but was sometimes dismissed or not even recognised because he was a one-man

Talented skier and cameraman Willy Bogner films a sledge-bound Diana Rigg.

band relying on little more than a single camera and a pair of skis. He would find a good position, rely on God for the lighting and come up with something innovative. Around 80% of it would probably be unusable, but the remaining 20% would be fantastic. Everyone responds to encouragement and Willy had not really been encouraged until I arrived.

Morale seemed to be lagging with the British unit and this was something I put down to what I now call 'mountain sickness'. This had set in because the crew had been frustrated by the mild weather and unable to get any work done, day after day and week after week. This enforced inactivity, combined with mounting studio pressure, had left everybody a little demoralised.

Having met the team and got to grips with the track, we separated from Anthony Squire, the existing second-unit director, and concentrated on completing the sequence ourselves using doubles for George Lazenby and Telly Savalas, who was playing Blofeld. Anthony Squire went off to shoot the stock car sequence that Bond and his wife-to-be Tracy become embroiled in, while Peter left to shoot the ice-rink sequence in a specially adapted car park in nearby Grindelwald.

The next morning, I held a production meeting with all my crew. The German production manager Hubert Froelich, who had found the film's major locations the previous year, was a key man because he was an expert on the area and was multilingual. With Hubert's help, we devised a system whereby a helicopter was used to hoist the bobs back to the top of the track after they'd completed their journey. A world championship bob team would probably only complete one run in a day. Thanks to our friendly helicopter pilot Bruno Bagnaud we could complete eight or nine. During our longest day on the bob-run, we shot for two-and-a-half hours continuously, filming 18 separate runs. We would shoot from around 9am to about 2pm, when Franz would usually call a halt to proceedings on safety grounds.

Sometimes we rehearsed the doubles with two or three bobs on the track at the same time. This was extremely dangerous, but I needed over-the-shoulder shots of Blofeld turning backwards and firing at Bond, so I really had no choice. We had a couple of accidents because the rear bob carrying the camera was much heavier than the one in front and tended to catch up with it. I discussed the problem of colliding bobs with Willy Bogner, who came up with the astonishing suggestion that he actually ski inside the track behind the bobs, filming the action with a hand-held camera. I was concerned about how he'd get out of the bob-run when he'd finished filming, so he built himself a little exit by cutting a ramp into the side of the track, just big enough for him to steer his skis up. We practised the plan, and even though Willy shot out of the side of the track at about 50 mph, he was still able to bring himself to a safe stop. The next problem was that Willy was obviously much lighter than the two bobs ahead of him, so had great difficulty in keeping up with them. We solved this by tying him to the back of the bob with a 20-foot length of cable that could be quickly released by knocking out a stick jammed into his belt. He thought this was a good idea and it worked perfectly. One bonus was that we could exactly measure the distance between Willy and the bob because he was in effect being towed by it, so he could keep his focus perfect. The cable also enabled him to get over-the-shoulder shots as well. From that point on, we stopped using the camera bob and instead used Willy skiing inside the track. Willy was a brilliant skier and only once got into trouble, dropping the camera and smashing the lens. There was a short hiatus while we waited for a new one to arrive from England.

The shots where Bond had to be seen firing at Blofeld also caused problems: Bond's Walther PPK never seemed to work properly, but I didn't let minor technical difficulties like this get in the way. I instructed the doubles to carry on and not to bang the weapons on the side of the bobs. Post-production sound effects completed the illusion that the guns were actually firing.

Working from storyboards that had already been prepared, I started to film the long and complicated sequence. The weather was bad on the first day of my schedule, so we erected a tent over the track and started filming insert shots inside it. Things like close-ups of the bobs' steering mechanisms and bullets ricocheting could be filmed regardless of weather conditions. We took Sun Guns, which are portable battery-operated lights, and used them for insert shots of the blades cutting the ice. The illusion of movement was completed by sweeping snow through with a broom and jiggling the camera. Shots like this were useful and kept the crew busy – I didn't want to risk another bout of mountain sickness by holing them up in the hotel, waiting for the weather to improve. The weather picked up after that, so while the sun shone I filmed all the wide shots.

It was only much later that I discovered the reaction my rushes were receiving back at Pinewood. When the first day's work came up on screen Cubby Broccoli – who I had yet to meet – watched intently. 'What a waste of time,' said someone, who was clearly expecting more than close-ups of hands and the odd ricochet. 'We could have filmed all this in the studio.' Apparently Cubby replied, 'At least this guy is giving me some rushes to watch. They've been out there three months and I've seen next to nothing.'

Harry Saltzman was in Switzerland while Cubby was at Pinewood. In those days, the two would alternate major responsibilities from film to film. *On Her Majesty's Secret Service* was Harry's picture and as such, he was the man on location. I had only a brief meeting with him when I was in Switzerland and I don't think he really knew who I was. My memory of him is as quite a stern man, although people have since told me that he wasn't like that at all.

I carried on working, unaware that my early efforts had found favour at the Pinewood viewing theatre. We got some great shots of the ice walls rushing past and I discovered that when Joe Powell, one of the British stuntmen, scraped the side of his helmeted head against the rushing ice, it had a rather interesting effect. By the time we'd dubbed the shots with an appropriate sound effect, we had another little innovation: the sound editors came up with something that sounded like rattling coconuts and it worked very well. Rydal Love was one of the sound editors and he used a piece of plastic and a scrubbing brush to simulate the sound of the bobsleigh blades scraping the ice. This was another important element of the sequence. The bobsleighs produced an awful lot of extraneous noise that sounded like rumbling, which is not really what we wanted. The skids beneath the bobsleighs were very sharp and dangerous, so we asked

The camera was
fitted to a turnover
mount in order to
accentuate the
angles while
filming in the
bob-run.

the editors to create sounds that suggested razor blades scraping the ice.

Eddie Stacey, another British stuntman, had an accident in one scene and fell off the bob, but clung on the back and was dragged along behind it. A Swiss guy called Heinz Lau doubled for James Bond in a yellow-and-black chequered bob and, although he was a bobsleigh champion, he also suffered an accident. He was firing his gun, lost control of the steering and went up the wall of a steep curve. He was thrown out of the bob, but wasn't hurt. Both incidents looked so spectacular that we used the footage from both in the film.

At one point, Heinz and Robert Zimmerman, who was doubling for Blofeld in a red-and-white bob, had to have a punch-up in the same bob. Like Heinz, Robert was no novice: he was a brake-man for the Swiss national bobsleigh team and an Olympic skier. It was difficult for them to make the fight look convincing and still keep control of a bob moving at over 60 mph, and unfortunately they had an accident trying. The bob turned over and they both got dragged along, trapped between it and the ice wall. We could see sparks flying, but they were tough guys and Heinz got up without a scratch. Robert was not so lucky and had to go to hospital to receive some stitches on the inside of his mouth. He was back at work two hours later, albeit with a rather swollen face. Both of them gave their consent to use the shot in the film and I hastily revised the script to incorporate it.

Willy Bogner finally convinced me he was a man without fear when he said, 'John, it's quite safe for me to stand in the track when the bob comes round the corner because the centrifugal force will send it to the outside of the curve. I can stand on the inside and get really close to the action.' It seemed too dangerous to even consider, but Willy knew what he was doing and the more I thought about what he said, the more I could see that he was making perfect sense. Willy was inside Stone Curve, the steepest curve on the track, when Heinz and Robert's accident happened. Willy got some great shots of the action.

Another of our cameramen was Johnny Jordan, who was absolutely excellent. Johnny specialised in aerial photography and lost his leg during the filming of *You Only Live Twice* in Japan in 1966. During the sequence in which Bond is being pursued in the 'Little Nellie' auto-gyro, Johnny was hanging from his Alouette helicopter filming the action. One of the Hillier helicopters chasing Bond got a bit too close to Johnny's Alouette and practically severed his dangling leg. Johnny was such a brave man that he filmed his own leg hanging by a thread before he passed out and was taken to hospital. The leg was eventually amputated back in London.

Johnny suggested a novel way he could come in useful shooting the bob-run action. He said that by taking off his artificial leg he would be able to squeeze into one of the bobs in front of Heinz, while Robert operated the brake behind them. I agreed to let him give it a go and he filmed much of the footage that was used as front projection plates for the actors' close-ups we would shoot at Pinewood. Johnny worked with our camera mechanic Ted Warringham to produce a turnover mount which we fixed to the front of his camera bob. The Swiss are wonderful engineers and the mount was constructed in the local blacksmith's shop. Two men worked through the night for our benefit, milling special rings and fitting them to our camera. Johnny used the mount to get some great angles as his bob raced around the track at speeds of up to 70 mph.

Johnny worked in partnership with pilot John Crudson and together they developed a circular harness that could be suspended from the bottom of a helicopter. It was known as the parachute rig. Johnny was suspended below the helicopter, which allowed him to film spectacular aerial shots without the blades creeping into shot. Johnny would sometimes hang as much as 50 feet beneath John's helicopter, and the pendulous effect of the harness could sometimes make taking off rather difficult. Johnny got some great overhead shots of the bob-run, but I was so short of time that I wasn't able to give him exclusive access. While he was filming, I asked the ground-based camera crews to wear white boiler suits and hide behind portable fir trees so they wouldn't show up on Johnny's footage. Later on, Johnny got some wonderful shots of the skiers in high glacial areas.

All the experts on the crew were leaders, not followers, and all of them were individuals with very high personal standards. Johnny was a perfectionist with a great love of film, and he would do anything to be in the right place to get his shot, even putting his own life at risk. Willy was the same, always breaking barriers in his attempt to get more and more realistic footage. He could ski backwards as well as forwards and crash

This stunning shot of Blofeld's skiers was taken by Willy Bogner.

through branches and all manner of obstacles to get what we needed. I never forgot what Willy could do and what a great asset he was. You occasionally had to read the riot act to these guys because they could get carried away and you had to remind them to stick to the script. Overall, however, there is nothing more stimulating than working with experts.

I first met Cubby while we were in the midst of shooting the bob-run material. He introduced himself to me and immediately said: 'I'd like to have a ride on the bob-run.' I soon realised he was serious and began to fill with dread – this would be the first run of the day, and they were always the fastest. We prepared a four-man bob for our producer – Heinz was in the driving seat and Robert operated the brake at the back. Cubby was a big man, and occupied the two seats in the middle. They set off down the track and I said a silent prayer in the hope everything would be OK. They got to the other end safely, following a hair-raising trip conducted at some 60 mph; Cubby never forgot the experience. As I got to know Cubby better, I learned that the request was typical of the man – he liked to experience what the crews were doing and become a part of it with them. It did wonders for crew's morale, to have Cubby sharing the risks they were taking. Cubby and Harry certainly complemented each other: Cubby was the affable one and Harry played the hard man. One was the father figure and one cracked the whip.

The sun suddenly started to shine with a vengeance and we had to rely on the sun sails once more to keep the ice on the bends intact. I made the decision to shoot the rest of the sequence with the sails still up, figuring that they would be very difficult to spot on film after some creative editing. Nobody would know which bend was which on the track and by cutting around the bends with the sails, I was able to make the track look twice as long. Ultimately, however, the decision to shoot with the sails still up was forced on me by the time factor: it might have taken an hour to get the sails down, by which time the corners would have been rendered dangerous by melting ice.

Overnight, trucks delivered more ice blocks from Bern, which we used to bolster the track. In the morning, Franz Capose made his usual daily inspection using his own little sledge. Franz was something of his own man and didn't communicate with the rest of us as much as he should have done. He didn't even carry a radio. I received a report that the track was clear and we did our first two-man run of the morning. Heinz Lau was driving, doubling for James Bond as usual. Lau came around a corner, and suddenly there was Franz in the middle of the track in his child's sledge. There was a camera on Heinz's bob, and you could see the look of horror on Franz's face as the collision loomed and his life flashed before him. Heinz reacted quickly and steered his bob up on to the side of the track, but he was moving extremely fast and he couldn't avoid striking Franz a glancing blow with the rear of the bob as he passed. We called for a helicopter and had Franz airlifted to hospital, where it was discovered he had sustained a badly bruised shoulder. This was probably the worst accident we had, but Heinz's quick-thinking saved us from something potentially tragic.

When I went to see Franz in hospital his shoulder seemed to concern him less than the loss of his favourite hat, which had been knocked off during the collision. We later found it at the top of a tree.

One particularly memorable sequence saw Blofeld lob a hand grenade behind him shortly after turning a bend on the track. James Bond follows him round the curve, spots the grenade on the track and jumps out of the run before the hand grenade detonates beneath his now-vacant bob. The first thing we had to do was construct a wall of snow inside the track to prevent the vacant bob running out control and getting damaged or damaging something else. Red markers were painted on the side of the ice wall to give Heinz an indication of exactly when to jump and we rigged remote-controlled charges to explode underneath the bob as soon as he was clear. The bob was ready to go at the start of the run when someone pointed out to me that the grenade wasn't showing up too well. Alex Barbey positioned a reflector to highlight the grenade on the track and I told Heinz to start his run.

As the sinister scraping sound of his bob approached, the two cameras filming the scene started rolling. Heinz came round the corner, searching for the red marks on the side of the wall. He was dazzled by the reflector, however, so couldn't tell when to jump. I had my finger on the detonator, ready to blow up the bob, but I could tell Heinz had missed his jump-off point. I made a split-second decision and pressed the button anyway. Heinz was blown out of the run. We rushed over to him, and to my great relief he

George Lazenby was enthusiastic and helpful during the short time he spent with my second-unit crew.

was fine. It was at that point I learned lesson number two: if you change anything on a stunt after you've briefed the stuntman, you have to call him back and tell him exactly what you've done, no matter how seemingly insignificant that change may be.

Fortunately, Heinz was fine and even told me he was glad I detonated the charge – if I hadn't, he would probably have gone 20 yards further and straight into the wall of ice.

The last stunt on my shot-list was the one in which James Bond, having left Blofeld dangling by the neck from an overhanging tree, leaves the track in his runaway bob. This was the most dangerous manoeuvre we attempted and we had three attempts at filming the sequence. Each time I used three cameras to capture it: two mounted on tripods and one hand-held camera operated by Willy.

Heinz was a professional bobsleigher, not a stunt man, but the stunt could be performed only by someone who was an expert at driving a bob. Heinz had an attack of nerves before the first attempt was due to begin. 'It doesn't feel right this morning,' he told me. 'I don't want to go through with it.' I respected the way he felt. The second morning he came to me and said, 'I had a few drinks last night, John, and I don't feel quite right.' When the third time came around, I told him that the weather was good and we really had to go through with it. It took two takes to get it, but Heinz manoeuvred the bob off the track at just the right moment (with a bit of help from an out-of-shot Robert) and gave us a great shot that Willy captured when he landed at his feet. We later cut in the shot of George Lazenby being attended by the St Bernard dog.

Up until this point, I had been working exclusively with doubles. The filming of the scene with Bond and the brandy-administering dog was the first time I met George Lazenby. We were slightly delayed when this huge dog and his handler disappeared into some sort of crevasse as they were making their way towards us. We managed to dig them out of this hole, but the handler was badly scratched by the dog, who had been trying to swim his way out. By the time we patched him up and got ready to shoot the scene, the light was fading fast. The sun went behind the mountain at about 4pm, so I decided to film the scene on the other side of the mountain and gain the benefit of another hour's sunlight. We all got into helicopters – including the dog – and flew around the mountain. I briefed George while we were on board. 'We'll probably only get one shot at this,' I told him, 'and we don't know what this dog is going to do. It says in the script that he rolls on his back and throws his paws in the air, like dogs do in the snow, but you have to be prepared to improvise in case he doesn't.'

We ran through his line – 'Never mind that, go and get the brandy!' – and we were ready to go. We touched down, set up the shot and the handler released the dog. He came trotting in, laid on his back in front of George and started pawing him. George delivered the line and Take One worked perfectly. I did the reverse shot on George without the dog and we were home and dry.

Peter arranged for me to shoot some skiing sequences with George and his co-star Diana Rigg near Grindelwald. The area was ideal because it got sunlight all day long. I spent the whole day with George and Diana filming Bond and Tracy skiing.

We had a lot of fun and the crew were crazy about Diana, who was a big star in England and America after her recent portrayal of Emma Peel in *The Avengers* television series. George, on the other hand, was not an actor and didn't pretend he was. He was a good-looking guy who had been a very successful male model, most notably advertising Big Fry chocolate. I'm aware of the controversy surrounding much of the filming of *OHMSS*, but I can only speak as I found – George had a nice personality and he was willing to try anything. He was always fine with me; we were an action crew and I think he enjoyed hanging out with us.

I think George's success in his previous career hung over him a little while he was shooting *OHMSS* and there were times when I got the impression that Diana was beginning to lose respect for him. She probably helped him a huge amount, but I don't think the feeling was great between them. Diana was never less than professional, however, and if there was a problem she just carried on as usual.

The insurance company insisted that our lead actors didn't actually ski during the production of the film (this was not a purely philanthropic request – any injuries would have had costly implications for the already strained schedule), so we constructed a simple sledge for George and Diana to kneel on. I'm not actually sure that George could have skied even if he had been allowed. I remember him trying it once, which made me very apprehensive because in certain respects he seemed undisciplined.

The sledge was pulled along and Willy Bogner followed on his trademark skis, which were specially adapted to have points at both ends. Expert skiers swooped around George and Diana out of shot, throwing up snow in the air to make it look more realistic. Willy filmed George and

I look on (far left)
as Willy Bogner
(far right) lines up
a shot with Diana
Rigg. Willy is
using his
customised skis,
curved upwards at
both ends.

Diana from the waist up, using his hand-held camera, and the results were wonderful. We used doubles for the long shots of Bond and Tracy skiing, so I had to adopt what I called a 'goggles up–goggles down' approach when I filmed George and Diana's close-ups. There was no point using the principals unless we could recognise them, so while the doubles were instructed to keep their goggles on, I began George and Diana's shots by asking them to lift their goggles over their eyes.

We had a great time and finished the day by breaking open one of a local farmer's sheds to discover a huge horn-sled inside. I think it was Heinz who put Diana on the horn-sled and organised a race between this and a couple of other sledges. While we raced down the mountain, Diana's suitcase, which contained a bottle of champagne, raced a good 20 yards ahead of us. The champagne probably had a few more bubbles by the time it reached the bottom. Before long, the irate farmer started pursuing us and I jumped on Willy's back for the journey down the mountain. Feeling a little sea-sick, I abandoned ship and made the rest of the journey riding on the back of Willy's skis, which was much more comfortable. I was reunited with the crew at Alpenrihe, where I spotted the farmer getting very drunk on the 60 francs compensation Heinz had paid him for writing off his horn-sled.

While I was still filming the bobsleigh-run sequence, Peter Hunt asked me to stand-by to shoot the sequence in which Bond and Tracy's escape from Blofeld is curtailed when they are engulfed in an avalanche. As I would discover over and over again, nothing was too much trouble where James Bond was concerned: the Swiss Army had planted explosive charges

A posed publicity
shot of George
Lazenby, who was
not permitted to
ski during
production of the
film.

in a hillside the previous summer. Peter had been waiting for the call to say that weather conditions were right to detonate the charges and trigger the ensuing avalanche. The 'right time' had to be very carefully judged: it would be when there was fresh snow on top of old snow, followed by two or three days of hot weather. This would have the effect of melting the snow on the surface, allowing water to run between the two layers and lubricate the top layer. The weight of the weakened snow would be tremendous, and we were looking forward to some spectacular results.

An old colleague called Les Hillman was in charge of this very special, special effect and deployed strong wires across the slope due to be engulfed. He then planned to slide three dummy skiers just ahead of the rapidly piling snow to a point where we would cut to human doubles trying to ski away. A special camera was due to be placed in the path of the oncoming snow, to be activated by remote control as soon as the charges were detonated.

One Sunday I had a day off and accompanied Les to look at the rig he'd had constructed for the tin skiers. 'I'm a bit worried about this,' I told him. 'Have you tested it?' He told me he had, but he recommended we did a rehearsal so we could prepare the five camera positions, ready to spring into action when we received the call from the Swiss Army. We had asked for 24 hours' notice before the charges were blown, but we were prepared for as little as six. We spent a whole morning rehearsing the sequence with the camera crews and I gave them instructions based on the points I anticipated the avalanche would have reached at various given times. When we were happy with the cameras, I gave Les the instruction to release the dummy skiers. He let them go and they went rushing down the wire. About 20 yards later, two of them fell off the wire and the other one accelerated off on its own. I went back to shooting the bobsleigh-run sequence and tried to figure out a way to keep these skiers upright.

A little while later, when I was working on the bobsleigh-run, I heard a deep rumble in the distance. I received a message with the bad news that the avalanche had inconsiderately triggered itself, leaving the hillside bare. To be honest, I had mixed feelings about this setback: the figures sliding down the wire clearly hadn't worked and Alex told me the remote avalanche camera had a habit of being activated by approaching cable cars. None of this had exactly filled me with confidence. Peter accepted the situation and asked me if I'd be prepared to come back and shoot the sequence in May, by which time more snow would have settled.

Peter encouraged me to film insert shots for the avalanche when conditions were bad, just as he had endorsed my decision to make the most of the bobsleigh-run when we were unable to film wide shots. We got doubles for Bond and Tracy and tumbled them down hillsides, throwing snow over them as they went. On one occasion, we used the rotating blades of a hovering helicopter to whip up showers of snow that rained down on the doubles while they pretended to have been toppled by the avalanche.

To simulate a tumbling motion, we used Johnny Jordan's turnover mount. By filming the doubles with this spinning camera, I was able to give the impression that torrents of snow had sent Bond and Tracy rolling head-over-heels. I was later able to perfect the shots with George and Diana, who were both great sports.

While Bond and Tracy are being pursued down the mountain, one of Blofeld's guards falls into a snowplough. The machine grinds him up and spits him out in a shower of entrails and blood-stained snow. In the script, the snowplough was originally being pulled by a train and the hapless assassin was supposed to fall beneath its wheels. I made a number of reconnaissance trips in an attempt to find a suitable location, including one particular trip to Andermatt, riding on the footplate of a train. We stopped just before a bridge which I was intrigued to notice had been swung to one side of a valley to allow snow and debris to fall down without damaging it. The location was appealing, but somehow we couldn't make it work. Hubert Froelich found the snowplough we ultimately used, the biggest one in Switzerland. The day before we filmed that scene in the Sustan Pass, we cleared a section of road and parked the snowplough in an adjacent tunnel so that it wouldn't be affected by any overnight slides or avalanches. We placed an Italian crew-member on watch to alert us to incoming slides – absolutely silent onslaughts of heavy, slushy snow that was like wet cement. We were working down the bottom of a hole when the look-out started waving frantically above us. We all clambered out of the hole in time to see a slide completely cover the snowplough. The engine was still running, and all we could see was the exhaust poking out of this huge pile of slush. We had to dig the machine out before we could continue. Luckily, Alex had retrieved his camera just in time, but the batteries had been covered.

We let some red dye soak into some ice and then moved the plough over

it to get the shot of the red snow shooting into the air. My wife Gina came up with the line 'He had a lot of guts!', which a smirking Bond says after Blofeld's henchman gets swallowed up and spat out to gory effect.

I dressed Diana Rigg in snow for the shots showing the aftermath of the avalanche.

We moved back to Mürren to complete the night-time ski-chase scenes. Peter had been worried about identifying Bond's different pursuers in the near-darkness. I hit on the idea of distinguishing Blofeld's men by having them fire a parachute flare while the other pursuers would carry hand-held flares. Peter was shooting in Portugal at this point, so I called him and got his permission to adapt the script accordingly before I embarked on five evenings of shooting.

My work in Switzerland had entailed much more than I had originally anticipated, but for the time being it was over and I returned to Pinewood. I went over the progress I had made with Peter and he was impressed. When I was editing the material I had shot, he paid me a visit. He explained that there had been a disagreement with Ben Rayner, the editor he had originally hired to cut *OHMSS*, who had left. Would I be interested in cutting the movie? I was very happy to step in and continue the job.

I had already adopted Peter's philosophy of editing and I was familiar with the previous films in the series, so I didn't ask to have any of them screened for my benefit. The Bond style was almost second nature to me and Peter and I had a good relationship, so it was a relatively smooth job. Peter worked in one editing room and I worked in another, so there was enough work for us both to be fully occupied. Whenever anyone from the distributor United Artists was around, Peter insisted the film would be two hours ten minutes long, but *OHMSS* had been the longest Bond shoot to date and it would go on to be the longest film.

Studio shooting and editing continued at Pinewood and in May I returned to Switzerland to film the avalanche sequence in a deserted valley near Mürren. By this time, the snow had completely disappeared and I was amused to observe cows grazing where the bobsleigh-run had been. My return had been planned to coincide with the period when Swiss experts cleared the snow from the high passes by dropping bombs from helicopters on to the mountainsides. This was an annual event, designed to shift the soft snow in advance of using the snowploughs to clear the roads below. These people purposefully started avalanches to save themselves extra work when they came to open the roads; I joined them for one of their bomb-dropping operations.

The conditions were perfect – approximately 6 feet of fresh snow had fallen before a few days of hot weather. We got permission from the Swiss authorities and went in by helicopter. Bruno Bagnaud and our guides began to drop strategically placed charges with two to two-and-a-half minute fuses. Hubert had been there before me and he was already in a good camera position. About 200–300 yards further on, I could see an outcrop that jutted out from the valley floor for about 300 feet. I asked the pilot to drop us off on the top of this outcrop and I had a look around. It offered us the possibility to shoot 360 degrees around the whole valley, and as such was perfect. I also figured that being 300 feet above the valley floor would offer us some protection from the avalanche. I changed the location to the outcrop and I'm very glad that I did – if we had used the place Hubert had scouted, we would have been wiped out.

We picked up Hubert and assembled the camera equipment. Alex Barbey positioned his gear on the outcrop and the helicopter got airborne. I was in radio contact with the guys in the helicopter and told them to drop the bombs while we started rolling the cameras. The bombs exploded, the avalanche started rumbling and we got some good footage from our precarious vantage point. By lunchtime, I noticed that there was a huge area of snow that hadn't been touched by the previous blast. By 2.30pm, the sun was high and it was getting quite warm – perfect avalanche conditions. The helicopter crew still had four bombs left, so I told them to drop the bombs. We didn't even bother turning over the cameras, as I figured we had plenty of good footage as it was. What happened next was amazing. The bombs exploded and I saw a huge wave that covered the width of the entire mountain like rippling sand. I quickly told Alex to start his camera and the next thing we saw was captured on film and used in the movie. An area approximately two miles wide, comprising what must have been thousands of tons of snow, gradually cascaded until it built into something awesome. As it gathered in intensity, the crashing noise became overwhelming. The growing avalanche hit our outcrop and loose rocks went flying into the air. Hubert's original filming position was swamped as the wall of snow hit the valley floor and flew over the top of us. We were trapped beneath a moving canopy of snow which was clearly 70 per cent air. It looked like thick white steam. Out of the corner of my eye, I could see my crew trying to run for cover, but many of them were already wading through four feet of snow. Alex emerged from the black cloth he had attached to the back of his camera to prevent any light getting in. He calmly assessed the situation and dived back under. As the sound subsided, the snow that was in the air began to settle and the sun began to shine through the haze. Alex ran out of film shortly after that, but not before we captured the most incredible scenes. The air cleared and I surveyed the devastation around me. The avalanche had created a wind so fierce that any loose objects were whipped away. Someone lost a jacket containing his passport and we had a bit of a job to retrieve it.

There was a big party that night, at which some of the locals told me that people two miles away were running for their lives at the sight of this huge avalanche. The Swiss are very fearful of avalanches because they have caused so many disasters. I had been in blissful ignorance of their power and was lucky to be alive. I have a lot more respect for avalanches now.

The footage was so precious that I flew it back to London in two batches in case the plane went down. I didn't tell anyone at Pinewood how good the avalanche had been, but waited for them to see the rushes. Peter was delighted with our results and I was later proud to see that the film's trailer opened with the line 'An avalanche of action!'

Only one thing spoiled the jubilant atmosphere. I was partying in a bar in Mürren when I heard that Johnny Jordan had been killed. He had been flying over the Gulf of Mexico, filming *Catch-22* for Mike Nichols, when he fell out of a B29 aeroplane. Johnny's assistant, Robin Browne, later related the story to me: Johnny had been tied into a harness inside the plane and was filming out of the door. He apparently couldn't get the shot he wanted, so took the harness off to give himself greater freedom of movement. There was suddenly a near miss and the pilot had to bank quickly to avoid a collision. Johnny effectively became weightless and drifted out of the door. It was a tragic end. Knowing Johnny, he probably filmed his descent.

With the avalanche footage in the can, the last piece of the location jigsaw was in place and I came home. When I started editing the sequence, I paid special attention to some long shots of skiers traversing the avalanche area. These were experts, but the terrain was so inhospitable that even they occasionally had accidents. One piece of film showed three skiers falling over one after the other in quick succession. I showed the footage to Martin Shorthall and asked him if he could create a model of the advancing avalanche which we could matte (partially superimpose) over the shots of the skiers so it would appear that they had been knocked over and finally engulfed. He said he would try, and came up with something remarkable which we used in the film. He even included some model trees that appeared to succumb to the weight of the snow and collapse in its path. If you analyse the avalanche shots, you may be able to tell where the original footage ends and the model shot begins, but I don't think you'd guess unless you'd been tipped off.

I continued editing over the summer of 1969. Cubby always seemed to be happy to wait until you were absolutely ready to run a sequence for him and didn't put any pressure on you. Harry, on the other hand, was a little more impatient and wanted to see things as soon as possible, especially if he had friends, guests or distributors visiting the studio. We had standard rushes and loosely cut sequences that we used to run for them, but after a while they got tired of looking at the same old stuff.

Shortly after I took over the editing, I re-cut Anthony Squire's footage of the sequence where Bond's Ford becomes embroiled in the stock-car rally. I got it looking pretty sharp and cut in a shot of a guy hanging upside down, which I tricked by simply inverting that piece of film. This got a big laugh from everyone I showed it to. One day, Harry had some visitors with him and asked to see something new, so I put some sound effects and a bit of music on this sequence and ran it for them. They loved it. When it finished, I went up to the projection box to collect the film and was confronted by an absolutely irate Peter Hunt. He was virtually blue with anger and had gone literally tight-lipped. 'Don't you *ever* do that again,' he shouted at me. 'Don't you *ever* run anything without my express approval.' He was quite right to admonish me – he was the director and I was an editor who had caved in under pressure from the producer. Peter soon forgave me, but I had learned another valuable lesson.

Towards the end of summer, I became involved with the music sessions for the film. Peter flew out to America to persuade the ailing Louis Armstrong to record 'We Have All the Time in the World'. It was a great performance of a great song, which is as popular today as it ever was.

John Barry wrote a fantastic score and conducted the orchestra himself. We spent a week recording the music and one day we had an unannounced visitor. A tall man sporting a thick black beard appeared at the back of the theatre and sat in the corner. While we were working, this stranger kept looking over at me and grinning. I thought, 'Who the hell is that?' Eventually this guy walked up to me and said, 'Hello John, you don't recognise me, do you?' It was George Lazenby. He looked like he'd spent the night sleeping in a doorway. Cubby was not best pleased because we were approaching the time when he wanted George to start promoting the film. I remember being quite surprised to see that he still had the beard when he went to the première in December. I think the actor playing James Bond really has a responsibility to try to look like the character at events such as these.

Stereo soundtracks were just being introduced in 1969 and we made a four or six-track version of the soundtrack of *OHMSS*. I don't think it was ever used, although the screenings at the Odeon in London's Leicester Square benefited from stereo during the avalanche sequence. We used the Odeon's ambient speakers, although I remember a trial run of the sound system revealed that they had material stuffed inside them in order to subdue the sound. I couldn't understand why this had been done, so we had the whole system overhauled and got a very exciting playback in the end.

The *Evening Standard*'s Alexander Walker gave *OHMSS* a resounding thumbs up and I received a phone call from Peter advising me to buy a copy. I was delighted to be mentioned in the review: 'John Glen, the man who edits this film, is also the second-unit director and presumably did the big action sequences. When the film moves, it moves like a jet-propelled cartoon-strip...There's a gold-medal ski-chase that ends with a pursuer being swallowed by a snowplough and producing red snow; a mammoth avalanche like half of Switzerland falling down...and a fight on a runaway bobsleigh to end with.'

I don't know whether Peter had mentioned me in dispatches, but I thought it was very generous criticism and I was deeply flattered.

By the end of 1969 we started receiving less complimentary feedback from United Artists, who were grumbling about the film's 139-minute running time.

UA complained that the film was so long that they were missing out on a whole screening per day in some cinemas, and this was having an adverse effect on their box-office returns. In Peter's defence, I feel I should point out that Ian Fleming's novel was a huge book with a plot that was very difficult to abridge. We cut a sequence where Bond, discovering he has been bugged, embarks on a chase through the streets of London. Another scene, in which Bond breaks into an office and cracks a safe, was minimised in the final cut. We shaved frames off all over the place to try to reduce the film's length, but there comes a point when you can take that process too far if you're not too careful. I personally felt that the bobsleigh sequence was edited a bit too harshly, for example, and ended up a little too tight. Throughout the editing process, Peter was adamant that we didn't lose any of the relationship scenes and we tried to retain as much of the action as we could because it was so good. Later on, when the film was out of our hands, it was edited down to around 130 minutes, and this was the version in general circulation until an uncut, home video version was released to celebrate the film's 25th anniversary.

*OHMSS* was the first and last time I worked with George Lazenby, who had already disassociated himself from the role of James Bond by the time the film was on release. I wasn't aware of this at the time, but he had informed Harry and Cubby of his decision to quit about halfway through

*OHMSS* was
running over-
length, and I left
this rooftop chase
on the cutting-
room floor.

filming. Cubby was philosophical about it, apparently saying, 'Well, there were 14 Tarzans.' Given the choice, I'm not sure he would have invited George back anyway.

I was reunited with George over 25 years later at a James Bond convention in Jamaica. He had matured into someone I liked a lot: still good-looking, but now with a refreshing modesty and an engaging sense of humour. He had learned his lesson and freely admitted it. We had both been newcomers to the James Bond films when we started work on *OHMSS*, but had both earned very different reputations from the experience.

# 007

## CHAPTER 6

### BOYS' OWN ADVENTURES

It was 1970 and my days of unemployment were over. If I had been hoping for a career working on Bond films, however, then it wasn't to be. At least, not yet.

After *OHMSS*, Peter understandably decided that six consecutive Bonds was enough and decided to turn his hand to other things. Had Peter decided to stay with the Bonds, I like to think I would have stayed with him, but he told me that instead he had ambitions to film a new version of *Major Barbara*. The film never came about, and we went our separate ways for a while. It is the prerogative of a director to choose his second-unit director and editor and when Guy Hamilton directed *Diamonds Are Forever*, the next instalment in the Bond series, he chose his usual editor Bert Bates to cut the film. Guy didn't much care for second units and preferred to shoot all such material himself, so I was out of luck in both departments.

I had made a name for myself as a second-unit director and editor, however, and I soon found another job. I moved on to *Murphy's War*, which was based on a novel by Max Catto and had a fantastic script by Sterling Silliphant. Peter O'Toole played Murphy, the sole survivor when his ship is torpedoed by a U-boat in the closing days of the Second World War. Murphy determines to take revenge on the U-boat and its ruthless commander (played by Horst Janson) and wages a one-man campaign – even after the German surrender is announced from Berlin. The film was directed by Peter Yates, with whom I had worked on *Danger Man*. Michael Deeley, the producer, asked me to stand by to direct the second unit and shoot a documentary about the making of the film, as well as co-edit the film alongside Frank Keller. Frank had won an Oscar in 1968 for his superb work on *Bullitt*.

The film was shot almost entirely on location along the Orinoco River in Venezuela and I took my assistant Robert Richardson out there with me. Our makeshift cutting room was the second-class dining area on an old Irish channel ferry that had been renamed *The Odysseus*. The crew, however, generally referred to it as *The Odious*. Frank, Robert and myself got to know the Greek crew quite well and spent many an evening drinking strong Greek coffee down in the engine room with the chief engineer.

There were a number of problems to tackle before we could start work. As soon as we arrived, the Venezuelan Navy impounded our passports and

Robert Richardson
and Oscar-winner
Frank Keller on
board *The Odious*
during the filming
of *Murphy's War*.

we had to hang around for a week waiting for official clearance. This had previously been given, but at that time, bureaucracy reigned. Then we discovered that the channel granting access to our intended location had become silted up and was too shallow for our boat. Our charts showed the area as being clear, but then again our charts had been printed in 1937. We scrubbed that location and purpose-built a village from scratch, which of course did our schedule no favours.

Soon after we started shooting, a storm whipped up out of nowhere and left us stranded in the jungle. We took refuge in an abandoned steamer and one enterprising soul produced some hammocks so we could at least try to get some sleep away from the mosquitoes. The following morning we attempted to re-board our ferry. One of the sound engineers slipped before he could get a foothold and was swept away by the tide. He popped up some 20 feet away and one of the Spanish boatmen staged a daring rescue. He swung on a rope, swooped down and grabbed him, hauling him on to the rubbing strip. Tarzan couldn't have done any better. From there, he was pulled to safety. Perhaps the most astonishing thing about the whole rescue was that the sound engineer was still clutching his Nagra recorder. That evening, Mike Sayle stripped the equipment down and dried it out, and it was working again by the following day.

Later on in the shoot, there was another accident that had more serious consequences. Our continuity girl, the lovely Helen Whitson, was returning from a shoot when she lost her footing on the gangplank connecting the boat to the shore. She struggled to maintain her balance, loaded down with her typewriter and papers, and she was in danger of falling in the river. Ira Anderson, the special effects supervisor, made a valiant attempt to grab her and succeeded in pushing her towards the shore. She fell heavily and fractured her hip, but we all felt that this wouldn't be a life-threatening injury for one so young. What we didn't know was that a blood clot was starting to circulate around her body. The day after she was repatriated to England, she suddenly died. Her death stunned us all and things were never quite the same afterwards.

My second-unit duties commenced with filming the German U-boat as it emerged from the river. The Venezuelans had come up with an old American sub from the Second World War, and after a lick of paint it passed muster. Once our cameras were in position on the shore, I asked the submarine commander if he'd know how to surface in the correct place. 'Don't worry,' he assured me. 'I'll know where you are.' The Orinoco was about two miles wide at this point, so I hoped he knew what he was talking about.

Gilbert Chomat, our helicopter pilot, was ready to film the sub breaking surface from an aerial perspective, so I wanted it to look as impressive as possible. I consulted Admiralty charts and sent the sub to the deepest spot in the river. Mike Sayle had asked to go aboard for the trip to record the noises the sub made as it went to the bottom, and he filled me in on what happened next. Mike said the submarine sank 90 fathoms and the commander lost control. They hit the river bed with a resounding crash, which shattered almost all the china on board. Apparently they hadn't allowed for fresh water buoyancy: the submarine was balanced for seawater, which is, of course, much more buoyant. After this hair-raising journey, the submarine began its ascent and we started filming.

Gilbert got some great footage of the periscope from his helicopter, and then climbed high enough to ensure that his shadow wouldn't spoil any of the shots we were taking from the shore. From a distance of about a quarter of a mile, we filmed the submarine breaking the surface and came away with some very effective footage. I later used the shot of the periscope breaking the surface to represent the trail of a torpedo fired from the U-boat, and later recycled it in *The Spy Who Loved Me* to once again double as a torpedo trail. Shortly after *Murphy's War* wrapped, I was saddened to learn that Gilbert had been involved in an accident while filming *Zeppelin* in Ireland. Both Gilbert and his fellow cameraman Skeets Kelly, who had survived the Pacific War, were killed.

The aerial unit shot some superb material used to represent Murphy's flight over the jungle in a salvaged seaplane. A talented one-legged pilot called Frank Tallman fearlessly swooped his Grumman Goose in and out of the jungle so that cameraman Ronnie Taylor could get the footage we needed. He once banked so low that the Goose ascended back into view with creepers trailing from its tail. Both Frank and his co-pilot Frank Mantz were also casualties in flying accidents: Frank Matz lost his life filming *The Flight of the Phoenix* and Frank Tallman disappeared on a routine flight in California during the making of the Bond movie *A View to a Kill*.

Later on, I accompanied the submarine for 60 or 70 miles to the mouth of the Orinoco, which was in a huge delta region that opened out into the Caribbean. It wasn't much fun sleeping on the submarine, even if you were in the officers' quarters. There were three bunks, all of which had head room of about one foot. You had to be a qualified contortionist to get into a bunk, and if you then found yourself unlucky enough to be sleeping above the second mate, his thunderous snoring would guarantee a sleepless night. One crew-member discovered that the most comfortable place to sleep was on top of a torpedo. Before long, we started sleeping on the support boat that followed the submarine down the river.

One night, the submarine crew asked us if we'd like to join them crocodile hunting. We picked out a lot of sinister red eyes in the darkness, but we didn't shoot at any of them. The Venezuelans were very trigger happy, however, and fired at anything that moved. They fired at quite a few things that didn't move – including one of the biggest owls I'd ever seen – which didn't strike me as much sport. On one occasion, I was in a conning tower filming a scene with a couple of actors when I heard the deafening noise of the crew taking pot shots at parrots in the jungle. I was treading on broken glass because I had to be nice to these people, but at the same time I needed to lay down the law. 'Excuse me,' I began, bracing myself for a confrontation, 'would you mind *not* shooting parrots while we're filming? I'm going deaf.'

A torrential downpour threatened to spoil our filming of the submarine passing into the delta region to its hiding place in the jungle. As we clambered from our launch on to land I decided to head for a rotten log cabin in an attempt to save us and the gear from the rain. We got inside, only to discover that the place was full of hornets' nests. We were plagued by the agitated occupants, who swarmed backwards and forwards in droves all the time, but the hut offered the only shelter available so we had to put up with it. I decided to stay in this log house with the precious equipment and the treacherous hornets, while the other boys preferred to take their chances with the rain. At about 4pm, the weather began to improve and as evening fell, beautiful shafts of yellow light pierced the dark clouds. The last light of the evening, just after a storm, presented the best possible conditions for filming. I had only half an hour before the submarine crew went off duty and commenced their leave, so this was my last chance to get the shot I needed of the U-boat arriving at the estuary at night. I asked the sub commander to steam through the shot, against this beautiful light, and then turn around and steam back the other way. I filmed the sub travelling in both directions, then flipped one of the shots and cut them both together to give the impression of a long journey in the same direction. With that little excursion crossed off my agenda, the submarine disappeared from sight and returned to base.

We were feeling quite pleased with ourselves, thinking we were free from interruption on one of the most remote areas imaginable. And then a native appeared out of nowhere and tried to sell us a parrot. Keith Jones, one of the crew-members, actually bought the bird, which became a feature of the production office from thereon.

Ingo Mogendorf, one of the German actors, lost a front tooth midway through our trip, so I asked him to hold his radio microphone in front of his face to obscure the gaping hole in his mouth. And then our pilot, who we relied on for bringing us supplies via the local air strip, broke his leg on a derelict railway track. He bravely flew himself to hospital in Caracas.

I was later sent to Portocabao to find a ship that had been bought for use in the film. I was accompanied by Roy Whybrow, one of the special effects experts whose job it was to explode and then sink this ship for the sequence representing the destruction of Murphy's vessel at the beginning of the film. The local harbour master was amazed when we told him we intended to

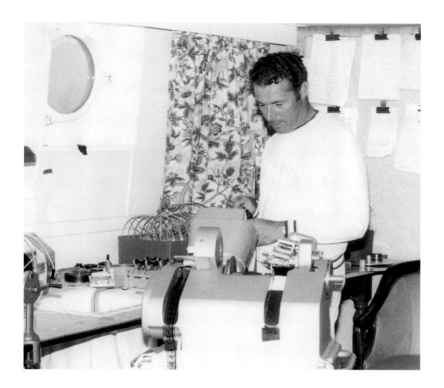

move this old wreck to the sinking site – he explained it hadn't gone anywhere for over 10 years and probably wouldn't survive the journey. When Roy put his foot straight through the rotten deck of this thing, I began to see his point. Roy pulled his foot out of the hole he'd made, then told me there was no way he was going down to the lower decks to plant the explosives. The poisonous gases that could be lurking down below would make it far too dangerous. I didn't need telling twice. It would be quite a big deal to plant explosives and blow the bottom out of this death-trap.

I conducted a reconnaissance around some nearby islands, in search of a good location in which to film the destruction of the boat. I made two major mistakes on that trip: the first was to pick a place full of cacti. The second was to wear a pair of soft shoes. When I looked at the soles of my feet, they were bristling with painful spines. I limped back to Caracas, where Roy and I checked into the Hilton. Roy alerted me to a telex awaiting transmission on the desk. I don't know how he did it, but from a distance of 10 feet he read the upside-down message. It was addressed to John Croydon of Film Financiers, the London company providing the movie's completion guarantee: 'HAVE ARRIVED INTO BIG TROUBLE – RENÉ DUPONT'. René had been sent from Film Financiers to join us because we were falling behind schedule, and his company obviously wanted to avoid stumping up if we ran out of money.

That evening, we were called into René's suite and subjected to a grilling over what we intended to shoot. Fortunately, Roy's eagle eyes had forewarned me of this cross-examination, and I was ready with all my maps, charts and plans. The exploding of the old wreck went straight out of the

*Murphy's War* was edited in a floating cutting room.

window (the sequence seen at the beginning of the movie was ultimately realised using a model) and René's reorganisation continued with a bit of hiring and firing. As was perhaps inevitable, not all the right people were hired and fired. While this was going on, we had to arrange a crucial screening for representatives of the production company London Screenplays, who were flying in to decide whether the movie was worth bailing out. Frank and I worked virtually all night to pull together what footage there was, sharing just one Moviola. We were saved by the fact we had the excellent aerial material; it was exciting stuff, and you could see its potential. I cut it together, adding some sound effects, and presented about 20 minutes of footage on the night. Frank cut together some dialogue scenes from the material that Douglas Slocombe, the director of photography, had shot with Peter O'Toole and Philippe Noiret, who played Murphy's reluctant companion Louis. It looked fantastic.

We had a projector on board our ship and while the footage ran for our guests from London, I remember thinking it was quite eerie to be screening a film about the sea on board a ship that was creaking and rolling on this huge river. The powers that be were sufficiently impressed to bankroll the rest of the film. I'm very glad they did, because *Murphy's War* turned into a great movie. It didn't do as well as it should have done when it came out, but it's subsequently gained a good reputation through numerous television screenings.

Shortly after I completed editing *Murphy's War*, Peter Hunt got in touch with me and asked if I'd direct the second unit on his next project, a Western called *Catlow*. I agreed, but then Peter fell out with the producer, Euan Lloyd, over the budget and some of the creative aspects. Peter was off the picture, but I had already committed. Sam Wanamaker was brought in to direct and things got off to a bad start between us. I asked Euan to arrange a meeting between Sam and me but he kept putting me off. I became increasingly frustrated and told Euan it was essential to get us together in the same room so we could discuss which sequences I was going to direct and get his agreement. It was only after I insisted on a meeting with Sam that we finally got together. It was an encounter I will never forget.

Sam was quite a powerful figure and his reputation preceded him. He greeted me civilly before asking, 'And what do you think you're going to be doing on this film?' I took Sam through the script, indicating all the action scenes. Sam went crazy and started jumping up and down in front of me. 'So I'm going to do the dialogue and you're going to do the action?' he shouted. I did my best to calm him down. 'Sam, it's going to have to come to that, or you're never going to make the schedule.' He wouldn't hear of it, and told me, 'No, no, no – I'll tell you what you're going to shoot!' 'Fine,' I replied, 'I'll do anything you want me to do,' and with that the meeting was over.

I'd seen this attitude before – Sam wanted to shoot everything himself, but this was a big action film and I knew he'd have to delegate. We started pre-production with a desert reconnaissance, during which Sam was very enthusiastic. He set his viewfinder up on top of a big rock and took three or four steps back without looking behind him. He took one step too many and teetered on the precipice. Luckily, our huge cameraman Ginger Gemmell was wearing a leather belt and if Sam hadn't grabbed hold of it, we'd have lost our director there and then.

Shooting got underway with a good crew and a cast that included Yul Brynner, Leonard Nimoy and Richard Crenna. Sam briefed me on what he wanted me to do, but unfortunately some of his instructions were a little difficult to follow. He would send me to a particular location and tell me he had marked the relevant spot with two crossed sticks and an oil drum. This was supposed to indicate the camera position. I'd visit these places only to find a whole mountainside covered in junk – Sam's crossed sticks and oil drums could have been anywhere. In desperation, I'd set the camera up in what I considered to be the best position. My footage just happened to be good enough.

With director Sam Wanamaker, on location in Almeria for *Catlow*.

Before too long, Sam was asking me to pick up close shots of actors in certain scenes that he hadn't found the time to finish. I was happy to do this, but I hadn't seen rushes of these scenes so had no reference. I had to ask the actors to try to remember which way they were facing and what the background was like before I embarked on each set-up. They were very helpful, and as I was editing the movie as well, I was able to blend my footage in with Sam's.

Leonard Nimoy had been cast as something of a mystery figure, who was fully revealed only in the final confrontation. He was consequently a little under-used during the main part of the shoot, so Euan asked me to direct some publicity footage with him as a ploy to get him out of his hotel room for a while. I was filming this material when one of the prop guns exploded close to Leonard's eye. Although he was in great pain, Leonard continued until he heard me say, 'Cut!'. I rushed over him to see how he was. 'How bad is it, John?' he asked through gritted teeth and I must say it looked gruesome – his whole eye was drenched in blood. I went to visit him in Almería Hospital that evening and I was relieved to see him sitting up in bed, with both eyes thankfully intact.

Despite Sam's insistence that it wouldn't be necessary, I had prepared the action sequences anyway. Sure enough, he took on too much and got behind schedule within the first few weeks. It was then that he realised that he did need me after all. Euan Lloyd was pleased to see me finally handling the action because he loved what I'd done in *OHMSS* and was keen to get more of the same in his own movie.

*Catlow* was a moderate success, but it had been hard work. I needed a holiday and returned to the scene of my crimes in Mürren. I'd been staying at the Eiger Hotel for about a week when I received a phone call from Michael Klinger, whom I immediately congratulated for being so enterprising in tracking me down. It turned out there was no time for small talk – he had run into trouble on *Pulp*, which starred Michael Caine and was directed by Mike Hodges, and he wanted me to take over the editing. I explained I was on holiday and had another week to go. 'I can't wait that long,' he replied. 'I need you to come back right away.'

At that time, England was not a good place to be. The country was in the grip of industrial unrest, we were restricted by a three-day week and the electricity supply was prone to disappear without warning. When the lights went out, there was nothing else for it but to head for the pub because there was no way to get any work done. Mike Hodges was a nice guy whose work on *Get Carter* I had admired enormously. 'How long do you think it will take you to edit the film?' he asked. 'At this rate,' I gloomily replied, 'at least a month.' His face fell. The film had been hacked around quite a bit by the time I started working on it, and I had to have the whole lot put back to rushes so I could start again. I thought the end result was quite amusing, but I had a problem with the fact that Mickey Rooney's character got assassinated halfway through. Mickey was a real live wire, and the film missed him desperately. It was interesting to see Lizabeth Scott, who I remembered seeing in films when I was a kid, and Lionel Stander was wonderful. Michael Caine did a great job, of course.

Then Douglas Hickox approached me to edit *Sitting Target*, which had its moments. *Sitting Target* starred Jill St John as a Clapham Junction

housewife, which took a stretch of the imagination, and Oliver Reed. Ted Scaife, who was the director of photography, had previously shot *Catlow*, and I remembered Dougie Hickox from my early days at London Films, where he had been an assistant director.

According to one of my nephews, who has rather highbrow taste, Patrick Garland's version of *A Doll's House* is the most important film I've ever worked on. I'm not sure I agree with him, but I'm certainly grateful for the opportunity it afforded me to work with Claire Bloom and Anthony Hopkins, both of whom were charming. I also have fond memories of Denholm Elliott and Anna Massey, but if there's one person I'll never forget meeting on that movie, it's the great Ralph Richardson. Poor Ralph was a little infirm, and he found it very difficult to stop his head shaking. He had to use extreme will power to keep still during close-ups, but he got through it and gave a very fine performance.

Sam Fuller was a director whose reputation preceded him. He was admired for such mid-Sixties classics as *Shock Corridor* and *Naked Kiss*, and I was excited at the prospect of editing his new Western, *Riata*. I found myself back in Almería, working alongside Fuller and leading man Richard Harris. Things seemed relatively straightforward at the outset, when Sam spent three days shooting the pre-titles sequence. He then surprised everyone by spending another three days shooting it again. I spoke to the producer Bernie Williams and suggested Sam would have been better off waiting until he got to the end of the schedule and seeing if he had the time for such a luxury, but we pressed on without a word. The next scene on the schedule involved a procession of hundreds of extras through a Mexican village. Shooting went on and on, and I became increasingly concerned that Sam had lost the plot – he spent all his time filming long shots, and I knew I'd have trouble making sense of this material in the cutting room.

One evening, I decided the time had come to have a serious discussion

Mickey Rooney, one of the stars of *Pulp*, with producer Michael Klinger.

Birthday
celebrations on the
set of *A Doll's
House*, with Claire
Bloom, Ralph
Richardson and
producer Hillard
Elkins. I'm
standing second
from the right,
wearing Telly
Savalas' jacket
from *OHMSS*. I
wish I'd kept it.

with Sam about the lack of progress. He was surrounded by admiring crew-members, all of whom were telling him what a magnificent job he was doing. I had been trying to edit the rushes, however, and I knew this wasn't exactly the case. After trying politely to get his attention so I could have a private word with him, I dropped any pretension and literally manhandled a reluctant Sam into my cutting room, shutting the door behind me. I told him we were seriously behind schedule and that I couldn't cut the material he was giving me. I hated doing it and I was shocked by his response. He was visibly shaken and became very emotional, apologising profusely and trying to explain that he was suffering a lot of pressure.

I later received a phone call from Warner Bros in Hollywood who wanted to know why we had fallen so far behind. 'You'd better take a look for yourselves,' I said, and that weekend I travelled to Madrid to screen the cut material and rushes for a group of concerned executives. After an hour, they'd seen enough and pulled the plug on the production.

My most vivid memory of *Riata* is not the disastrous filming, but the riotous party Richard Harris organised for the crew. It took place during a thunderstorm in Almería and the canopy covering us collapsed under the weight of the rainwater. The next day I was surprised to see that Richard and company were still in town – they were stranded, unable to return to their hotel because the coast road had disintegrated under the onslaught of rain.

Warner Bros salvaged *Riata* the following year. Sam gave way to director Barry Shear, who remounted the production with Richard Harris under the new title *The Deadly Trackers*.

In 1973, Peter Hunt came back into my life to offer me the jobs of second-unit director and editor on *Gold*, an adaptation of the Wilbur Smith novel that he was directing. Michael Klinger secured the best part of the film's £1 million budget from private South African backers, and the movie

– which was set against the back drop of South African gold mining – was naturally shot on location there. This caused enormous problems, as this was still very much the era of apartheid. The British technicians' union, the ACTT, did not allow any of its members to work in South Africa and forbade us from participating. We defied them and went anyway because we figured that it was better to work in that environment than to isolate people who were already suffering at the hands of a racist government; our script, written by Wilbur and Stanley Price, dealt with neither racial nor political concerns. We started work amid ultimately unfounded threats from the ACTT that the film would be boycotted in the UK.

*Gold* starred Roger Moore, who had already made a great impact in his first James Bond film *Live and Let Die*. Throughout the 1960s, Roger had been filming *The Saint* at Elstree while I had been working with Pat McGoohan on *Danger Man*. We had been rivals in a way, and our careers had run along parallel paths for quite some time. This was the first time I had worked with Roger and it was a very pleasurable experience. It was the start of a fruitful working relationship that lasted so long that by our fourth or fifth picture together he asked me, 'Are you in my contract or am I in yours?'

Many of the sequences I shot were filmed deep underground in a real gold mine. We chose the Buffel's Fontein gold mine in the Orange Free State, one of the largest and most efficient gold mines in the area, and getting there from our base in Johannesburg was very difficult. There were petrol restrictions in South Africa at that time, and the pumping stations were open only every other day. To get to Buffel's Fontein, Michael Klinger and I had to drive some 250 miles on a Sunday, carrying spare cans of petrol in the boot of our car. During the journey, the car ground to a halt and our African driver got out to retrieve some of the petrol cans stashed behind us. Petrol was a precious commodity, and I was horrified to see it splash all over

Discussing a scene from *Gold* with Michael Klinger, Roger Moore and make-up artist Paul Engelen.

the road while he tried to fill the tank without a funnel. Ever-resourceful, I found an old plastic water container in a ditch and sliced it in half with my Swiss Army knife. The remnants of the water container made a handy funnel and saved a bit of petrol.

When we got to Buffel's Fontein, we stayed at a comfortable hotel run by an enormous man who must have been nearly seven feet tall. His name was Tiny. One evening, at 10 o'clock, I heard the wail of an air raid siren outside. I immediately reacted, possibly prompted by my wartime memories, but Tiny put a reassuring hand on my shoulder. 'Don't worry about that, Mr Glen. It's only the curfew.' No black man was allowed on the streets after 10 – it was a striking reminder of the miserable political climate.

In the morning, we donned miners' overalls and wore helmets with lamps in preparation for our descent into the mine. We joined the African miners, squeezing into the three-tiered cages that made the 3000-foot journey down the shaft. We then got into something that looked uncomfortably like a steel coffin for the journey along an incline shaft. Roger Moore made a real effort to conquer his claustrophobia so that he could join us.

We shot the underground mine sequences at a depth of 6000 feet, which funnily enough was almost exactly sea level – the entrance to the mine was about 6000 feet above. I borrowed Alec Mills, who was usually the cameraman with the main unit, for our jaunts underground because the second-unit cameraman Jimmy Devis suffered from such bad claustrophobia that he refused to accompany us.

One scene involved an actor drilling too far through a rock face and tapping an underground lake which bursts through, flooding the mine. Production designer Syd Cain constructed three huge water tanks in the training area of the mine, which was on the surface but looked underground enough for our purposes. Syd specially designed these tanks so he could pull the plugs on all three of them and thousands of gallons of water could rush down, sweeping the hapless driller away. I sat down with this actor and earnestly persuaded him that the stunt was perfectly safe, even though I must admit I wasn't 100% sure about it myself. At the appointed moment, the signal was given and we heard an ominous rumbling. Shortly afterwards, torrents of water came bursting through the rock face, picking up this miner and his pneumatic drill and throwing him yards. He was fine. We even did another take.

We couldn't do a lot of the flooding stuff on location because we couldn't control the water. Later on, at Pinewood Studios, we were able to pump the water around continuously, matching the new shots with the material filmed on location the previous year. Syd built a brilliant mineshaft set where we filmed the rescue attempt with Roger.

Location filming continued through Christmas 1973 and it felt strange to be away from my family, spending winter in such a hot country. As a second-unit director, I didn't enjoy the same privileges afforded to a main unit. My cast often had to work without the relative luxuries of attendant hairdressers and make-up artists, but everyone mucked in. Peter let me have Bradford Dillman for half a day so I could shoot the sequence where Tony Beckley chased him around the gold dump, trying to run him down in a Rolls-Royce. We were working in incredibly hot and dusty conditions, but

Bradford gave it his all and was very professional. In fact, I think he was so engrossed in what he was doing that he lost track of time. After a few hours, he exhaustedly said to me, 'That's it John – that's the last shot I'm doing today,' and staggered back to his hotel.

Shooting *Gold* in South Africa with co-star Bradford Dillman (right).

The stunt arranger on *Gold* was Leslie Crawford, with whom I had worked on *OHMSS*. He was very good at his job, but like all stunt drivers he liked to frighten you a bit when he got the chance. Frankly I'd rather not have my nerves shredded in this way, but there was one instance I was grateful for his expertise. When we finished shooting, Les drove us back back to Jan Smuts Airport. We must have been doing almost 100 mph in the Rolls when one of the tyres suddenly blew. Time seemed to slow down as a I looked out of the window and saw the hub cap fly into the air and bounce into a nearby field. Les handled the car beautifully, steadying it and bringing it to a gradual stop. A little while later, I retrieved the errant hub cap while he was changing the wheel.

When the titles for *Gold* were prepared, I was reunited with Maurice Binder, with whom I had last worked with on *OHMSS*. Maurice was an expert at filming opening title sequences, and was of course the man responsible for devising the opening 'gun barrel' shot in *Dr No*. The sequence is probably as well known as the James Bond theme it accompanies, and has opened every official Bond film ever since. Maurice produced some Bond-style opening credits for *Gold* using footage I shot with the second unit. Maurice was an extraordinary man with an extraordinary talent, but he reminded me a little of Ossie Hafenrichter because he was also incredibly disorganised. He didn't know what he wanted for his title sequences until he saw it, and was one of those people who was so vague that he could never seem to tell you exactly what sort of footage he needed. He could drive you mad with frustration, but it was only after he completed his sequences that you realised he had been working towards something specific all the time, he just hadn't been able to verbalise what it was. A number of producers tried to tame Maurice over the years, but none of them ever succeeded. He wasn't the sort of guy you expected to start at eight and finish at six. But he was a genius.

We did the dubbing for *Gold* at Twickenham Studios, where Gerry Humphries, my old friend from Nettlefolds, was the chief sound mixer. Gerry recommended me to Tony Richardson, who was due to direct a Dick Francis thriller called *Dead Cert*. Although Tony's groundbreaking films *Look Back in Anger* and *The Entertainer* had been produced by Harry Saltzman, they were gritty black and white dramas that were about as different from the Bonds as it was possible to be. They nevertheless played just as important a part in revolutionising the style and subject matters adopted by British film-makers. Many people had copied Tony's approach and the business had moved on in the intervening years. Tony had achieved a lot, but when I met him I got the impression that he no longer knew where to take the medium.

Tony was a pleasant man who liked employing odd characters – maybe that's why he hired me to edit *Dead Cert* – but before we hit it off, I had to get used to the little games he liked playing. At my initial interview with him and the producer, Neil Hartley, Tony told me he intended to shoot most of the film on location. 'I don't want to see any rushes until I've finished shooting,' he said, 'and I don't want you to cut anything until I've finished.' A quick glance at the very tight schedule before us indicated that this was madness. I suggested a compromise whereby I would cut the major sequences together, but also join up the material I hadn't used so he could look at everything – used and unused – when he finished. He agreed and I got the job.

On my first day of editing, I ran into problems straightaway. I called him and said, 'You haven't completed that sequence inside the car have you?' He invited me to discuss it with him face to face, so I rather reluctantly drove down to Bognor Regis, where he was shooting, and went to his hotel room. I didn't know him well, so I was all the more perturbed to have to wait while he had a shower. He emerged wearing a towel and pair of red-and-white striped socks. 'So what do you feel was missing from that car sequence?' he asked. 'You're going to need some close shots,' I said, still faintly incredulous of the fact I'd driven to Bognor Regis to have a conversation with a virtual stranger wearing little more than a pair of stripy socks. 'You've done seven or eight takes on a two-shot in a car. It's a three-and-a-half minute scene and you're going to want to shorten it. You won't be able to achieve that unless you splice in some close shots. And you haven't got any.' 'I don't think you're right,' he said, before pausing. 'But you might be.' He did shoot the close-ups and he did ultimately need to shorten the scene, so I hadn't made a wasted trip. I still, however, don't know why he made me feel so uncomfortable about it.

That evening, we were having dinner together and he explained how he wanted me to cut that day's footage. 'Have you got a script?' he asked me, and I reached into my bag to give him my copy. He opened it up and pointed to a particular scene. He told me he wanted to play the whole scene in a close shot of one particular actor. He then turned the page over and told me he wanted the next scene played entirely in a close shot of another actor. I stared at him, but he remained impassive. This must be some sort of bizarre test – no one in their right mind would cut a film that way. The next day, I returned to the cutting room and recounted the previous evening's conversation to my assistant Ron Saunders. 'What are you going to do?' he asked me. 'I'm going to cut the scene the way I would normally cut it, and if he doesn't like it he can fire me,' I replied.

When Tony finished filming, he did exactly what we'd agreed and looked at the cut sequences before inspecting the material I'd discarded. When the lights were raised he turned to me and complimented me on a job well done. I then realised that he had been testing me during our strange meetings. It would have been a mistake to have argued with him. I had done the right thing by listening to him and then disregarding his ideas. Editing is a very important aspect of film-making: in searching through the material for the best performances, you can greatly improve a movie's chances. An editor must focus in on the narrative and sometimes make a bad cut in order to better the scene. A film should be shot in such a way that you can edit it without making a bad cut, as there should always be sufficient material for you to cut to. You must not allow yourself to be dictated by the continuity of the scene – you must control the scene with your scissors.

Although Tony had behaved in some unpredictable ways, I quite enjoyed working on *Dead Cert*. My amusement at his antics lasted up until the very end: before the first screening for the press he said to me 'I hate the titles – take them off!' This eccentric whim was a misjudged gesture that left the assembled reviewers strumming their fingers. And Tony needed all the help he could get from *them*.

I went on to edit and shoot some second-unit footage on a Shepperton-based film called *Conduct Unbecoming*, which was directed by the very talented Michael Anderson. There was a good cast, which included Richard Attenborough and Christopher Plummer. I then heard from Peter Hunt, who was gearing up to direct Michael Klinger's next Wilbur Smith adaptation – *Shout at the Devil*.

*Shout at the Devil* starred Lee Marvin as the improbably named rogue Flynn Patrick O'Flynn and Roger Moore as his upper class accomplice Sebastian Oldsmith. The story was set in 1913 and unfolds when the hard-up Oldsmith is reluctantly roped into helping Flynn smuggle poached ivory. Lee and Roger made a great double act and both indulged their respective screen personas to the hilt. I was thrilled to meet Lee Marvin, who was a rugged character with some nasty scars in nasty places following his experiences in the Pacific War. I thought he had been excellent in *Cat Ballou* and *Paint Your Wagon*, and in 1970 he had even scored a number one record with the classic *Wand'rin' Star*. He was nothing if not versatile.

Peter asked me if I'd be the second-unit director and I expected to edit the film as well. We were based at Port St John on the Transkei coast of South Africa, and the apartheid situation was just as bad as it had been when we shot *Gold* almost three years before. Port St John was a beautiful area, but a lot of white-owned businesses had pulled out and we were greeted by scenes of desolation on our arrival. Driving through town, we saw closed garages and shop after shop with smashed front windows.

I stayed in a beach bungalow, which I shared with camera operators

On location for
*Shout at the Devil*
with rugged star
Lee Marvin.

Jimmy Devis and Alan Hume. I was the first person to arrive and the maid asked me what I'd like for breakfast. I told her that egg and bacon would be very nice. The next morning I woke up to the sound of frying from the kitchen and sat down to eat with eager anticipation. I was dismayed by the sight on the plate before me – the egg had been fried, but it had been smashed and the yoke was all over the place. 'This is no way to cook an egg,' I told her, and took her into the kitchen to explain how it should be done. The next morning, I awoke to find another mangled egg on my plate. By the third day, I'd had enough. Some of the local children would come to the door selling undersized crayfish. These the maid *could* cook, so I decided to buy one and had crayfish breakfasts from then on. Jimmy arrived a week later. When the maid asked him what he'd like for breakfast, he replied: 'Egg and bacon, please.' I left them to get on with it.

Near the port itself was the airstrip perched high above the town. As the film was set in 1913 and the script called for a bomber plane of the period, we used a Vickers Vimmy, a First World War crate with a hopeless safety record. We didn't dare try to use the airstrip to get the thing off the ground in case it ended up plummeting over the cliff. We flew it from a makeshift runway on the beach instead, and we managed that only after Alan Hume volunteered himself as human ballast at the front. The pilot was Nick Turvey, a South African aerobatics champion, and as he got into the air Jimmy Devis started filming. Seconds later the engine died and Nick had to put the thing down in the water. Luckily, it stayed afloat and we managed to drag it ashore before anyone was hurt or the plane was badly damaged. The guys worked on it overnight and we got it flying the next day, but it persisted in conking out at crucial moments.

Peter and I had a conference and decided we couldn't rely on the Vickers any more. We hired an Agcat, a tough crop-spraying aeroplane that we

My second-unit crew adorn the wreck of the *Agcat.*

could use to tow the Vickers. I would have to be careful to keep the Agcat and its camouflaged tow-rope out of shot so as not to spoil the period atmosphere. While filming the sequence where the Vickers bombed the German battleship the *Blucher*, I discovered that I didn't have to be as careful as I anticipated. I shot into the sun and the backlit Agcat passed for the Vickers. Another challenge was presented by the weight of the Vickers, which was making the Agcat struggle a little. We took it to a place called Margate (I was even more amused to note that it had a sister town called Ramsgate), where there was a useful little operation at the local airfield. There I met one Ziggy Harris VC, who had been a fighter ace during the war. His team stripped the Vickers down to its bare bones in an effort to make it as light as possible. Every pound was crucial, and Ziggy's team even drilled out the tops of the internal screws in an effort to reduce the plane's weight. While they did this, I availed myself of the nearby crayfish restaurant, which was one of the finest on that side of the coast.

The *Blucher* itself was the handiwork of production designer Syd Cain, who built it into the bank of the river. This convincing, but stationary, replica was constructed from hardboard stretched over scaffolding.

My other work on the film continued at the Kruger National Park, where I had to film the shooting of some elephants. We didn't kill any elephants during the production of *Shout at the Devil*, but we were present during one of the Park's regular culling sessions so it probably looks as though we did. The gamekeepers would cull certain elephants in a bid to keep the population down. To do this, the unfortunate animals would be herded to the designated area by a pursuing helicopter. I had a double for Roger Moore in the foreground, while the Park marksman stood behind him out of shot. The marksman fired and the double made it look as though he had downed the elephant. The chap doubling for Roger did so well that I congratulated him when we finished. 'It was amazing how you appeared to fire your rifle at precisely the right moment,' I told him. 'There was nothing amazing about it,' he replied. 'I felt a bullet whistle just past my ear – I nearly jumped out of my skin!'

We needed a shot of a herd of elephants rampaging past the camera. I found what I thought was safe place – a rock split by a huge fig tree. I figured that if things went wrong, we could drop down this split in the rock. I was accompanied by an armed ranger, Jimmy Devis and his assistant. We had a radio link to the pilot of the helicopter hovering nearby. We started filming as the elephants got closer to us; as they approached, I was astonished at how quiet they were. As they ran past us I started to wonder whether they were wearing carpet slippers because they barely made a sound. As they rampaged past, I saw the mothers reach their trunks down their throats to suck up water that they then sprayed over their youngsters to keep them cool. Encouraged by the fabulous shots we got of these huge creatures at such close quarters, I got the pilot on the radio and asked him if he could herd them back towards us again. This was a mistake. The matriarch of the herd must have smelt us because she ran up to our rock and reared over us on her hind legs. She was as big as a house. The ranger froze with fear, unable to aim his rifle. The helicopter tried to scare the animal away from us. Then I realised the matriarch was trying to grab the helicopter to bring it down. We got some wonderful shots and eventually the elephant was driven away by the helicopter. We didn't need to drop into the split in the rock, but the ranger later explained it wouldn't have done us much good if we had – she would have winkled us out of there in a trice.

Second-unit directors tend to get the dirtiest jobs and *Shout at the Devil* was no exception. I had to shoot a sequence featuring the German District Commissioner (played by Rene Kolldehoff) aboard a fog-bound boat. We spent most of the morning laying down this thick mist that promptly blew away as soon as the cameras started turning over. When the wind eventually dropped, we tried again. I gave the 'Action!' instruction to Rene. The outboard motor of our boat had been kept under cover to preserve the period atmosphere and he had been sitting on the casing. I gave him the instruction again, but he didn't respond to any of my directions. Alan Hume started jumping up and down in front of Rene, flapping his arms and shouting 'I am the *Blucher*, I am the *Blucher*!', but still nothing would rouse him. It turned out he hadn't responded because he'd spent so long breathing exhaust fumes from the encased engine that he was virtually unconscious.

It's no exaggeration to say we almost lost our lives filming Flynn and Oldsmith being shipwrecked on a rocky coastline. I did a deal with a local boat man, offering him two new mercury engines for his boat if he agreed to take us. I took a minimum crew with me and told the continuity girl that she had to stay behind – it was simply too dangerous to take her. As we sailed out, I began to wish I'd stayed behind with her. Huge breakers the size of double-decker buses loomed over us and we gripped the side of the boat tightly while we waited for the right wave to appear before we gunned the engines. Our captain waited until the boat was almost vertical before he chose his moment and any equipment that wasn't tied down went overboard. Once we were out at sea, we turned around and started taking trips on the surf in order to film the approaching shore. On our third

attempt, I looked behind us and saw a huge creamer which I knew wouldn't let us go. Sure enough, it picked us up and threw us about 50 yards up the beach. My first thought was for Jimmy Devis, who was tied to the bow of the boat while he filmed the huge wave as we chased it inshore. A lot of his equipment was damaged or lost, but Jim at least was OK, if a little waterlogged.

We were marooned on a skeleton coast miles from anywhere. We dried the equipment out and after a few hours resolved to make the journey back. We launched the boat back into the surf and got back to Port St Johns by the evening. At least the results of our labours looked good on screen.

Although there was never enough bad weather to induce the South African equivalent of mountain sickness, we did experience the odd thunderstorm and one of them gave me a good idea. We were driving through torrential rain one night when we spotted a load of land crabs scuttling across the road ahead of us. I told the driver to stop and jumped out of the car, dragging a reluctant prop man with me. We grabbed a large crab, stuck it in a box with a lettuce leaf and put it in the back. I knew exactly what it would come in useful for.

I had read Wilbur's novel before we started filming and the passage where he describes Oldsmith opening his eyes and being stared out by a seemingly massive crab had stuck in my memory. We were due to film another scene when a cloudburst sent us hurrying for shelter in the nearest hut. 'I know what we can shoot,' I announced. 'Get the crab.' Everyone looked at me as though I'd lost my marbles. The box was retrieved and an old carpet was spread on top of a table. I was careful not to release the crab until we were absolutely ready to shoot, so we focused the zoom lens on a strategically placed cigarette packet which we then removed in preparation for the crab's grand entrance. I looked at Jimmy Devis and said, 'Turn over,

Roger Moore and I keep our distance from a drugged elephant while the second unit films a scene for *Shout at the Devil*. The elephant was pretty angry when it woke up!

Jim,' while signalling to the prop man to release the crab. We plonked it on the dusty carpet, where the cigarette packet had been. The creature adjusted to the light with two windscreen wiper-type arrangements revealing its eyes. That shot, filmed in a beach hut during a downpour, is the first thing Oldsmith sees when he comes to.

Towards the end of the schedule, Peter's main unit went to Malta, leaving us to complete a crocodile sequence that had already been attempted and aborted. A South African stuntman called Rio Riata had been sewn into a crocodile skin for a scene which was supposed to show him emerging from the water and menacing an injured Flynn, who has half-swum, half-crawled away from pursuing Germans. The first time we attempted the scene, Rio started getting nervous as soon as we sewed him into the suit. When the last stitch was in place he became quite tense, and when we placed him in the water he descended into hysterical claustrophobia. We had to cut him out quickly. One of the special effects technicians ultimately did the shot himself and waddled out of the water without any problem. But now we needed to find a real-life crocodile to complete the shot.

I scoured South Africa for a suitable reptile and ended up at a zoo near Johannesburg where the owner tried to convince me that his smallish specimens would be up to the job. Standing outside their cage, I said to him, 'We're really looking for something bigger than six or seven feet.' He insisted that if I joined him inside the cage and had a good look at them, I would change my mind. I don't know what possessed me to do it, but I got inside the cage. 'If they go for you, all you have to do is keep perfectly still,' he told me. 'They have very bad eyesight.' I didn't need any persuading to keep still and the docile animals paid no attention to me. This clearly frustrated the zookeeper, who perhaps thought his crocodiles weren't making a good impression. To remedy the situation, he grabbed the tail of one of them and whipped it backwards and forwards. The agitated animal started snapping and I decided it was time to go. I closed the door behind me and went to look elsewhere.

I'd heard there was a particularly large crocodile in Zululand, so I went to the government office in Pretoria and camped outside until I was seen. The head of the parks commission was very much against film units, but I cajoled him into letting me see this huge crocodile so I could evaluate its suitability. We flew to a remote crocodile farm and I was taken to ring-fenced area dominated by a small lake. 'They're hungry today', said the ranger. 'When I heard you were coming, I decided to delay feeding them.' He clattered a pale of fish, and the lake suddenly seemed to boil with activity. Out swarmed half a dozen small crocodiles, followed by a monstrous crocodile that must have been about 16 feet long. This creature could have fitted at least two men in his mouth should the mood have taken him. I sent a telegram to the main unit in Malta telling them that I had found a ferocious crocodile that would be perfect for us. Unfortunately, I never got the opportunity to film the sequence as I was recalled straightaway.

I was aware that Michael Klinger and Peter Hunt had fallen out over the budget of the film and the atmosphere had been sour for quite some time. I was friends with both of them; as such, I was caught between a battling producer and director. I was expecting trouble when I flew to Malta, but nothing prepared me for the news that I wasn't going to edit the film. I

would edit the second-unit material I had shot, but the majority of the work would be undertaken by Michael Duthie, who had acted as an assistant to both Peter and me on previous films. I realised that I had been kept busy on the fruitless crocodile sequence in order to avoid an embarrassing confrontation in Malta.

I recalled that many years before Peter had told me he often felt betrayed by the people with whom he'd worked. 'Why does everyone always turn on me?' he asked. I was baffled by what he was saying and now I was baffled by his attitude towards me. The situation between Peter and Michael Klinger had been difficult, but I had never given any indication of disloyalty to either of them, and I certainly never did anything sneaky or underhanded.

While Michael Duthie cut the film, I came back to London feeling pretty low. A friend of mine called Roger Cherrill had a cutting shop in Dean Street and I called him to see if he had any work going. He wasn't able to offer me much money – in fact, the wages barely covered my train fares and lunches – but I've always believed that working is good for the soul. Indeed, I've always held the slightly irrational belief that as soon as you start work, other offers begin to come in.

I received a call from Michael Klinger, who was in Munich working on *Shout at the Devil*. By this time, his relationship with Peter Hunt had reached crisis point and he wanted me to fly out to Germany and take over the film. I refused because I didn't think it was ethical. Although Peter hadn't been very kind to me, I still felt a great deal of respect for him. Besides, there were only a few days of shooting left anyway.

Later on, there was a private screening of the film for the cast and crew, and I was invited. When I arrived at the cinema, I was met by Michael who greeted me warmly. A short while later, Peter Hunt arrived and glared at me in the same fearsome manner I recalled from our brief

A lighter moment with director Peter Hunt during the filming of *Shout at the Devil*.

confrontation over *OHMSS*. 'And what are *you* doing here?' he demanded. Everyone in the cinema heard this insult and they all looked around. Michael quickly intervened and asked me to sit next to him. While the film played I kept my thoughts to myself, but by the end I felt it could have done with a bit more editing work.

I decided to share my opinion of the editing with Peter, so I called him at Elstree Studios the next day. I thought he might appreciate some constructive criticism from a friend. His response was surprising: 'Oh, that Michael Klinger has got to you,' he said. Peter was convinced I was in Michael's pocket and there seemed to be no way to change his mind. I put the phone down, regretting that our friendship had come to an end on such a sour note. I haven't spoken to Peter since that day in 1975, but I remain grateful for the opportunities he gave me and for the huge contribution he made to my career.

I continued working at Roger's cutting shop and my depression deepened. Peter Beale, who was then head of Twentieth Century-Fox in London, tipped me off that an American director was about to shoot a movie at Elstree Studios and was looking for an editor. He told me the director's name was George Lucas and arranged an interview for me. Lucas was a scholarly-looking young man who asked me a few questions and told me a little about his new film *Star Wars*, but I soon got the impression that I was perhaps too experienced for him. I didn't get the job, but I wasn't too upset, as I later found out that Lucas's wife was an editor and I may well have found myself shunted around a bit. When filming on *Star Wars* was completed, a lot of the technicians who worked on it assured me that it was a load of rubbish, which just goes to show how much technicians know.

I was living in Chalfont St Peter at the time and I remember one evening in December when my superstitious tendencies were re-awakened by the sight of a grasshopper on the kitchen boiler. I knew that this could be read as a sign of imminent good luck. Out of the corner of my eye, I could see our cat prepare to lunge for the insect. 'No!' I shouted, holding up my hand just in case the cat hadn't understood me. 'Leave it alone – it's lucky!' Disturbed by the commotion, the grasshopper disappeared under the skirting boards, never to be seen again. I left the rather bemused cat in the kitchen, while I mentally crossed my fingers for good fortune.

The phone rang. It was Bill Cartlidge, Lewis Gilbert's associate producer. I asked him what he was up to. 'I'm in Paris at the moment,' he told me. 'We're cutting Lewis's new film.' The film was *Seven Nights in Japan* starring Michael York. I knew Lewis was familiar with the Land of the Rising Sun because he had shot the Bond film *You Only Live Twice* there in 1966. 'Lewis is going to give you a ring,' Bill continued. 'I just thought I'd call you first to check your availability.'

Gina and I were supposed to go to a neighbour's party that night, but I told her to go on alone while I awaited the call from Lewis. An hour later, I heard the phone ring and dived for the receiver. It was Lewis calling from Paris. He began the message with some bad news – his editor Thelma Connell had died of cancer. Thelma was a popular and highly respected figure within the industry and I had fond memories of her from when we worked together on *The Four Just Men* back in the mid-1950s. Thelma died before she completed *Seven Nights in Japan* and Lewis told me that while she was on her deathbed, he'd asked her who she'd like to finish the film. Perhaps remembering how she'd had to let me go from *The Four Just Men* and wanting to honour an old debt, she'd said, 'Lewis, I'd like you to ask John Glen.' When Lewis told me this incredible story I was transported back 20 years and sat in stunned silence. 'Are you still there?' asked the anxious voice on the other end of the line. 'Yes…yes I'm here.' I replied. 'Well,' said Lewis, 'would you like the job?'

I had an arrangement with Roger that I could leave at short notice if a 'paying' job came along. Three days later, I was on my way to Paris for my first collaboration with Lewis Gilbert since my sound editing days. Lewis took me to Thelma's cutting rooms and I met her assistants. It soon became clear that Thelma's ill-health had prevented her from doing very much work at all because there was film stacked up everywhere. Together with Patricia Ninny, Thelma's chief assistant, Lewis and I decided the best thing to do would be to break over Christmas and reconvene in Paris on 2 January 1976.

I knew from the outset that *Seven Nights In Japan* would be a real struggle to get together because there was so much to be done in such a short space of time. Patricia could see that we were up against it and came to me one morning with a suggestion. 'Why don't you do what French directors do?' she said. 'Simply mark the film and let us cut it.' This would have been an unusual practice in a British studio, but the more I thought about what she said, the more I realised that this wasn't so different from what I used to do in my sound editing days. I decided to give it a go and she stood beside me while I marked up the first sequence. At the end of the process, we wound the film back into rolls and she disappeared next door where her girls began cutting. I moved on to the next sequence, already having saved time.

That afternoon, I inspected their handiwork on a French machine called a Moritone. We trimmed up the sequence to make it respectable and I had to admit that it didn't work too badly. The biggest problem seemed to have been that the French girls couldn't decipher the marks I'd made on the film. They diplomatically suggested that I might like to list my marks on paper in the future! I have Patricia to thank for pointing the way to a procedure that allowed me to edit twice as quickly.

The next person to feel the benefit of this innovation was Lewis, who was impressed at the time we were saving. I have many happy memories of the time I spent with Lewis in Paris. I had always admired him as a director, but during this time I came to know him better as a person. He is a very likeable man with refreshingly modest tastes; at night, we would visit the Left Bank and eat some fantastic meals in the sawdust-strewn cafés frequented by the local artists. One evening, I met Lewis at his flat before we embarked on another night out and noticed there was a slight leak coming from one of the radiators in his bathroom. Lewis, not being technically minded, brushed my concerns aside: 'I'll get somebody in to fix it tomorrow,' he said. I decided to wrap a towel around the pipe nevertheless. When we returned from our meal, we were alarmed to notice that fellers in steel helmets and fire engines were outside the block. The little leak from Lewis's radiator had developed into a gushing torrent that was pouring through the lobby. Lewis's flat was relatively OK, but I don't think the people who lived beneath him were best pleased.

Lewis Gilbert, the director of *The Spy Who Loved Me*, with associate producer Bill Cartlidge.

Towards the end of editing *Seven Nights in Japan*, Lewis told me that he wouldn't be able to make our usual lunch appointment because Cubby Broccoli was coming to visit him. 'Give him my best.' I said. While Lewis and Cubby went to the Ritz, I went out for lunch with the girls. Lewis returned at around 3.30pm and called me aside for a word. 'A little while ago, Cubby asked me to direct the next James Bond film,' he revealed. 'It's called *The Spy Who Loved Me*.' I offered him my congratulations. He continued. 'Cubby's very impressed with you, John. He thinks you did some excellent work on *OHMSS*. He's just told me he'd like you to be involved with the next picture.'

There was already a buzz back at Pinewood about the next Bond film: Cubby had recently split from Harry Saltzman and was producing the next film alone for the first time. The budget for *The Spy Who Loved Me* was going to represent a significant increase compared to the money spent on the previous picture, *The Man With the Golden Gun*, and there was a lot of expectation riding on the new film.

Lewis had already asked Ernest Day to direct the second unit on *The Spy Who Loved Me*. He explained that it was probably just as well because he wanted me to edit the film and he didn't think I could do both. I don't think Lewis was aware of how well I organised my work and delegated certain responsibilities, but it didn't matter – I was glad of the opportunity to edit another Bond film, and excited that it was going to be such a lavish one. A compromise was ultimately reached when Lewis and Cubby decided I should shoot the pre-titles sequence. This, of course, turned out to be the ski-parachute jump – which is where we came in.

In early 1977, I went to St Moritz in Switzerland to oversee the remainder of the skiing footage in the pre-titles sequence. I was joined by Ed Lincoln, a freestyle world champion who performed a spectacular backwards somersault

Willy Bogner films
Sergei (Michael
Billington) as he
pursues Bond in
the pre-titles
sequence of *The
Spy Who Loved
Me*.

twist, along with various other skiing experts, including Jake Lombard, who I would go on to work with numerous times on subsequent Bond movies. My cameramen were Willy Bogner and Alex Barbey, both of whom were old colleagues from *OHMSS*. I didn't realise that there was ill-feeling between Willy and Alex that dated back to 1969. While this simmered away, I asked them to bury their differences for the sake of the movie.

Willy and I stayed at his father's house, but were almost prevented from getting in by a six-foot high wall of snow. We ploughed through it as best as we could and swam the rest of the way to the front door.

Michael Billington was cast as Sergei, the leader of the Russian agents pursuing Bond, but unfortunately he couldn't ski. The first thing I did was rehearse him on the children's slope while he was attached to a special sledge, just as I had filmed George Lazenby and Diana Rigg's close-ups in *OHMSS*. While we were rehearsing, I learned to ski myself by keeping up with the sledge.

The main location was a mountain in Italy and we used a cable car station some 10,000 feet high as our helicopter base. We wanted crevasses carved out of the glaciers so that our skiers could weave in an out of the them during the chase; it took the Italian team nearly a week to dig these areas out for us. We shot those sequences with Willy's hand-held camera and when the light hit the ice on the glacier walls, it produced some beautiful reflections.

As so often happens in these environments, bad weather overcame us surprisingly quickly. I reluctantly abandoned shooting and ordered that everyone be evacuated. First to go were the visiting press photographers. There was one huge chap who took up two seats. By the time the helicopters had returned from ferrying the press off the mountain, the weather had really deteriorated. I made the difficult decision to leave the most experienced mountaineers behind – they were the ones most likely to survive the night – while Willy, Ed and myself bundled on to the last helicopter. I felt like a captain deserting a sinking ship, but the ones left behind insisted it was for the best and we left them warm clothing, shovels and chocolate.

The helicopter struggled through the blizzard and as snow crashed into the windshield, it became difficult to tell which way was up. Our pilot Bruno tried one mountain pass and then another, but everywhere he steered he was faced with an impenetrable flurry of snow. I looked behind to the passenger seat and I could see that Ed was starting to turn a pale shade of green. We were all becoming quite scared. Eventually, Bruno found a relatively clear path through the blizzard. What seemed to be a small town or village loomed ahead, but it was only when we put the helicopter down that we realised we had landed in a mental hospital. The inmates peered out of the window, most amused to see a helicopter land in their midst. By this time Ed was in a perilous state and we left him at the hospital overnight while we returned to St Moritz by train.

The following morning, Ed was collected from the hospital and we returned to the mountain to collect the people we'd been forced to leave behind. They had made themselves a snow house and had spent the whole night walking up and down in an attempt to keep warm. We had lost a whole day's shooting, which grieved me a little, but at least everyone had survived.

We continued shooting the following day, but the bad weather continued intermittently and we finished up on the roof of the cable car station, shooting the close-up showing Bond's ski-pole missile hitting Sergei's chest. We were rehearsing the scene and Alex was following the small missile with his zoom lens, when there was an argument that led to a fight. Alex and Willy began thumping each other and I had to hold them apart, giving each of them a stern lecture. The fight seemed to clear the air a bit and bring this long-standing dispute out into the open. They calmed down and we went on to do seven or eight takes, which made productive use of the day.

The weather eventually cleared and we continued shooting the ski sequences. The large press photographer rejoined us and at one point came close to causing a serious accident. One of the skiers took a corner at 40 mph and all he could see round the other side was this photographer in his path. He leapt up and his skis hit a rock with a loud crunch. From that point on, I made sure this photographer was relegated to the sidelines.

When my contribution to the pre-titles sequence was complete, I returned to Pinewood to begin editing the first unit's material. I had been working in the cutting rooms for a couple of weeks when I got a call from Lewis, who asked me to join the location shoot in Cairo. Roger Moore's co-stars in *The Spy Who Loved Me* included Barbara Bach as the Russian agent Anya Amasova, the lover of the murdered Sergei, and Richard Kiel as the towering steel-toothed villain Jaws. Barbara was a famous model who had appeared in some Italian films. She was recommended shortly before filming started by United Artists' Danny Reisner, who was her boyfriend, and when Cubby and Lewis looked at some of her movies they decided they liked her. This left Danny a little bit nervous because he didn't want to be accused of nepotism in case she didn't work out. A few weeks into filming, I showed Danny a cut sequence featuring Barbara. As

Sergei (Michael Billington) falls victim to Bond's ski-pole missile. I filmed this scene on the roof of a cable-car station.

the seconds went by, I could see him become visibly relieved when he realised that she was doing a good job. He needn't have worried – I think Barbara turned out to be one of the best leading ladies in the whole series.

Lewis Gilbert did a superb job. *The Spy Who Loved Me* saw Roger completely assured in a role he now played with ease. He was at his most handsome and his confidence showed through in every scene. Barbara had to get used to Roger's sense of humour: I remember one particularly amusing prank while Bond and Anya are trudging through the desert. Bond is wearing his tux and Anya is wearing a long evening dress. Roger was walking slightly behind Barbara and he quietly undid his trousers so they started to loosen. By the time she looked behind her, Roger was standing there with his trousers around his ankles. She didn't laugh.

Many of us thought the catering on *The Spy Who Loved Me* was diabolical. When one day the food simply failed to arrive, Cubby got stuck in and cooked up a huge tank of spaghetti. That endeared him to everyone and reminded me that Cubby was a hands-on producer who liked nothing better than sharing the experiences of his crew.

Back in England, I raced to edit the film in time for its scheduled release date. I first met composer Marvin Hamlisch at Pinewood, on one of the soundstages, where he sat down at a rather out-of-tune piano and apologised in advance for his singing voice. As I listened, he played and sang the theme song 'Nobody Does It Better'. I just wish I'd had a tape recorder with me because it was a very special moment hearing that superb song for the first time. Carole Bayer Sager wrote the lyrics and at the time she and Marvin were an item. He was looking forward to her joining him in England, but was fretting a little because he knew that she couldn't stand flying. During one of the rehearsals, there were a number of false starts before he could begin. After the fourth attempt failed, he looked up at me and said, 'I've just heard John Barry is on the way!' Carole eventually arrived, which put him out of his misery.

The legendary 007 Stage was specially constructed for *The Spy Who Loved Me*, based on a design by Ken Adam. It cost well over $1.5 million, but we got good value from it over the years. In *The Spy Who Loved Me* Lewis very cleverly used it as the inside of the submarine-swallowing *Liparus* supertanker, which Stromberg (played by Curt Jurgens) uses to set East and West against each other.

I started to compile the first ever 'wanker reel' of bloopers to give everyone a good laugh at Christmas. It later became a tradition to screen the out-takes at the end of shooting on each of my Bond films. I included such scenes as the moment when Roger let his trousers down, and another which took place during the final confrontation between Bond and Stromberg. The two face each other at opposite ends of a long table in the underwater base. Unbeknown to Bond, there is a long-barrelled gun fixed to the underside of the table pointing right at him. As Stromberg squeezes the trigger, Bond quickly ducks out the way and the bullet slams into the chair behind him.

On the first take, however, the special effects supervisor John Evans was a little too quick with the detonating button and Roger dived off the chair with his bottom on fire. I don't think he ever forgave John for that, but it made a priceless inclusion in my collection of humorous gaffs and blunders. These mishaps ran to the sound of 'The Wanker Song', with music provided by Roger. Ken Adam was another victim, with a special section dealing with the construction of the 007 Stage. There had been a documentary about the building of the stage and I borrowed some footage from it, intercutting certain scenes with Ken saying 'I did that' at the end of each one, so it appeared he was taking credit for everything. To this I added propaganda footage of Hitler building the Third Reich, to complete the good-humoured wind-up. I wanted Ken to be present the first time I screened the wanker reel, and of course we got a bigger audience than were usually present at the everyday rushes screenings. Ken was surprised to see the viewing theatre full to bursting, but soon understood why as the rushes finished and Roger's song came on. At first I don't think Ken was very impressed, but he soon saw the funny side and later asked to borrow the film for a party. Unfortunately, I couldn't let him have it – the film was potential dynamite and I couldn't risk it falling into the wrong hands.

Like the bobsleigh sequence in *OHMSS*, the ski parachute jump in *The Spy Who Loved Me* got me noticed and boosted my reputation in the industry. I continued to lay the foundations for a career in directing and was able to pick and choose second-unit jobs while I waited for the opportunity to helm my own movie.

Euan Lloyd asked me to be the editor and second-unit director on *The Wild Geese*, which was yet another Roger Moore film due to be shot in South Africa. Reginald Rose's impressive script was based on a novel by Daniel Carney. Here was a thundering *Boys' Own*-style yarn that promised to bring together Roger, Richard Burton, Richard Harris, Hardy Kruger and Stewart Granger. I'd have been mad not to say yes. The director was Andrew McLaglen, a huge American with strong Irish roots. We got on very well.

Richard Burton had recently remarried and his new wife Susie was trying to straighten him out. Richard Harris was also on his best behaviour and as far as I'm aware, neither of them touched a drop while we were filming. Richard Harris also brought his wife, Ann Turkel, who I remember thinking was one of the most beautiful women I'd ever seen. All the crew knew Harris and were pleased to see him, but I think they were even happier about meeting his missus.

Richard Burton's health had begun to fail – I think his liver was probably on the way out even then – and he was in such a state that he could barely walk into his close shots. The stunt arranger Bob Simmons was a wonderful double for Burton. He performed the scenes in which Burton's character Colonel Faulkner carries the African leader on his back. Burton stepped into shot for the scenes showing Faulkner put the guy down. I'm aware of the stories about Burton's behaviour, but he was never less than a perfect gentleman in my company. He had a beguiling charisma and was a patient and considerate listener – he never dominated conversations, but rather led you into them. I loved working with him.

The main location was at a place called Tshipse in the northern Transvaal. We were housed in some kind of government holiday camp which was served by a hot spring with supposedly therapeutic qualities. I found the water so hot I could hardly bear it, but the sulphur was certainly invigorating. At the beginning of the shoot, we celebrated Roger's birthday in a natural amphitheatre that had a dance-floor made of hardened cow dung. I finally got to bed in the early hours, and I remember the moonlight illuminating the monkeys swinging in the distant trees. I was rudely awakened the following morning by the sound of the South African air force flying their jets at virtually ground level. 'Why do they do that?' I asked one of the locals over breakfast. 'It's a demonstration of white power,' he replied. I winced at my hangover-induced headache and made a mental note to stock up on Aspirin.

Andy McLaglen was used to directing the big John Wayne-style action picture and had a good concept of the broad canvas this type of film was painted on. I think he was a little suspicious of me at first because Euan had rather dumped me on him – 'You've got to use John,' he said. 'He did a great job on the last Bond film and he's done some wonderful action material.' I was on probation as far as Andy was concerned and for the first few days of filming, he asked me to shoot back-to-back with the first unit so he could keep an eye on what I was doing. This never really works because you're always having to do things like keeping quiet in case any noise you make comes through on the first unit's recording. You invariably end up getting under each other's feet.

Despite the slightly restrictive conditions, I was able to get some satisfactory stuff in the can during that week. One shot involved Hardy Kruger shooting a guard using a crossbow loaded with a cyanide bolt. The guard is killed without a sound. The challenge was this: how could our camera operator Dudley Lovell follow this fast-moving bolt into the distance and keep it in focus? We solved the problem using a high-speed camera and a bit of lateral thinking. I got Hardy's double to position the crossbow in the foreground of the shot and we pre-determined the focus on the zoom lens using an educated guess of the bolt's trajectory. I told Dudley to begin zooming as the crossbow was triggered. We knew there was no way of knowing whether it had worked or not until we saw the rushes, so we did seven or eight takes to give us a good chance of getting it right. I counted in the double and he fired the crossbow. Shooting at 72 frames per second, Dudley filmed what he hoped was the speeding cyanide bolt. Over the following takes he sometimes shot at 120 frames per second so we would have an option when we came to check the rushes. When the rushes came back from the lab two or three days later, we were relieved to see that there were two takes that worked perfectly: you could actually see the bolt barrelling towards the guard, and when it hit its target, the figure in the distance dropped. Andy watched the rushes with us and at that point I think he realised he needed me.

I was left to get on with it after the first week and I probably did some of the finest second-unit work of my career. I was especially pleased with the parachute drop, which featured a huge squad of troops and mercenaries descending en masse. We filmed the scene from a twin-engined Cessna, not an ideal aeroplane for filming purposes because its design makes it difficult to keep its wings out of shot. The scene was shot at 72 frames per second and we had only relatively small magazines on the cameras. We were looking at about three minutes tops before we ran out of film, so it was crucial that there was precise co-ordination between the Cessna and the C130 transport plane carrying the parachutists. We were in radio contact with the C130, where another cameraman was suspended on a stretcher above the door, but two-way radios weren't terribly reliable in those days and I didn't feel confident enough to trust to them alone. I asked the jumpmaster to radio us when he was about to lead the descent, but also to throw a newspaper out of the plane so we'd have a visual signal in case we didn't get his message. Sure enough, the radio let us down, but I did spot the flying newspaper. I told Dudley to turn over and instructed the pilot to bank slightly to the right so we could film the scene without the wing getting in the way. Just as Dudley's camera got up to speed, the parachutists came into view like a string of pearls. It was a glorious shot and we got it on the first take (which was just as well because Euan had already warned me that he wouldn't let me have another). I also had the camera on board the aircraft, filming at 32 frames per second. When this footage was combined with the footage of the descent, the main unit's shots of the troops landing and close-ups of the leading actors, we had a very successful sequence. I can't think of a better way to illustrate how different units on a film can work in harmony to create seamlessly blended action. The only person who seemed less than happy was Dudley, who had ignored my advice to wrap up while he was in the air and came back an alarming shade of blue as a result.

Back in England, Andy and I edited the film together. The climax of the movie with our heroes only just making it on to the departing DC3 was very exciting and my sound editor Colin Miller did a first-rate job, imaginatively embellishing the sequence with some very clever work. I was astonished when I heard the rough dub he'd put together, initially just for presentation purposes.

I'd hardly got my bags through the door when the phone rang – it was Bob Simmonds calling from Pinewood, asking if I was free to come over and talk about a new project. Bob's nickname was 'Bob the petty' because it was always his job to issue petty cash vouchers on movies. His near namesake

Bob Simmonds was always called 'Bob the leap' because of his energetic stunt work. Over a drink, Bob Simmonds revealed that he was working on *Superman*, which Richard Donner was directing on location in Canada. Would I be interested in directing some of the second-unit sequences? The buzz surrounding *Superman* was enormous and the expectation that this could be the biggest thing since *Star Wars* would prove justified. While I was at the *Superman* office at Pinewood, I met the composer John Williams, who had written the score for George Lucas's epic space opera. John Williams was something of legend with both *Jaws* and *Star Wars* under his belt and it was a real thrill to meet one of my heroes.

Within a couple of days, I was in Canada, preparing to shoot a complicated sequence illustrating the effect an earthquake had on parallel rows of telegraph poles. Margot Kidder, who was playing Lois Lane, was due to drive down the road between these poles, initially oblivious to the fact they were collapsing like dominoes in her wake. Canadian special effects technician John Thomas had rigged the telegraph poles so they were on hinges loaded with explosive charges and packed with Fuller's Earth – they could be collapsed or erected on cue. At least, that was the idea. I asked him if he could rehearse just two or three poles for me, just to reassure me that everything would be OK before I started filming. He obliged and I watched in dismay as the poles collapsed in the wrong order. I went back to my hotel and he went back to the drawing board.

I also had to film the petrol station exploding after Margot filled up her car and the close-ups of her driving away. I had four cameras on the scene, the best-placed being the remote inside the car itself. This filmed what Margot would have seen as she looked over her shoulder at the explosion behind her. When the petrol station blew, the resulting ball of flame filled the whole of the car's back window. Dick Donner was especially pleased with that shot.

Margot had to drive through a load of chickens in a Native Indian village and the birds were supposed to flap around and get out of her way. 'What if I flatten any of them by accident?' she asked me, a look of genuine concern on her face. 'It'll be fine,' I reassured her. 'They'll get out of your way.' Unfortunately, she came in a little faster than I expected and there were a few casualties. Margot was very upset, but was consoled by the genial Indian Chief Tug Smith. 'Don't worry, my dear,' he said. 'Just a few feathers.' Tug had worked with Euan Lloyd before and gave me a message to pass on to him: 'Tell Euan I'm not on the firewater any more!'

Dick Donner took his unit back to England and left me with quite a lot of work to do with Margot at the Montana border. *Superman* marked the beginning of a good relationship with Dick, who was always ringing me up asking me to do second-unit work on his films. Dick's not a man to mince his words and I remember receiving a typically forthright call during 1979: 'Hi, John. It's Dick. Get your arse down to Louisiana and get me out of the shit!' At the time of this call I was working on my third Bond picture, *Moonraker*, so I recommended Jimmy Devis instead.

Later on, however, I was available to help out Euan Lloyd and Andy McLaglen on *The Sea Wolves*, a semi follow-up to *The Wild Geese* set in India. *The Sea Wolves* was a charming story, again from a script by Reginald Rose, about a group of old soldiers who decide to make a glorious last

From left to right:
Trevor Howard,
Gregory Peck,
David Niven and
Roger Moore on
location in Delhi
for *The Sea
Wolves*.

gesture. They sabotage some German spy ships on the unofficial behalf of the British government, whose hands are tied in neutral territory. Gregory Peck was the star and he was ably supported by Roger Moore, Trevor Howard, David Niven and Patrick Macnee, to name but a few. David worked hard for us, but he was sadly not in the best of shape and was nearing the end of his career.

I was hired to edit *The Sea Wolves* and didn't do very much filming on the picture. Euan said he wanted me around, however – possibly as a back-up to Andy – and I stayed with the crew in Goa and later Delhi. Even before I started editing the film back in England, I was apprehensive about Gregory Peck's performance. Greg delivered his lines in a measured manner and with great authority, but he could come across as a little slow. I decided to speed up some of his sequences and nervously awaited his arrival in the dubbing theatre for the post-synchronisation of his lines. As the film played, I looked over to gauge his reaction. When it had finished, he came up to me and congratulated me. Euan had once again assembled a first class cast and Gregory Peck was one of its most professional and gracious members. I couldn't have picked a better film to bring my career as a second-unit director and editor to an end.

# 007

## CHAPTER 7

### OUT OF THIS WORLD

There are relatively clear subdivisions in my working life: following an apprenticeship in the 1950s, I really got to grips with my craft working in television in the 1960s. I spent the 1970s building a reputation as a second-unit director and editor of some of the biggest action movies of the era. In the 1980s, I directed five consecutive James Bond films – a record that is so far unbeaten.

Just as I had to serve an apprenticeship in the film industry, I also had to pay my dues in the Bond films before I earned my directing stripes. *On Her Majesty's Secret Service* was my big break, and *The Spy Who Loved Me* featured probably the greatest action sequence I ever committed to film. Between *The Spy Who Loved Me* in 1976 and my first directing assignment in 1980, I contributed another sequence to the Bond series. The film was *Moonraker* and the sequence was a spectacular and highly dangerous stunt which saw Bond kicked out of an aeroplane without a parachute.

*The Spy Who Loved Me* had a been a huge success, putting Bond back on the map and cementing Roger Moore's popularity in the role that many people had believed Sean Connery had made his own. Cubby Broccoli was delighted with the film and invited Lewis Gilbert back to direct the follow-up in 1978. At $13.5 million, *The Spy Who Loved Me* had cost twice as much as *The Man With the Golden Gun*. At $30 million, *Moonraker* would cost twice as much again. Lewis coolly accepted the responsibility of the huge budget, but joked that when he started out in the industry he could make an entire feature for less than *Moonraker*'s telephone bill.

As had been the case with *The Spy Who Loved Me*, the plot of Ian Fleming's novel was discarded. *Moonraker* told the story of an audacious plot to hijack space shuttles and use them to launch a germ warfare offensive from an orbiting space station. The influence of *Star Wars*, which had been such a huge hit around the world in 1977 and 1978, was all pervasive. *Moonraker* would present James Bond as the star of a lavish space epic. The pre-titles sequence would set the mood for the off-world adventures to come by being almost totally set in mid-air.

The sequence had been devised by Michael Wilson, Cubby's son-in-law. Michael was being groomed to assume ultimate responsibility for the James Bond series (a position he now occupies with great success) and he cut his teeth as executive producer on *Moonraker*. As well as being a

highly efficient producer, Michael is also a talented writer, and I was impressed by the ideas he presented to me for *Moonraker*. It went something like this: a pilot sabotages a plane carrying Bond, then jumps out of the door after a scuffle. Bond is then kicked out of the plane by his *Spy Who Loved Me* nemesis Jaws *(played* by the huge Richard Kiel). Bond skydives towards the pilot and steals his parachute from him in mid-air. He then has to shake off the pursuing Jaws, who has followed him out of the plane. The pilot hurtles to his death, Jaws forgets his own strength and breaks his parachute cord, while Bond lands safely. Cue credits.

The sequence would have to be a tapestry of numerous fragments from a lot of jumps, but a technical question threatened the whole venture before we began. Bond films are shot using an anamorphic process. Anamorphic lenses shoot an apparently distorted image that resolves itself as a correctly proportioned widescreen image when projected properly. The process was first defined by Leonardo Da Vinci, who taught his students anamorphic principles by getting them to draw distorted images that would appear normal when reflected on to a polished metal tube. I was privileged to see some of Da Vinci's original sketches when one of the Samuelson brothers, who owned the Panavision franchise, showed me his private collection.

The 35mm anamorphic cameras we used could be very heavy. Freefall footage is generally shot using 16mm lightweight cameras, but even these can weigh around seven pounds. We decided very quickly that a camera would have to be mounted on the skydiving cameraman's crash-helmet, but we were concerned that the G-force of the sudden upward rush could place a fatal pressure on his neck when he opened his chute. Michael discovered a plastic anamorphic lens in a second-hand camera shop in Paris. We used this as the basis of a specially manufactured camera with a titanium body. After some tests, Continental Camera Systems developed an anamorphic camera that could carry 100 feet of film and was light enough to mount on to a crash-helmet with a makeshift drop-down viewfinder attached. Cubby remained dubious about the whole affair and ensured that filming took place some months before principal photography, giving us time to substitute another idea if the sequence proved untenable.

In the spring of 1978, I went to California to meet up with the skydiving team charged with the responsibility of starring in and filming the sequence. We were based at a small town called Yontville (population 902). I was billeted in the sort of motel where most people are reluctant to spend more than one night. I stayed there for over a month. Every morning, I would drive up the Silverado trail to this airfield in a remote area of the wine region and meet the team, who more often than not had been camping overnight with their girlfriends. They were very young skydiving enthusiasts and I found their approach a little amateurish at the outset. The first morning I got there, I was horrified to discover that they didn't emerge from their tents until about 10am. I read them the riot act and explained that they were being presented with an opportunity to become professionals. We had to work with the available sunlight and that meant they had to be ready to begin by 8am. These guys were pretty laid-back and the news hit them hard, but we managed to get a routine going.

The cameraman was called Rande Deluca. He had done some experimenting with the helmet-mounted camera and had devised a way of

James Bond (Roger Moore) looks understandably nervous aboard Drax's space station in *Moonraker.*

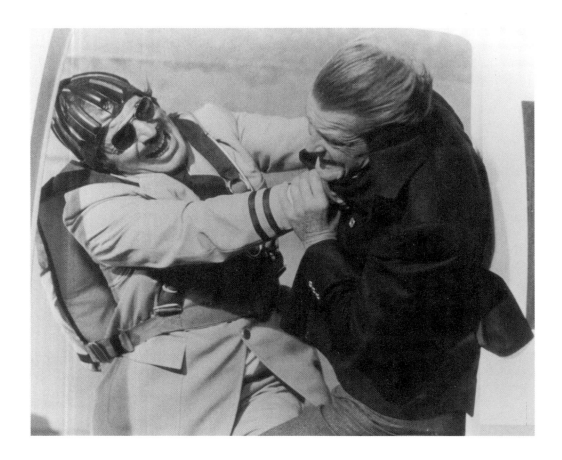

In the pre-titles
sequence of
*Moonraker*, a pilot
(BJ Worth)
struggles with
Bond (Roger
Moore) in the open
doorway of an out-
of-control plane.

wrapping rope around his parachute so it would open two to three times slower than usual. This minimised the potentially damaging upward jolt, but meant he was dangerously close to the ground when his parachute finally unfurled.

The sequence had been drawn up as a storyboard and each skydiver had a copy which he studied. Storyboards play a crucial role in directing action sequences. A writer can dream up a great sequence and the first or second-unit director must interpret that dream. A good storyboard artist can act as an essential bridge between the two. While his work may never be seen by the public in its original form, a director's interpretation of it can often be a close reflection. I have always found it quite simple to envisage a scene and break it down into a shot list, which I can then realise as rough sketches. A good artist can take those sketches and imbue them with an inspiring dynamic quality in an effective storyboard. Certain storyboard artists seem to be able to create movement and excitement that everyone can interpret. Storyboards are also useful because they give you something tangible to pin on the wall while you're preparing a film and they can give crew-members a degree of confidence if they feel uncertain about a particular shot. The problem with my rough sketches is that only two people ever seem to be able to interpret them – me and a trained artist!

Directing second units taught me that you also have to be flexible, however, regardless of what is depicted in your storyboard. If an opportunity presents itself, I will embrace it, unlike some directors I have worked with who resist new ideas and can't cope when plans change. My experiences on *OHMSS* showed that you can sometimes be lucky enough to capture fantastic moments of action that you wouldn't dare ask a stuntman to repeat.

Each particular shot was rehearsed on the ground and I watched while they crawled around, devising a way to get the parachute off B J Worth (who was doubling for the pilot) and on to Jake Lombard (who was doubling for James Bond). Of course, both B J and Jake had two concealed parachutes beneath Velcro panels which they could activate to bring them back to earth safely. Their specially made costumes looked pretty ropey on the ground, but in the air they looked fine.

B J was a world champion skydiver and captain of the US team. Jake was very versatile and was such a remarkable double for Roger that the finished sequence features some relatively close shots of his face that don't give the game away. The team asked if they could wear goggles because free-falling at 150 mph is obvious pretty rough on your eyes. I explained that the whole point of the sequence was that Bond was supposed to seem unprepared for his freefall and therefore shouldn't be seen wearing them. They reassured me, however, by showing me a pair of rimless Perspex goggles that they claimed wouldn't be picked up by a slightly vibrating camera travelling at the same high speed as its subject. I agreed to let them use the goggles. When the guys felt confident enough to go for Take One, Jake was carried to the aeroplane (to avoid getting his shoes dirty and spoiling the shot) and they took off. Their twin-engined Cessna seemed to take forever to get up to the 7500 feet altitude they needed. I waited with baited breath on the ground. I heard on the radio that they had bailed out and were descending in formation while Rande signalled to them to get in the right position.

We encountered an unforeseen problem on the first day. The skydivers let go of BJ's dummy parachute pack and it fell on to private property. The owner was irate and refused to give the dummy parachute back, which was awkward because we didn't have that many props. I managed to placate him with a bottle of whisky and the parachute was returned, but we soon developed a mini-parachute for the dummy parachute so that at least it wouldn't hurt anybody if it did fall away.

The jumps resumed on a regular basis and this is how we continued: I only ever attempted to get around three seconds of film in the can on any particular jump. I had little choice because they were only ever in freefall for between five and seven seconds. The film was developed in San Francisco and I viewed the previous day's rushes on an editing machine I had installed in the airfield hangar. The skydivers would gather round and we would discuss how we could improve the shots.

After two weeks, I had ticked off quite a few of the shots on my storyboard so I went to San Francisco on Sunday, my day off, and hired a cutting room to edit the material together. The guys were impressed with what they saw on Monday morning, and one week later, we had got everything we needed. It took a total of 88 jumps to shoot enough footage for a sequence that lasted just over two minutes, but it was worth the effort.

We would use BJ for action work on a number of subsequent films. In a

James Bond
(Roger Moore)
heads for firm
ground – with
somebody else's
parachute.

way, I regretted that he became a stunt man because he later got quite badly hurt when he was caught in an explosion. Jake was someone else we would come back to – his likeness to Roger came in very useful. I never got the chance to work with Rande again, and I was deeply saddened to hear that he later died of cancer. I sometimes wonder if the numerous jolts his spine endured may have contributed to his illness.

Like the studio work, the editing of *Moonraker* was undertaken in Paris. Eon had made the unprecedented move of taking principal photography away from Pinewood for tax reasons. The production was split between three studios in the Paris area: Billancourt, Boulogne and Epinay. I arrived in Paris during the pre-production period and one of the first people I saw was Claude Renoir, who had been the director of photography on *The Spy Who Loved Me*. He was on the phone when I went into his office and I was shocked to see that he was on his hands and knees trying to read the numbers on the dial. He immediately came clean and told me he was having terrible problems with his eyesight and was due to go into hospital to fix a detached retina. He resigned from the production that same day. Another French cameraman called Jean Tournier took over. I felt desperately sorry for Claude – the disease affecting his eyes was a terrible tragedy to befall such a fine cameraman. Unfortunately, after Claude underwent surgery he suffered a fall and dislodged his retina once again.

Lewis began principal photography on *Moonraker*, with Ernest Day once more directing the second unit, in August 1978. I was editing the movie when I got a call from Lewis, explaining that Ernie's wife had been taken ill. He asked me if I'd be prepared to take over some of the second-unit shooting in Venice. Lewis and I had a good working relationship, and I knew he trusted me. 'You know what to do, boy,' he told me. 'Go and do it.'

I went to Venice and worked with the main unit on the scene where Bond's gondola-shaped hovercraft glides through St Mark's Square. Roger got dunked in the lagoon a few times while we tried to manoeuvre the outlandish vehicle on to dry land, but the biggest problem I remember was controlling the huge crowds of tourists. We gave up in the end and simply filmed their naturally bemused reactions as they parted to make way for James Bond on a gondola-shaped hovercraft. Fortunately, I had been privileged to have been invited along to the reconnaissance of Venice with Lewis some months before, so I was familiar with the location and what needed to be done. I went on to shoot the gondola chase through the canals.

The French studios couldn't offer the same facilities that were available at Pinewood, which was why work had to be split across three sites. The French crew were every bit as good as the technicians back home and it wasn't long before they started playing the sorts of practical jokes Bond crews are famous for. One scene that definitely hit the cutting room floor featured Bond and Holly Goodhead (played by Lois Chiles) aboard the villain's space station, staring out at the stars. Just as Lois goes to walk away one of the French prop men – with his face painted green and two antennae protruding from his head – appears on the other side of the glass and starts cleaning the window!

While editing the film, I began to have more and more to do with Michael Wilson. As well as acting as executive producer and contributing ideas to the screenplays, Michael wanted to try his hand at directing. He went to the United States to film the scene that shows Bond being attacked by the villain's pet python. He came back with some interesting material, but there is a limit to how much you can achieve without the involvement of the principal artists. I gave the sequence to my assembly editor Alan Strachan and ran the result for Michael. This was his first time behind the camera and he was a bit disappointed with the result. I suggested he went home and wrote out a progressive shot list, illustrating how he'd like the scene to play. I believe an editor should give a director every opportunity to view a scene in the way he envisaged. Alan recut the scene and screened it for Michael, this time with Cubby in attendance. When it was over, the lights came up and Cubby said, 'Put it back the way it was!'

In reality, the scene was not particularly good, and the underwater action with the snake was fairly restricted. The sequence didn't feature very prominently in the finished film, but I think Michael's imagination had run away with him and he had come to regard it as more important than it actually was. Michael is very versatile: he is a qualified lawyer, an engineer and one of the world's foremost experts on early still photography. At this stage of his life, I think he wanted to get into the creative side of film-making a bit more. He ultimately achieved that ambition by playing a major role in the scripting of the Bond movies throughout the 1980s.

While we worked in Paris, Derek Meddings directed the demanding miniature effects sequences at Pinewood. Derek had a lot to live up to in the wake of *Star Wars*, but he did a wonderful job and I was absolutely amazed by what he produced. I'd originally recommended Derek to Lewis for *The Spy Who Loved Me* and he went on to become a key member of the Bond production team on a number of subsequent films. Another of the special effects supervisors on *Moonraker* was John Richardson – I had known and worked with his father Cliff. John is a good friend of mine and I admired the work he did on the boat chase sequence shot in the Florida Everglades. He even performed one of the stunts himself when one of his explosions threw him over the side of a speeding launch.

*The Spy Who Loved Me* was relatively fresh in my memory while I was editing *Moonraker* and one day I noticed something that I decided to use to tease Lewis. Bernard Lee had been flown to Paris and the set of his office had been retrieved from storage at Pinewood and driven over on the back of a lorry. When Lewis finished filming the scene, I was given the footage to edit. I was immediately struck by how similar Bond's briefing in *Moonraker* looked to Bond's briefing in *The Spy Who Loved Me*. This wasn't terribly surprising really – both films had the same scriptwriter and the same director and both scenes shared the same actors. It just happened I had the cutting copy of *The Spy Who Loved Me* with me, so I tagged the scene in M's office on to the rushes from *Moonraker*. I ran the footage for Lewis and he laughed uproariously, but nevertheless requested I didn't try the joke out on Cubby – the scenes were indeed similar and our producer might not have seen the funny side.

*Moonraker* marked the welcome return of John Barry, who composed the score after a bit of break from the Bond films. John's music is very much the sound of the Bond series and there is a timeless quality to his scores – they always sound fresh and up-to-the-minute, however old they are. Together with Cubby, Harry Saltzman, Terence Young, Peter Hunt and production designer Ken Adam, I think John can be included as one of the chief architects of the Bond film-making style.

*Moonraker* was an ambitious and expensive film and it proved a great success at the box-office. In retrospect, it's possible that we got a bit carried away with the humour – maybe Jaws' romance with the girl on the space station was a bit much – but it's easy to be wise about these things with hindsight. With a long-running series such as the Bond films, you can progress a long way in one direction before you realise you've gone too far. After *Moonraker*, there was a feeling at Eon that it was time for a new direction and time to get back to Ian Fleming's original style.

The only other regret about *Moonraker* was on the publicity front. We had carefully timed the film's release in June 1979 to coincide with the first flight of the American Space Shuttle. The US space program suffered some delays, however, and the Shuttle program was put back to 1980. After our hard work over the previous year, we all felt NASA had let us down.

The 1970s had seen a consolidation of my career as a second-unit director and editor. At the close of the 1960s my career was in the doldrums and my confidence was in tatters. Ten years on, I was able to look back on a substantial body of accomplished editing and second-unit work that I was proud of. Understanding the mechanics of effective editing, I had developed an economical method of second-unit shooting

that occupied itself only with footage I knew would be useful. I always directed my second-unit sequences with editing in mind, so had the jigsaw of footage already mapped out in my head. This enabled me to shoot out of sequence, which was a great asset when weather conditions were poor or technical challenges called for a last-minute revision of the shot list.

This will sound immodest, but by 1979 I felt it was inevitable that I would become a main unit director. My career had developed a momentum of its own, but I was aware of the generous patronage of such figures as Peter Hunt, Michael Klinger and Euan Lloyd. I think Michael would have offered me *Gold*, were it not for the fact that having Peter Hunt – an experienced Bond director – on board helped him convince his backers. During the mid-1970s, I had met Michael and Wilbur Smith to discuss the possibility of directing *Shaka Zulu*, but the opportunity became another near miss.

I had another champion among the producers who had supported me over the previous decade. Cubby Broccoli had remembered me from the bobsleigh sequence in *OHMSS* and been especially impressed by my work on *The Spy Who Loved Me*. I wasn't aware of this at the time, but Cubby had already earmarked me for a promotion to the next and most exciting stage of my career.

Meeting Princess Anne at the premiere of *The Spy Who Loved Me*. To my left are Peter Lamont and Derek Meddings.

# 007™

# CHAPTER 8

## SPYMASTER

When my work on *The Sea Wolves* was complete, I was invited to Pinewood Studios to have lunch with Cubby Broccoli. It turned out to be quite a gathering of James Bond luminaries: Cubby and his wife Dana were joined by Michael Wilson, Derek Meddings and Peter Lamont, who was about to be promoted to become Ken Adam's replacement as production designer. Following a very pleasant meal, someone mentioned Roger Moore's intimation that *Moonraker* would be his final Bond picture and there was some discussion over the next film in the series, *For Your Eyes Only*. The identity of the new Bond was not the only subject of speculation. 'Have you chosen a director for the new film?' Derek asked Cubby. 'I might ask Guy Hamilton to do another,' Cubby replied, after a long pause. 'Or I might ask Lewis to come back.' I listened to the conversation, not really paying any attention to the fact that Cubby appeared to be stalling. 'What about me directing it?' asked Derek. He said it jokingly, but I could tell that he actually meant it. A peal of embarrassed laughter went around the table and nothing more was said.

Three or four days later, I received another invitation to have lunch with Cubby at Pinewood. This time I was met by just Cubby, Dana and Michael. Over conversation, I deliberately avoided the subject of the new film's director and answered all sorts of questions about the work I'd done outside my previous three Bond films. Deep down, I was beginning to get the impression that something was afoot.

We retired to Cubby's office and after a short while, I popped out to wash my hands. When I returned, Cubby was seated behind his desk. 'Sit down, John,' he said. There was a dramatic pause. 'What would you say to directing the next James Bond film?' I sat in a stunned silence, my mind racing at the proposition. I pinched myself mentally and did my best to make an intelligible response. Cubby held up his hand, 'If you want time to think about it, that's absolutely fine.' He barely had time to finish before I said, 'I don't need time to think about it – that would be fantastic.' Cubby added that he'd have to clear it with his partners at United Artists, but he was confident there wouldn't be a problem. We shook hands and I left his office walking on air.

When it was confirmed that I was to be the director, we had a celebration in town. I remember the startled looks on some people's faces when they

From left to right: Peter Lamont, Michael G Wilson, Cubby Broccoli and me on location in Greece for my first directing assignment.

learned I'd got the job. No one seemed more surprised than Jerry Juroe, Eon's publicity director, who was visibly shocked at the news. I'm sure a number of people felt the same way – here was a humble editor and second-unit director elevated to the rank of director on one of the biggest movies of the year. I kept my insecurities very much to myself: although I had considerable experience as a film-maker, particularly on the James Bond movies, I felt I hadn't gained much experience with actors. I had worked with actors quite a lot, but rarely in the capacity of directing them in the way I knew I would have to on *For Your Eyes Only*. I would have to trust my instincts – I had always got on very well with the actors as long as I was honest and straightforward.

One thing I was absolutely sure of in those heady days was that I felt enormously privileged to have been entrusted with something as important as a James Bond film. The ski-parachute jump was Cubby's favourite Bond sequence and I think he'd earmarked me as a future director from that point on. He'd obviously watched my progress, testing me here and there to see if I had the right stuff. I think he knew I'd make a few mistakes along the way, but he was also aware that I knew the Bond films inside out. I had always felt that if I was to get a break as a director, I would want to cut my teeth on a James Bond film. I had the necessary experience and I knew exactly what was required.

*For Your Eyes Only* would be the first James Bond film adapted from one of Ian Fleming's numerous short stories. The film's screenplay would ultimately draw on elements from *For Your Eyes Only* and another Fleming short story, *Risico*, and in doing so prove a great deal more faithful to Fleming's work than *Moonraker*, which had been (nominally) based on a full-length novel. By the time I was brought on board in early 1980, Michael Wilson had already begun work on a story outline with Richard 'Dick' Maibaum. Dick had written or co-written almost every James Bond film to date and his knowledge of Bond history and successful story structure was unparalleled. *For Your Eyes Only* marked the beginning of his long and fruitful collaboration with Michael, who contributed some fresh and very modern ideas.

I had spent some time with Dick during the shooting of *OHMSS* in 1969 and met up with him again on both *The Spy Who Loved Me* and *Moonraker* (on the rare occasions he wasn't called on to script or co-script a Bond movie, he was usually consulted on the screenplays). I was reunited with Dick in Hollywood, where we discussed *For Your Eyes Only*. I contributed ideas for a number of action sequences early on in the scripting process; those that met with the approval of Dick, Michael and Cubby were incorporated. Dick and Michael were of course the main collaborators on the screenplay, but on certain pages they would leave a space indicating that an action scene should take place between certain characters. They would usually leave me to devise a suitable sequence.

The James Bond formula is a bit of a mystery really; we would look at the early films and study their structure, but to be honest, we were sometimes left none the wiser over why some of them worked so well. One of the 'rules' was that after a couple of dialogue scenes there had to be an action sequence. Cubby would describe this best when he asked me, 'Where are the bumps?' – the idea being that the traditional pre-titles sequence provided the first big bump. A number of subsequent 'little bumps' would lead to the 'big bump' finale. The trick was to orchestrate carefully the action, or bumps, and develop the story in equal measures, while always keeping the film moving. I think it's fair to say that the James Bond films are not renowned for their story content (with the notable exceptions of the earliest pictures in the series), but rely instead on delivering an eyeful of action. The public aren't sure when they're going to get it or how it's going to arrive, but they know there's going to be great excitement. I think this is built in to people's expectations.

We were always attempting to strike a fine balance between preserving a tried-and-tested formula and treading new ground, which we recognised as an essential way to ensure the longevity of the series. One thing that remained constant during my years as a James Bond director was that we tried to stay faithful to the spirit – and where we could, the writing – of Ian Fleming.

I had enormous respect for Dick Maibaum: he was always the perfect gentleman, but at the same time he always spoke his mind. On one occasion, I was about to play a round of golf with him at the Brentwood Country Club when someone approached him and said, 'Hey Dick, what about a game of golf?' He turned around and replied, 'I will never play golf with you for as long as I live!' Dick registered my surprise and replied matter-of-factly, 'I don't want to play golf with him because he's a horrible man,' and that was that. You could always rely on him to be honest.

Dick had a delightful wife called Sylvia, who is still as beautiful as ever. Every time he created a leading lady for one of his scripts it was always based on her, or more specifically, his romantic view of her as a fairytale princess from Austria. Cubby knew he was doing this and I also came to recognise the disguised Sylvias in Dick's scripts. If Cubby ever asked Dick to remove anything from his scripts, he would recall his days as a stage actor by dropping to one knee, throwing his arms out and making an impassioned and theatrical plea to preserve the scene. Dick and I would often have heated arguments over scenes either of us would want to introduce, remove or change. Cubby would watch us and roar with laughter, knowing that the script would inevitably have to be rewritten at some point anyway. He enjoyed being the mediator, and sometimes the protagonist, during these little conferences.

Dick, Michael and myself had known each other for quite some time. None of us had an axe to grind and we could be quite critical of one another. When we were working on the script, there was a lot of constructive criticism and a lot of arguments, but we never actually fell out.

*For Your Eyes Only* had the shortest pre-production period of any recent Bond film – the story called for predominantly European locations and I knew that in order to get the right weather conditions we would have to start shooting by September. If we missed that date, we would have to shift production back to 1981, and nobody wanted to do that.

Michael and I went on a reconnaissance to find a location for the early part of the film where Mr and Mrs Havelock are murdered aboard their yacht. Greece was a place the Bond films hadn't been to before and, after a spell of bad weather that prevented us flying, we took a series of ferries to Corfu. As soon as we stepped ashore, Michael and I knew we had found the

Richard Maibaum
was a major
contributor to the
Bond series for
almost 30 years.

place we needed: Gerald Durrell was right when he said the place seemed magical and enchanted. The light was good and the island seemed to offer all the locations we needed for that part of the film. We drove around the island, which didn't take very long, and then visited Meteora, which boasted some imposing rock formations with monasteries perched on the top. Because the monks were inaccessible by car – there were no steps or stairs, let alone a road – they would lower baskets from their rooms to receive the food and other supplies they needed. We were struck by this unique location and decided to incorporate it into the script.

Casting was a relatively novel experience for me, although I had been involved in casting my episode of *Man in a Suitcase*. The process was very much a collaborative effort: Cubby's daughter Barbara was an established assistant director on the Bond series and she helped us, alongside casting director Debbie McWilliams. Fleming's *For Your Eyes Only* featured a good female lead in the shape of Judy Havelock, who used a bow-and-arrow to avenge the murder of her parents. We changed the name Judy to Melina and gave her a crossbow, but apart from that, she remained much the same character Fleming had created. The role required a beautiful girl who could also act well enough to meet the demands of a very dramatic part. Jerry Juroe recommended a French actress called Carole Bouquet, whom I had met briefly when she visited the set of *Moonraker*. She had appeared in Luis Buñuel's *That Obscure Object of Desire* and I thought she made a good impression. Cubby, Michael, Jerry and myself had dinner with Carole in

Rome, where she lived, and I was immediately impressed. The first thing that struck me was her long, thick hair, which hung very straight. She spoke good English with a slight French accent and was undeniably a striking-looking girl. I could immediately picture her wielding that crossbow. Although she was only 22 years old, I felt sure she was right for the role.

Chaim Topol, one of my favourite actors, was Dana's choice to play the villainous Columbo. In some ways, Topol has been the victim of his own success, as he will forever be associated with the film and stage play *Fiddler on the Roof*. He must be absolutely tired of it by now. The teenage ice-skating champ was played by the fresh-faced Lynn-Holly Johnson, who was a skater with some acting experience. She had recently appeared in a film called *Ice Castles* and we felt she could carry the role. The alternative would have been to hire a professional skater and give her a wig and whatever else she needed to double the actress we chose, but we did the right thing in casting Lynn – someone who could play the part and do the skating as well.

Julian Glover played the main villain, Kristatos, and brought with him the steely, intense quality I had admired in his previous work. Jill Bennett played Brink as quite a butch lady, which was absolutely the opposite kind of person she actually was. She enjoyed appearing in the movie and did a great job. Debbie found Michael Gothard, whom we cast as the assassin Locque. Michael was a captivating actor, perfect to play an inscrutable and ruthless killer. He suggested that Locque should wear the thick octagonal glasses that somehow made him appear even more sinister.

Chaim Topol as Columbo in *For Your Eyes Only*.

Janet Brown and
Roger Moore on
the Downing
Street set, which is
seen briefly at the
end of *For Your
Eyes Only*. Even
the Iron Lady left
notes for the
milkman.

An important part of the casting process in any Bond movie is the selection of the obligatory 'Bond girls' – the beautiful decoration for poolside parties, casino scenes and so on. I spent a whole week in town interviewing beautiful girls. I must admit I failed to spot the potential in one particularly attractive 16-year-old by the name of Elizabeth Hurley and she didn't get the job. Many years later Liz collared me over the incident and I protested that at 16, she seemed too young! Luckily she didn't hold it against me.

One of the most beautiful girls I interviewed was Tula, a model and game-show hostess in her late 20s. Tula had a very small role, lounging around by a swimming pool. When we were filming in Corfu, Roger and I went to a discotheque accompanied by some of the girls and I spent a lot of time dancing with Tula, who I thought was stunning. I knew that Tula's real name was Caroline, but it came as a considerable shock when I discovered she'd actually been born Barry. None of us was aware during filming that one of our best-looking girls had been born a boy and had undergone a sex-change operation in her teens.

They say there's no such thing as bad publicity, but we only narrowly avoided a more serious casting mishap. Dick and Michael wrote a humorous scene involving an encounter with Prince Charles, which we thought would be a good way to close the film. We hired a guy who at that time made a living as a Prince Charles look-alike in clubs and on television, but about four weeks before we were due to film, it was reported that he had been arrested and had a previous conviction for something unseemly. We dropped the scene and paid him off.

Rather than using the Prince Charles look-alike, we decided to poke some gentle fun at our new Prime Minister Margaret Thatcher and her husband Denis. At that time, Janet Brown and John Wells used regularly to pop up on television playing the bickering couple, and Dick and Michael quickly wrote a scene where the Iron Lady congratulates James Bond on his success while simultaneously preventing her husband from picking at food in the kitchen of No. 10 Downing Street. I contributed a gag of my own to the scene – I have an addiction to Brussels sprouts and regularly get slapped for stealing them, so I decided that Denis should get a wrap on the knuckles from Maggie for doing the same thing. Of course, when the phone call from Downing Street is patched through to Bond, Mrs Thatcher ends up having a discussion with Melina's parrot. I don't know if Mr and Mrs Thatcher ever saw it, but if they did, I hope they saw the funny side.

The cast came together over summer 1980, but as the shooting date loomed, there was still one question that remained unanswered: Who would play James Bond? I had been told categorically that Roger Moore was out of the picture. He was getting quite expensive and had been suggesting to the press that *Moonraker* would be his final Bond film. Looking back on what ensued, I can now see that I became embroiled in what was in fact an elaborate game of poker. Cubby asked me to test some potential Roger replacements, but I'm not sure whether he was seriously considering any of them, or whether the tests themselves were a means of calling Roger's bluff. Cubby and Roger were as astute as each other and negotiations went on between the two of them for quite some time. I was the innocent caught in the middle.

I spent two or three days shooting screen tests for a new James Bond at Pinewood Studios. We knocked up a small set and I got a copy of the script of *From Russia With Love* from the Eon archive. We used the famous scene where the Russian agent Tatiana is in bed and James Bond seduces her, while soliciting the information he needs. Bond is unaware that they are being filmed from the other side of a two-way mirror. I more or less copied the way Terence Young had shot the scene all those years before, testing various actors to see if they could handle the love scenes. I also recreated the scene from *Dr No* where Bond waits until Professor Dent has emptied

his gun before shooting him in cold blood ('That's a Smith and Wesson…and you've had your six'). I also shot a number of shorter scenes, such as Bond ordering breakfast in his hotel room and getting into a punch-up with some heavies. All these scenes were designed to test an actor's suitability for the different types of scene that generally crop up in Bond screenplays.

One unexpected candidate for the role of Bond was Julian Glover, who wrote to Cubby nominating himself after I'd cast him as Kristatos. I'm sure Julian would have made a good job of it, but it wasn't to be. Cubby let Julian down gently. During their discussion, Julian asked if we'd seen a young Irish actor by the name of Pierce Brosnan. I wasn't familiar with Pierce, but we looked at a television series he'd done in Ireland and I could see he was going places. I later met Pierce during filming, when he accompanied his wife-to-be Cassandra Harris, who was playing Columbo's mistress Lisl.

We looked at the footage from the screen tests and I started to feel a little downhearted. We hadn't found anyone who could replace Roger and I left the viewing theatre secretly hoping that Cubby could persuade him to make the picture. As the poker game continued, my anxiety mounted. *For Your Eyes Only* was due to be my first film as a director and the idea of working with Roger again was very appealing. I knew that we'd get on well, as we always had done before, and I couldn't be sure that a new actor would be as accommodating to a first-time director. I was in the middle of turning the situation over in my mind for the umpteenth time when the phone rang:

Roger had finally struck a deal with Cubby. It was an enormous relief.

When it came to picking a crew, I had some definite ideas about who I wanted. Cubby and Michael allowed me to choose, but only after a bit of a fight. Alan Hume was the perfect man to photograph my first film: he was experienced, full of energy, absolutely fearless and possessed of a great sense of humour. Alan had not yet done any big films as a director of photography – his career had largely been taken up with shooting *Carry On* movies and similar low-budget pictures – and he had yet to reach the pinnacle of his abilities. I was a big advocate of Alan, but Cubby was initially reluctant to go along with me. I persisted and I'm glad to say I eventually prevailed. I think Cubby came round to my point of view because he had been impressed by Alan's photography on the ski-parachute jump sequence.

The man I really wanted as my camera operator was Alec Mills. Alec had been the camera operator on *Shout at the Devil* and *Gold*, and I recalled how he'd photographed the mine sequences for me when Jimmy Devis was unable to overcome his claustrophobia. At this time, Jimmy was spending more time as a second-unit director than an operator and I felt I owed Alec something for helping me out. He certainly didn't owe *me* anything and I was fortunate to secure his services. I thought he was one of the country's best camera operators, if not the best. Alan and Alec brought their usual guys with them, including the focus puller Mike Frift, so that was a big pre-production concern crossed off my list.

The next role I had to fill was the second-unit director. I understood the demands of the job very well and the person that immediately sprang to mind was Arthur Wooster. Appearances can be deceptive: if you'd never met Arthur before, you'd think he was the least likely contender to sit behind any sort of camera. I'm sure Arthur won't mind me saying that he's a slight fellow with extremely thick pebble glasses. Despite this, I knew Arthur was a formidable one-man band and an expert documentary cameraman. He was prepared to fly in fast fighter aircraft, ski and mountain-climb, plus he was a terrific underwater cameraman. I called Arthur and broached the idea of working on the new Bond film. He was delighted because he hadn't done a feature film of that stature before. Cubby was rather less delighted when I mentioned Arthur's name – as far as he was concerned, Arthur hadn't worked on anything of any note, and he had two or three other people in mind. I asked Cubby to meet Arthur before he made his mind up and arranged a quick interview in Cubby's office. While Arthur waited outside I had a brief chat with Cubby and then we called him in. The door opened and in came Arthur, who promptly tripped over the carpet. There was a dreadful silence. Cubby looked at Arthur, and then looked up at me. Arthur recovered, but was so nervous that he began stuttering when replying to Cubby's questions. The interview was a disaster. I had to work overtime to convince Cubby that first impressions counted for very little in Arthur's case. It was only after several weeks that he relented and let me hire him. Arthur's been part of the Bond team ever since.

While I was working on Cubby, I found an ally in associate producer Tom Pevsner. Tom was a good logistical man who became a great friend. He knew what Arthur was capable of and supported my decision. Arthur was absolutely right for a Bond crew: he was a self-sufficient and self-reliant cameraman who would not stand on ceremony when we needed high quality results in a hurry.

I was glad I finally got the crew I wanted. My experiences on *OHMSS* were very much at the forefront of my mind when I selected the team: in 1969, we had placed cameramen in situations that were arduous and sometimes life-threatening. I knew that someone like Arthur could be slung off a mountain top at the other end of a rope and be quite happy to shoot a scene without even thinking of any personal discomfort or danger. One of the best things about my crew was that I felt we could be entirely frank with one another. No one was frightened to speak up and be critical, and I think this was a very healthy working environment.

We had a budget of around $28 million to shoot *For Your Eyes Only*. This was only slightly less than Lewis had for *Moonraker*, but inflation had taken its toll and the money didn't go quite as far. I set out to make *For Your Eyes Only* a turning point in the Bond series. It was time to get back to the spirit of Ian Fleming's books and time to make Bond seem a little harder than he had been in the previous few films. Roger's portrayal was unashamedly light-hearted and it worked very well within the context of the more humorous films. *For Your Eyes Only* was a story with a harder edge, however, and I felt Bond had to respond to these new situations in an appropriate way. Where there was inherent humour, I decided to let it emerge naturally, and where there were action sequences, I endeavoured to make them as realistic as possible. In September 1980, it was time to begin.

We filmed in various locations in Corfu from September through to October. Things got off to a bad start with the scene in which Lisl was pursued and eventually run down by a pair of hit-men driving dune buggies. The buggies were extremely temperamental and the slightest splash of salt spray would bring them grinding to a halt. It couldn't have happened at a worse time – the whole of the United Artists' hierarchy were observing my progress from the edge of the beach and I imagined them shaking their heads in dismay under their sun umbrellas. At one stage, I got so desperate I was forced to move the camera past a stationary buggy to give the impression the thing was actually in motion. We got two or three days over schedule and I'm sure Cubby was starting to get a hard time over the budget. He took me to one side to give me a mild rebuke and told me to get on with it. Throughout my whole experience with the Bond films, Cubby was always wise enough not to try to influence the director in front of the crew – if he had something to say to me, he would always take me to one side or speak to me in private in his office. On the floor, the director has to be king and nothing should undermine the respect you earn from your crew. If there is a dispute or a problem between the producer and the director, the worse thing that can happen is for it to be resolved in front of everyone – morale can rapidly diminish and this can have serious implications for the rest of the shoot.

One of the hit-men was played by a striking young actor called Charles Dance. This was Charles's first film and he didn't have very much to do except get out of his dune buggy, point his gun at James Bond and say, 'Get your hands up' or something corny like that. When we came to shoot the scene, I had to stop and tell him to try it again, this time holding his gun straight. A couple of takes later, I told him, 'Never mind about the line –

we'll drop it.' He wasn't very happy about that, but I was up against it and I didn't think it was much of a line anyway. I didn't realise I had hurt Charles's feelings so much until I was later told what he said about me in a bar in Cortina: 'Who is this John Glen anyway? First he tells me I'm holding my gun like a poof and then he drops my line!' Of course, Charles went on to be quite a big star, and a few years later he repeated the story during a television interview. By pure coincidence, it was around this time that I recommended Cubby should test Charles to play James Bond. He was considering my recommendation when Charles came on the television, repeating this story. It didn't bother me very much, but Cubby didn't like it one bit. I think Charles might have made a very good James Bond, but after that incident Cubby wouldn't even consider him.

Cyd Child doubled for Cassie Harris at the moment of impact when Locque's buggy collided with Lisl. Cyd was one of the greatest stuntwomen around and also happened to own Krone, the parrot that was featured in the film. The buggy hit her with such force that she rolled onto the bonnet, smashed the windscreen and bounced off onto the ground. I cut the cameras and rushed over to where she was lying. She said she was all right, but I could tell she was putting a brave face on it.

I met Pierce Brosnan for the first time while we were shooting in Corfu. He visited Cassie on the set and stayed with her for about a week. I think it's fair to say that Julian Glover was the only person who recognised his potential to play Bond at that stage – I knew he was a good

Charles Dance holds the gun straight.

actor, but thought he looked far too young. Cassie was a delight to work with and we had a ball. She got on very well with Roger, who I remember came up with a great idea to help us out when I was trying to figure out how to get Bond to follow Lisl out of the casino. I was discussing the scene with Roger and Cassie and Roger said, 'Why don't we use the old stage trick where she drops her handkerchief and I follow her after picking it up?' It was on old gag, but it worked well.

By the second week, we were three days behind schedule. I said to Alan, 'Well, it's Friday and we haven't got the sack yet, so things can't be that bad!' Every Friday after that, we'd say the same thing to each other. I clawed back the days we lost on the beach and before long I got the production back on schedule. When we finished the Corfu location work, Cubby paid me the greatest compliment when he told me: 'John, I'm going to California for three weeks. You know where I am if you need me.' He took off and left me to it. Knowing he had sufficient faith in me to leave me alone boosted my confidence, and I think it was good for Michael as well – he gave us a chance to get on with it by ourselves.

Another scene that was shot at the beginning of the schedule was Melina's assassination of Gonzales, the man who murdered her parents. Gonzales falls into his pool with a crossbow bolt embedded in his back. A chase commences and when Bond's Lotus is destroyed by an exploding burglar alarm, he and Melina pile into her old banger and make their escape through the winding mountainside roads.

The poolside assassination was shot at the Villa Sylva in Kanomi and every time I watch that scene it's a pleasure to see Alison Worth, who played one of the girls walking past in the foreground. Alison had a magnificent bottom and looked so good in a swimsuit that I used her in a decorative capacity for several other movies.

The exploding Lotus was a response to a recent wave of car thefts in New York. We put a sticker on the Lotus window that said 'burglar protected'. One of Gonzalez's goons, played by Bob Simmons, unwisely ignores the warning and smashes the window of the car to gain entry to it. As soon as he breaks the glass the car explodes, taking him with it. I understand the gag got a huge cheer when the film opened in New York. The exploding Lotus also made it symbolically clear that we were leaving behind much of the high-tech gadgetry seen in *Moonraker* and forcing Bond to rely on his wits. Or in this case, Melina's Citroen 2CV.

Corfu is a very mountainous island and it just so happened that we were filming at the time of year when the local farmers collected the olives from the trees by spreading their nets beneath the branches and shaking the trunks. It immediately struck me that the opportunity to incorporate winding roads and cascading olives in our car chase was too good to miss. This was also a good opportunity to integrate the local olive-pickers with the action. It's always a good idea to involve people with action scenes because quite aside from adding an extra element of perceived danger, it also disqualifies any suspicion the audience may be harbouring that the stunts have been performed using optical effects or models. In my opinion, the famous corkscrew river jump in *The Man With the Golden Gun* (where Bond's car drives off one end of a collapsed bridge, flies over a river and lands on the remnants of the bridge on the other side) is compromised by

Michael Gothard played the sinister Locque, seen here observing the assassination of Gonzales.

the fact that no one is visible on either bank. An incredible stunt is somehow as a result.

I first met Remy Julienne in 1968, when his team did the amazing car stunts in *The Italian Job*. When we discussed the car chase in *For Your Eyes Only*, I immediately thought of Remy and invited him over to London. He spoke very little English at that time, but my storyboards spoke louder than words and he understood perfectly what we were trying to achieve. Remy had a top quality team, which included his sons Dominique and Michel, and they did a great job for us. Arthur's unit filmed the chase with Remy and his drivers for the first few weeks, and then my unit came in and shot the little incidents you saw in the seemingly devastated village of Danilia.

I enjoyed shooting the scenes with Topol as Columbo and was especially impressed by the way he could pour a drink, eat a bag of nuts and deliver his lines, all at the same time. Columbo's habitual pistachio-munching was Topol's idea and it came in useful during the warehouse scene when the sound of someone treading on the scattered shells alerts him to approaching danger.

During the filming of the scene where Columbo and his men are attacked as they come ashore, one of the charges exploded near Topol's face and cut his eyebrow quite badly. If it had hit him an inch lower, it would have caught his eye. Such charges, more properly called squibs, are always unpopular with actors because they tend to cause injuries however careful you are. Topol was very good about it all and didn't complain, but Derek Meddings was very upset. Topol assured him that he was OK to go on and once we'd

Locque is sent to his death by a vengeful Bond (Roger Moore).

applied a dressing and some make-up, we continued with the scene.

The next scene in the film showed Locque escaping in his Mercedes and Bond chasing him on foot. Bond has to scale a huge staircase to reach Locque, but Roger took one look at these three or four hundred steps and said 'No way.' Martin Grace, who was our main double for Roger on this film, was terrifically fit and shot up the steps like a rocket. At the top of the steps, Bond fires at Locque, whose car goes out of control and ends up delicately balanced on the edge of the cliff. I knew that the confrontation that followed would be one of the most important scenes in the whole film and crucial to the new direction I wanted to take the series. I wanted Roger to kick the car, tipping it over the cliff with Locque inside it. When I came to shoot the scene, Roger was adamant that he wouldn't do it, arguing that something so cold-blooded just wasn't in his character. Roger is a personality actor and is always mindful of how children and his other admirers see him. He was well aware that James Bond was a hero-figure to many people and felt uncomfortable about portraying him in this light. On the other hand, I was aware that we were at a crossroads in the depiction of the character and I fought hard to show Bond kick the car. Locque was a ruthless killer who had murdered Bond's friend Ferrara – I wanted Bond to act in a similarly ruthless way in return. Roger wanted Bond to simply throw Locque's dove-emblem badge into the car, its extra weight toppling the car over the edge. In the end, I recall that we shot both scenes, but we went with the take where Bond kicked the car over the edge. Roger ultimately agreed that it was the right decision.

Roger Moore is a much better actor than he ever gives himself credit for and although it's hard to believe, he has little confidence in his own abilities. There were occasions when I had take him to one side and give him pep talks, saying, 'Roger, you can do this, you really can.' The scene with Locque proves what he's capable of and illustrates what a great professional he is. During the early part of the *For Your Eyes Only* shoot, Roger was suffering considerable discomfort. He had a painful bout of kidney stones and had to drink a lot of water to keep going.

In mid-October, we moved to Meteora and found ourselves at the mercy of some appalling weather. Luckily, the sun would emerge through the clouds in the evenings and we were able to light our scenes in its warm glow. Before our arrival, we had struck a deal with the Orthodox Church in Athens and paid the fee to film the monastery perched atop the 2000-foot outcrop. When we got there, however, we discovered that the monks wouldn't co-operate and did their best to spoil our shots. Aware that we were trying to film them, they placed oil barrels on the roof and hung their laundry from the windows. Peter Lamont decided to improvise and built his own dummy monastery instead. Alan carefully chose a time of day when the real monastery was backlit by the sun, which made the monks' protest rather less obvious. For close shots, we filmed Peter's pre-fab monastery on the adjoining rock.

When we came to the mountain climbing sequence, Roger took me to one side and said, 'John, I absolutely hate heights.' I understood how he felt. 'That makes two of us!' I replied. Luckily for Roger, we had Rick Sylvester on hand to double for him. Since performing the ski-parachute jump on *The Spy Who Loved Me,* Rick had become part of the team. I decided to call on his expert climbing skills for the scene in which Bond scales the sheer face of the mountain leading to the monastery. Cubby's son-in-law Pat Banta was a good climber and stuntman and he joined Rick's team. Rick doubled for Roger for the scene in which Bond makes a spectacular fall from the sheer face, is jolted when the rope suddenly halts his descent and then slowly makes his way back up to the monastery. Rick had to drop 300–400 feet before coming to a sudden halt. The shock of suddenly stopping after such a swift descent would quite probably kill you, so Derek Meddings constructed a special rig which consisted of a 30-foot trough partially filled with sand. He fitted sandbags to the end of Rick's rope and embedded them in the trough. When Rick came to the end of his fall, the sand in the trough acted as a kind of restrainer. The sandbags took the weight from the fall and were dragged through the trough, softening the jolt at the end of the fall. There was still a perceptible jerk, but it wasn't as great as it would have been if the rope had been taut. Rick had absolute faith in Derek and it worked perfectly. We only needed one take.

After Rick had dropped from the mountain face, we had to get him back up the rope and up to the top of the mountain. We all know it's not really possible to hoist yourself up any significant length of rope using your arms, so we had him remove his shoe laces and use them to create a makeshift mechanism which would enable him to 'climb' up the rope. There was an

added element of tension as Apostis, one of Kristatos's heavies, is waiting for Bond, rapidly loosening the clamp holding his rope in place. With some creative editing, Bond scales the rope fairly quickly and then dispatches Apostis, ready for the film's dramatic climax. Throughout this whole process, Arthur Wooster shot some amazing footage for me, securing some great angles by hanging off precipices and other such precarious positions.

Apostis was played by Jack Klaff and in an attempt to heighten the film's realism, I elected to show his body actually hitting the ground. With the camera running at just 12 frames per second, I filmed an empty patch of ground, stopped the camera and cut to a shot of Jack lying, apparently dead. With a suitably gruesome sound effect, we created the impression that he fell into shot. While Jack was lying on the ground for us, a snake appeared from under a bush and slid under his neck. 'Keep very still,' I whispered, while the snake slowly made its way back under the bush. When he got up, I told him what had happened and he nearly fainted.

There was no way Roger could get out of the close-ups and he was game enough to do what was necessary. At one point, when Roger is seen climbing the mountain, he puts his hand into a cavity he thinks is a natural hand hold. Some pigeons fly out of the cavity, startling Bond and hopefully the audience. I've used pigeons flying out at unexpected moments as a kind of 'trademark' in all my subsequent films. I like to wait for a particularly quiet or tense moment, then make the audience jump out of their skins. All good, clean fun.

We began shooting the studio material at Pinewood from the end of October. Bernard Lee had been in poor health during the filming of *Moonraker*, but he always managed to pull himself together for the actual takes. Towards the end of 1980, his health had declined even further and he was unable to make his customary appearance as M. I was very disappointed, as I had been looking forward to working with him again. Bernard had played M in all the Eon-produced movies since *Dr No*, but I had first come across him when he played Sergeant Paine in *The Third Man*. Even then, one of the second assistants was charged with finding Bernard's hidden booze and removing it. Despite liking the odd drink, Bernard was a fine actor, a true professional and a most generous man.

We didn't look for anyone else to play M at that stage, but instead gave most of Bernard's lines to the character Tanner, who appears in Fleming's novels but had yet to make an appearance in the films. We interviewed a number of different actors for the role, but Roger suggested James Villiers and we went with him. Bernard was irreplaceable and I didn't envy James one bit.

Shortly after Christmas, I was saddened to learn that Bernard had died. My last memory of him is a fond one: on location for *Moonraker*, Bernard and Geoffrey Keen, who played the Minister of Defence, shared a boat from the Lido to the main town of Venice. It was wonderful to eavesdrop on these two old actors sniping away at each other but actually having an awful lot of fun. None of us realised that this would be Bernard's final Bond appearance.

In November, we filmed the pre-titles sequence, which was my way of maintaining continuity with some of the Bond adventures of the past. Bond is visiting the grave of his wife Tracy when the vicar meets him in the

Roger overcame his fear of heights to film the close-ups of Bond's arduous ascent.

cemetery to tell him that his office have called and have sent a helicopter to pick him up. Bond is in the helicopter when the pilot is electrocuted and it is flown by remote control. Bond soon discovers that the helicopter is being manipulated by a familiar-looking wheelchair-bound villain with a neck brace and a white cat.

I was walking around Pinewood with Cubby one Sunday when we saw that one of the workmen had invited his son to join him for the afternoon. The little boy was playing with a remote-controlled car, which was quite a novelty for 1980. This is what gave me the inspiration for the remote-control helicopter.

We filmed the graveyard at Stoke Poges Parish Church, near Pinewood, and Bond's struggle to regain control of the helicopter above the Becton Gas Works in East Ham. The gas works were in the process of being demolished, but there was still enough of Europe's biggest coal-powered gas station to form an impressive backdrop of tall chimneys, huge sheds and railway lines. I inspected the site with Marc Wolff, a pilot we had used on *The Spy Who Loved Me*, and Derek Meddings. I asked them if it would be possible to fly a helicopter into one of the huge depots and out through the other side. They both said, 'Absolutely not!'

Derek constructed a foreground miniature, which in this case took the shape of a fake wall placed before the camera in a position that helped it merge with the distant depot so it appeared to be a part of the building. Marc then flew the helicopter in front of the hangar but behind the foreground miniature, thereby giving the impression that he had actually flown through the building. Inside the depot, there was a railway track which had originally been used to receive wagons of coal. The great thing about foreground miniatures is that you can evaluate their success by simply looking through the lens – you don't have to wait weeks and weeks to see whether a more complex optical effect has worked or not.

Derek constructed a full-size helicopter body to run on the tracks, complete with an engine to spin dummy rotor blades. The helicopter was placed on a tilting device, so we could appear to change its angle from left to right. Roger sat in the recently vacated pilot's seat and we filmed the helicopter's journey from inside the depot as well as from outside. It was relatively easy to do and it worked very well.

The second-unit director for the helicopter sequence was Jimmy Devis, who jumped at the chance to film some aerial action. Marc performed some superb helicopter aerobatics for us, and Martin Grace clung to the side of the helicopter, doubling for Bond. For the climax of the scene, he succeeded in using the helicopter to skewer the villain's wheelchair and drop it down a tall chimney stack not once but five times. He would have made a great bomber pilot. My only regret about that sequence is that we wanted to end it by showing a cloud of dust emerge from the chimney followed by a spinning wheel lying discarded on the ground. Unfortunately, we ran out of time and I had to abandon the ideas.

In January 1981, we arrived at Cortina in northern Italy to shoot the ski sequences. Once again, Willy Bogner was on hand to direct the second unit. Willy was now an accomplished film-maker in his own right and I think he continued working with us simply because there was such a good atmosphere. I spent about three weeks there with the first unit, while Willy

shot the sequence where Bond is chased through the bobsleigh-run by two assassins riding motorcycles. At one point, three units were shooting simultaneously in the area. Cortina had experienced a particularly mild winter (*déjà vu*!), but this didn't cause as many problems as it had on *OHMSS*. In fact, the thin covering of snow made it easier for the steel-spiked motorcycle tyres to get around. Willy once again used a hand-held camera to film the breathtaking chase through the bobsleigh-run.

In Cortina with the beautiful Robbin Young, Roger and Carole Bouquet. We nick-named the driver 'Amore' because that's all he kept saying!

John Wyman played Eric Kreigler, one of the villains on Bond's tail, and he had a real problem playing the part of an experienced cross-country skier. This was largely due to the fact that he couldn't ski. John did his best to master the sport on our behalf and spent quite a lot of time falling over as a result.

In February, I was in the cutting room at Pinewood when Tom Pevsner told me there had been an accident in the bobsleigh-run. The four-man bob had come out of the run at the wrong place and hit a tree. One of its occupants, a young stuntman called Paolo Rigon, was killed. The footage was impounded by the Italian authorities and they held an inquiry which took nearly a year. I was never able to see the footage, nor did I want to, quite honestly. Filming should never cost anyone their life, but however many precautions you take when shooting, high-speed action accidents happen. It was tragic that someone had lost their life in this way.

*For Your Eyes Only* featured quite a lot of underwater material, most of

Hitching a lift on
Roger's skis in
Cortina.

which was shot in the clear water of the Bahamas while the rest was shot in the underwater tank at Pinewood's 007 Stage. The Bahamas shoot was supervised by underwater specialist Al Giddings, whom I had recently met in his home town of Berkeley in California. Al was so at home in water that when he was on dry land he appeared to have difficulty in keeping steady. The underwater material included the submerged Roman villa that Melina's father, played by Jack Hedley, is investigating when he is killed. We built the components of the villa at Pinewood and had them shipped over to the Bahamas. Filming explosions underwater can be a tricky business: you can't use real charges because they can damage people's ears, so we used old photographer's flash bulbs and dubbed on an appropriate sound effect instead. You have to be similarly inventive when filming blood underwater – for some reason it appears green when you see it on film.

At the beginning of the film, we see a British Navy spy ship disguised as a trawler. It hits an old Second World War mine and sinks, taking its top secret ATAC computer with it. It was important to me that the audience was left in no doubt about the fate of the ship, so I made sure that the mine had a slightly caricatured spiky appearance. Rogue German mines used to turn up quite a lot after the war. When I was a young Sea Cadet, I was taken out on patrol in the Channel, looking for mines to machine gun. I never found any mines, but when we saw objects that looked like mines, the crew let us shoot them anyway.

Al used a wet submarine, which was constructed at Palm Beach. Wet submarines aren't pressurised like normal submarines, but filled with water. The people inside obviously wear wet suits and breathing apparatus. Wet submarines sometimes have trouble maintaining stability, especially when they're unfortunate enough to encounter sudden chasms in the sea bed. On several occasions we lost control of our wet submarine and had to struggle to recover it as it plunged into the depths.

Although Roger is an excellent swimmer, both he and Carole remained bone dry when we shot their underwater scenes at Pinewood. Carole had a problem with her inner ear and couldn't spend any time underwater, which caused a major problem when shooting the extensive sequence where she and Roger had to dive into the wreck of the *St Georges* and retrieve the coveted ATAC computer. Derek came up with an ingenious way to solve the problem: I got Arthur to shoot the underwater sequence in the tank using doubles, and I shot Roger and Carole dry. We used a wind machine to blow their hair, and turned the camera over at 72 or 84 frames per second, to simulate an underwater inertia when played back at normal speed. Alec Mills placed a series of crosses on graph paper to indicate where Roger and Carole's mouths were on the film we had just shot, and gave the graph paper and the wound-back negative to Derek. Derek then dipped two air lines into some water and filmed the streaming bubbles directly on to our negative. Once the film was processed I could look at the rushes and see whether bubbles seemed to be coming from the actors' mouths. We needed the odd retake, but most of the time the bubbles were superimposed perfectly and it worked very well. Not only was Derek a brilliant technician, he was also a very nice person who loved to help everybody, not just the first unit.

There is a scene in Fleming's *Live and Let Die* which sees Bond keelhauled over razor-sharp coral. The scene wasn't included in Guy Hamilton's film of the book, although Dick had been keen to use it ever since. It had been in and out of Bond scripts for as long as I could remember, each successive director reluctantly concluding that it would be too difficult to film. I must admit that this was my initial reaction when it cropped up in the screenplay of *For Your Eyes Only*, but nothing is impossible and I decided we should try it. Al got some remarkable results with doubles for Carole and Roger crashing through the coral heads.

I filmed the surface shots of the doubles tumbling into the sea in Corfu, while simultaneously Al was shooting the underwater elements of precisely the same scene in the Bahamas. We once again shot the close-ups dry at Pinewood. I was glad that we were able to include another scene of original Fleming action in the film and I was especially pleased that it showed another instance of Bond having to get out of trouble by relying on his wits. Gadgetry will always play a part in the Bond movie formula, but I never lost sight of the fact that Bond is super-intelligent and extremely resourceful. He is a professional who falls back on his skill and regards gadgets as merely tools of the job.

By the time principal photography was over, there was relatively little time to cut the film. I promoted my assistant John Grover to editor and when shooting was finished, I worked alongside him in order to meet the deadline.

The music for the film was composed by Bill Conti, who contributed a wonderful score. The title song was performed by Sheena Easton, who was

Roger and Carole
share a joke before
the keelhauling
scene.

enjoying a lot of success in America at that time. The timing was perfect. When she came to Pinewood to meet me, both Maurice Binder and I were struck by how pretty she was. Maurice came up with the idea of including her in the title sequence, which was the first time a singer had been used in a Bond film in this way. Quite aside from anything else, time and other logistics would have made this impossible on previous films (indeed, it's never happened since). The title sequence looks like a very stylish pop video and the song is terrific.

Cubby always liked to hold special screenings for one of his favourite charities, a boys' club in New York. This was the film's first public screening and for this prestigious event we all arrived looking very smart. Cubby was sitting on one end of an aisle and I was sitting on the other. As the film appeared on the screen, I couldn't shake the feeling that something was wrong. As soon as Sheena started singing, it dawned on me that the film was running about 20 per cent too slow. I jumped out of my seat and bounded towards the projection box, only to see a furious Cubby coming at me from the opposite direction. Being America, there was so much security surrounding the projection room that we had great difficulty getting in.

When we finally got through the door, we saw that the projectionists weren't even watching the screen but were chatting to each other. 'The film's running slow!' I said. 'That's impossible,' one of them replied. 'The projector motor runs at a constant speed.' Cubby and I went over to the projector itself and persuaded the reluctant projectionist to open the spool box. The problem was obvious: the belt driving the projector was running on the flange, not in the groove. Cubby asked me if we should stop the show; I told him I didn't think that was a good idea. So we waited 20 minutes for the first double reel to run through the projector, poised to fix the problem before the second reel started. As this was the first screening of my masterpiece, I was naturally upset. I'll never forget peering out of the projection room during the agonising wait for the first reel to end. I think it was the longest 20 minutes of my life.

As brilliant as Maurice was, he was a continual source of embarrassment because his titles were always cut into the print at the last minute. On the film's opening night in Los Angeles, he called me from London. 'I've sent you another version of the titles with some changes in it,' he told me. 'Will you cut them in to the print for me?'. I couldn't believe what I was hearing.

Cubby Broccoli, myself and Michael Wilson with the diminutive Sheena Easton. Sheena sang the *For Your Eyes Only* theme song, and appeared in the title sequence.

'Certainly not,' I responded. 'It's going out as it is!' We did change the titles later – Maurice was a real perfectionist and the anguish in his voice was a terrible thing to hear. Part of Maurice was never satisfied with his work, but there was only so much slack we could cut him.

The London première was almost as dramatic, but for entirely different reasons. The event was a benefit for the Royal Association for Disability and Rehabilitation. One or two critics had pointed out that to kick off the film by scuppering a villain in a wheelchair showed rather poor taste. Of course, that was never intentional and the fact we had a villain in a wheelchair was just an unfortunate coincidence. There were 30 or 40 disabled guests at the première who watched the film from the first two rows in the stalls. I was glad that when that sequence came on, they were the ones who laughed loudest.

They say ignorance is bliss and it's certainly true that the more experienced you become, the more challenges there are. I was very single-minded on *For Your Eyes Only* – I had a very clear picture of what I was trying to do and uncompromising in how I tried to achieve it. At the same time, I hope I was open to opportunities when they presented themselves and if something came along that was more exciting than my original concept, I grabbed it. When you listen to other people, you learn very quickly, although you don't necessarily adopt all their suggestions.

I don't really look at any of my movies after the night of the première, but I am fond of *For Your Eyes Only* and it remains one of my favourite films. While I was in the middle of filming, a journalist from *Screen International* asked me about my ambitions for the future. I told him that I would like to direct some thrillers and then after that a drawing room comedy or a love story.

What I really wanted more than anything else, however, was another Bond picture.

# 007™

# CHAPTER 9

## ALL TIME HIGH

'Oh great,' I thought, as I stood staring at the empty place where my briefcase had been. I had attended a short meeting at Eon's Mayfair office and emerged to discover that my car had been broken into. The missing briefcase contained my script and my passport, both fairly essential to the location filming I was due to join the next day. I sometimes wonder what happened to that briefcase. I can't imagine what use anyone could have made of my passport, although I suppose an original *Octopussy* shooting script might fetch a few quid in certain quarters.

I immediately went back inside and initiated a series of small miracles that enabled me to fly out the next day after all. I was intimately acquainted with the staff by this point and I enjoyed the friendly atmosphere in the office. Cubby had offered me the job of directing *Octopussy* while I was still in post-production on *For Your Eyes Only*. I was flattered to be asked – quite aside from anything else, it was Cubby's seal of approval on the work I'd done on *For Your Eyes Only*. During the course of my contract negotiations in early 1982, I spent quite a lot of time at Eon. One unexpected highlight of trawling through the contractual paperwork was a beautiful Australian secretary called Janine, who was a ray of sunshine in the gloomy dungeon of an office. We became friends and I invited her out for a drink.

A short time later, I was in Cubby's office when I heard a knock on the door. It was Janine, who announced she was about to throw herself out of a plane as part of a parachute jump for charity. She produced a pen and a piece of paper and asked if anyone was prepared to sponsor her. She looked at Michael Wilson, who flatly refused because he didn't want her to risk her life in such a reckless manner. Janine turned to me and I decided to pledge some money. We were already friends, but I think the sponsored parachute jump was the first thing that really endeared her to me. I admired her courage and I subsequently discovered that she thought I was a rather charming older man. As time went by, we got closer and closer and we eventually collided. I'm glad to say Janine survived the jump in one piece and at the time of writing has survived 16 years as my wife.

My blossoming relationship with Janine had put me on a high and I was thrilled to be working on the follow-up to *For Your Eyes Only*. The screenplay for the new film was inspired by two of Ian Fleming's short stories: *Octopussy* and *The Property of a Lady*. The events of *The Property of a Lady* featured in the screenplay, but the events of *Octopussy* were cleverly incorporated into the script as back-story.

There were a number of clouds on the horizon during pre-production in spring 1982. The first was that Cubby's distributor United Artists had suffered a near-terminal financial setback with the disastrous movie *Heaven's Gate*. Fortunately, MGM rode to the rescue in 1981 and the new company, MGM/UA, promised a secure distribution and financing foundation for the Bond series. We nevertheless had to watch our budgets more closely than ever, but the only way this really affected me as a director was in the choice of foreign location for the new film. Cubby and Michael never burdened me with any of the business problems they may have been facing at this or any other time. I appreciated this and respected them for it: the producer does the money and the director does the creative stuff. That's the way it should be and that's the way it worked for us.

The first draft screenplay was written by George MacDonald Fraser, who is best known for the *Flashman* historical adventure novels. I met George in Hollywood and about an hour later we were joined by Cubby and Michael. Cubby and Michael had some business to take care of with Eon's legal chief Norman Tyre, so they left me and a perplexed George to sketch out a scenario and some ideas for a script.

George and I ultimately spent a whole day working on ideas. We were both great students of Ian Fleming's work and would often run sequences from the early movies and leaf through the novels looking for passages or chapters that hadn't yet been committed to film. George's script was all his own work, but there is a collaborative element to every James Bond screenplay and I think a lot of people had suggested ideas to him. I had been back in London for only three days when Cubby and Michael called from Hollywood and told me that George's screenplay would have to give way. Richard Maibaum was brought in and he and Michael collaborated on a new script that retained only a few elements of George's work. Once Dick returned, it was business as usual and we proceeded as we had done on *For Your Eyes Only*. The scripting problems had squeezed our pre-production and, as on the previous film, we had to work doubly quick to meet our August principal photography date.

By this stage, Roger Moore was negotiating his contracts on a picture-by-picture basis, so I had to go through the process of conducting screen tests for a new James Bond all over again. This time round, however, Cubby seemed to have a definite actor in mind. He found this fellow who had been born in England, but now lived in America. He flew him over from the States to meet us, saying that he thought he could be a contender to play Bond. When we met him, we weren't sure whether Cubby was being serious or not – the guy had quite a fun personality, but he wasn't particularly tall or handsome. In fact, he didn't look anything like Bond at all. Over lunch, it became clear that Cubby really liked this actor. Michael and I grew increasingly horrified, unable to work out whether we were witnessing just another round in the casting poker game or whether Cubby was serious about offering this man a contract. We were privately trying to figure out ways of changing Cubby's mind when this man dug his own grave. 'So, Cubby,' he said after lunch 'is it true that you're the Godfather round here?' The Mafia allusion didn't go down terribly well with Cubby, who shot this man a withering glare. Our would-be Bond was obviously out of the picture. Michael and I left the restaurant enormously relieved.

In early June, I went back to Pinewood to shoot artists' tests with a number of actors, re-enacting scenes from the early Bond films as I had done before. I tested men who were household names and I tested virtual unknowns, but I was left with the feeling that Cubby would once again make Roger an offer he couldn't refuse. Roger was a pleasure to work with because he was so professional – I don't think he ever fluffed a line. I asked him one day if he'd developed a photographic memory through spending so many years working in television. He just laughed, but I still suspect that he employs some top-secret system for absorbing his scripts. The Bond films don't always use the most experienced actresses – looks can be just as important as ability – and there were occasions when Roger would patiently feed the girls the lines off camera while they tried to get it right for their close shots. Sometimes this could continue for take after take, and I should think Roger was mentally exhausted at the end of some days. It wasn't always possible, but I tried to shoot his close shots first so that he didn't get too bored. When I discovered that Roger had been persuaded to return for 'one last time', I was very pleased.

Over the summer, we were also searching for a replacement for Bernard Lee, who had created the role of M as far as every Bond fan was concerned. Bernard was irreplaceable, but we interviewed a number of actors who, we hoped, could bring their own interpretation to the role. We were close to the point of shooting and getting pretty desperate when Roger suggested we take a look at Robert Brown, an actor he had worked with in the *Ivanhoe* television series. I put the idea to Cubby, Michael and Barbara and we went to interview him. Robert understood the unique relationship M shared with Bond – although he could be quite scathing of 007's behaviour and attitudes, he held a special affection for him, almost as though Bond was one of his children. We agreed that it would be impossible, and quite wrong, to replicate the performance Bernard had given. At the same time, we felt restricted over how much we could do with such a well-established character. Robert did an absolutely splendid job over the next four James Bond films, but in retrospect I think it was a smart move to be brave enough to cast a woman in the role in *GoldenEye*. We had discussed the possibility of casting a female M, but the idea had been quickly dismissed. I don't think a female M would have gone down well with Cubby at any point during my 10-year tenure, but I think Eon have been fortunate to get Dame Judi Dench for the most recent films. She is, of course, a superb actress and the time is right now. In the early 1980s, however, we weren't quite ready.

Lois Maxwell was reaching the end of her secretarial career and we felt that Miss Moneypenny was about due for retirement. Lois had done a wonderful job in the role of M's secretary and had been absolutely perfect for the part. Terence Young, who had cast her in *Dr No* over 20 years before, described her as looking 'like she smelt of soap' and I think I know what he meant – she was the pretty girl-next-door. Miss Moneypenny was always playful and charming, and Bond always promised to take her out for dinner, but of course he never did. Miss

Maud Adams as
the mysterious
Octopussy.

Moneypenny always looked out for Bond and I thought Lois had been especially good in *OHMSS*, where she takes Bond's letter of resignation and fakes a request for a holiday instead.

We were very reluctant to say goodbye to Lois, but we felt the time had come to start looking around for someone new. In the end, we came up with a compromise which enabled Lois to stay on for a bit longer. Cubby knew the novelist James Clavell and had met his daughter Michaela. She was a very pretty girl and an aspiring actress, so we decided to cast her as Miss Moneypenny's new assistant. We gave her the name Penelope Smallbone, which was actually the real name of Perri Small, a model Maurice Binder had used in the title sequence of *For Your Eyes Only* and whom I had used in my artists' tests back in June.

Lois cherished the role of Moneypenny. She lived in Canada and enjoyed making the trip over to Pinewood every two years to make her brief appearance in each new movie. Desmond Llewelyn was in a similar position – he would wait two years for a few weeks' work as Q, but enjoy every minute of it. Moneypenny and Q were both extremely well-known characters and I'm sure this damaged the careers of both

Lois and Desmond. Their pay was not that great, probably not enough to compensate them for their typecasting and certainly not enough to keep them in any kind of luxury. Unfortunately, casting directors everywhere passed them over for roles because they feared their faces were instantly recognisable to the public. I don't know about Lois, but I know that Desmond used to make a bit on the side as an after-dinner speaker. He would attend such functions as firemen's conventions and bring his *From Russia With Love* briefcase with him. Of course, the gadgets didn't work and Desmond was never very good with technology anyway, but over the years he developed quite a repertoire of gags that were guaranteed to make people laugh.

We cast Maud Adams as the mysterious Octopussy. Maud had appeared opposite Roger before in *The Man With the Golden Gun*, and it was unprecedented for us to cast the same actress as a leading lady twice in her Bond career. Maud is a brilliant lady and the most beautiful and elegant woman I have ever seen. One day she invited her mother, who was in her 70s, on to the set. I could see immediately from whom Maud had inherited her beauty. Maud was great fun and I enjoyed working with her.

Louis Jourdan, who had been a heart throb in Hollywood for many years, was cast as Kamal Khan. Cubby suggested Louis after he attended one of his parties in Beverly Hills. Louis had a dark complexion and certainly carried the necessary authority to make an arresting villain. Louis didn't feel at all at home on a British film set, however, where the relaxed atmosphere and continual practical jokes threw him slightly. I had to keep reassuring him that we did know what we were doing and that everyone was professional when the time came to shoot a scene. I think he had been used to the adulation of the Hollywood system when he had been a big star at MGM, but now his career was on the wane and he was finding it difficult. In my opinion, you have to learn to adapt or you fall by the wayside, but Louis did a very good job for us and delivered the funniest line in the movie – when Bond is clinging to the outside of his plane, Kamal turns to his incredulous henchman and says, 'Go out and get him!'

We started filming in Berlin in August with Roger and Robert Brown. We spent only three days in Berlin, which included scenes shot at the Berlin Wall. The Cold War was still very much a reality and as our crane-mounted camera ascended, we could see the armed East German guards taking photographs of us from the other side. We hadn't asked permission to film over the wall and it suddenly struck me that they may have thought we were trying to distract them from some sort of escape attempt. I imagined the East Germans' photographs going back to the KGB and them trying to figure out what the hell was going on. I had heard that the staff at the Kremlin were big James Bond fans and probably the only people in the Soviet Union who had access to the films. I hoped they enjoyed the scenes where we showed General Gogol, M's KGB counterpart, with his secretary on his knee – we tried to humanise the Russians whenever we could.

After a brief sojourn at Pinewood, our next location was the RAF base at Upper Heyford in Oxfordshire, which doubled for a US air base in Germany. We had wonderful co-operation from the American Air Force personnel, and the women camped outside to campaign for

Kamal Khan
(Louis Jourdan)
with the lethal
yo-yo he used to
intimidate his
opponents. The
yo-yo was
presented to
Cubby Broccoli at
the end of filming.

nuclear disarmament left us alone. We put up the tents and big top of Octopussy's travelling circus in the midst of this very busy aerodrome, while all these fighters and bombers were buzzing around in the background. This was the height of the Cold War and I don't know whether any of the planes were armed with nuclear devices or not. I was quite happy not to know at the time.

While we were at Upper Heyford, we filmed the exteriors of the climatic scene where Bond, disguised as a clown, locates and defuses an atomic bomb that has been hidden inside the big top. It was a bit of a struggle to persuade Roger to dress up as a clown and wear the garish face paint – at the time, he thought I was going a little bit too far. It turned out to be the perfect disguise, however, and I was pleased with the scene when he came face to face with his double, who is also dressed as a clown.

Bond's location and disabling of the bomb comes in the midst of one of the circus acts. Francisco the Fearless is waiting to be fired out of the cannon when Bond calls a halt to proceedings while he deals with the bomb. Francisco is inside his cannon, unaware of the drama outside until he angrily emerges when the drama is over. Francisco was played by

legendary stuntman Richard Graydon. Dickie is a lovely guy and good stuntman who turned up in the Bond films all the time – most notably when he almost lost his life hanging from a cable car without a harness in *Moonraker*. He has an elegant, aristocratic air and always smokes his cigarettes through a special holder – no wonder he's earned the nickname 'Lord Graydon'. I immediately thought of Dickie to play the man with gossamer wings who got shot from the cannon. I called him into the office and he loved the idea. After many attempts, we got the costume right and he really looked the part with his outlandish clothes, flying helmet and goggles. The cannon Dickie was stuffed in didn't fire, of course, but carried explosive charges and expelled a dummy on a wire. We bounced Dickie on a trampoline for the finale when he flies through the air and lands on the net. Dickie was a great sport – a real extrovert and one of my favourite characters.

Bob Simmons and Martin Grace, with Richard Graydon (centre), on location for *Octopussy*. Dickie played Francisco the Fearless in the circus scenes.

The next thing on my schedule was the pre-titles sequence, which saw Bond undercover in South America. This was the era of the Falklands War and no one much fancied the idea of going anywhere near Argentina, so we asked the ever-resourceful Peter Lamont to knock up a few fake palm trees

James Bond
(Roger Moore) is
exposed by the
real Colonel Toro
(Ken Norris) while
sabotaging South
American fighter
planes.

and headed for an aerodrome in Northolt.

We filmed the sequence at RAF Northolt in Ruislip. The aerodrome had been used in numerous Bond films from *Thunderball* onwards and we had a good relationship with the staff there. We always made a donation to their benevolent fund and promised to behave ourselves. It was understood that we had to work around their flying operations, which continued while we were filming. This was where Peter's palm trees came into their own – the ones on the runway were constructed in such a way that they could be collapsed every time an aircraft landed. When the planes had landed, a tug on a rope ensured the trees swung back into place. It so intrigued the locals that somebody in a nearby pub claimed the fake trees had been installed by the RAF in order to make the Argentinian prisoners of war feel at home.

The story begins with Bond impersonating one Colonel Toro and planting a bomb in a high-security airbase. He is caught in the act by the real Colonel Toro, however, and is taken prisoner. With the help of an attractive young ally, Bond escapes, captures a tiny jet aircraft and takes off. The South Americans launch a heat-seeking missile in pursuit of the

Bianca (Tina Hudson) distracts the guards, and Bond's escape attempt begins.

jet, but Bond cleverly evades it in such a way that that the missile destroys the base itself.

Back in the 1960s, Roger had used a double called Ken Norris on *The Saint*. Roger suggested that Ken – who really did bear a quite remarkable resemblance – would be good for the role of Toro, so we got him in and gave Roger a fake moustache to match Ken's. It was very funny when they came face to face in the aircraft hangar – a lot of people thought we had used trick photography to have Roger playing both parts.

Bond's attractive ally Bianca was played by model Tina Hudson, who was only 17 years old. The part required her to drive a Range Rover alongside the truck in which Bond was held prisoner. She admitted she couldn't drive when I first interviewed her, so as a semi-wind-up I asked our production controller Reg Berkshire to teach her. He spent the whole morning with this beautiful girl, teaching her to drive in Black Park near Pinewood. She learned quickly, but while we were filming I noticed that she wasn't keeping the Range Rover in a straight line and on occasions was veering dangerous close to the truck. She had to keep looking over at the soldiers keeping Bond captive, gradually hitching up her skirt to distract

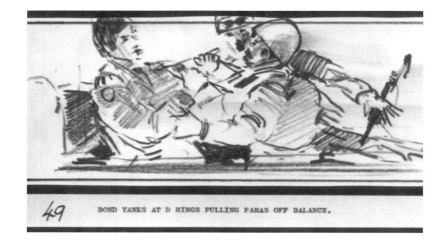

49  BOND YANKS AT D RINGS PULLING PARAS OFF BALANCE.

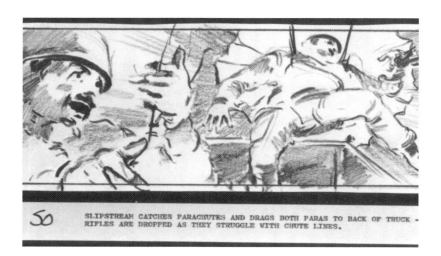

50  SLIPSTREAM CATCHES PARACHUTES AND DRAGS BOTH PARAS TO BACK OF TRUCK –
RIFLES ARE DROPPED AS THEY STRUGGLE WITH CHUTE LINES.

Precise
storyboards were
used to prepare for
this potentially
dangerous scene.

51  LONG SHOT AS CHUTES OPEN AND PARAS BECOME AIRBORNE.

them. While she was doing her best to drive and look sexy for the camera, I was frantically shouting 'Tina! Steer left! Steer right!' and so on. She did very well under the circumstances.

While the soldiers are distracted, Bond pulls their parachute cords and they go flying out the back of the truck, enabling him to initiate his getaway. This was a very dangerous stunt, the idea for which was born while I was filming the skydiving sequence in *Moonraker*. The skydivers were a wild bunch of guys and after a day's shooting, they would drive back from the airfield in a truck. They would find it highly amusing to reach over and pull one of the other's parachute cords, making them fly out of the back of the truck. I thought this was a terrible thing to do and when we came to replicate it in *Octopussy*, the stuntman Chris Webb and special effects supervisor John Richardson had to work quite hard to ensure no one got killed. As with all the stunts performed in James Bond films, we would never advise anyone to try them for themselves – it could have fatal consequences!

The next stage of the pre-titles sequence saw Bond make his escape in a Bede jet and evade the missile by flying through an aircraft hangar, emerging just before its doors close. The closed doors block the missile's path, and the hangar is destroyed in the ensuing explosion. We had originally intended to use the Bede jet in *Moonraker*, but the sequence was dropped from the film before we started shooting. While we were scripting *Octopussy*, Bede pilot J W 'Corkey' Fornof came to London to show us a Japanese television commercial, which featured him flying the jet through an aircraft hangar. Corkey flew through this empty hangar at about 250 mph and it was the most boring thing I'd ever seen – there were no people in the shot to relate to the size and speed of the aircraft, and to my mind, it may as well have been a model. The Japanese clients were obviously aware the shot wasn't terribly exciting because they had matted on a pair of rapidly closing doors at the far end of the hangar in an attempt to add some much-needed drama to the situation. This gave me an idea – we could finally get to use the Bede jet, but we would fly it through a hangar full of people and have it turn on its side in order to squeeze through the gap in the closing doors. It was an insane situation, but I knew it would make a great action sequence. Corkey agreed that it was lunacy and quickly added that it was also impossible. John Richardson suggested flying a model Bede on wires and said this would enable him to change the pitch of the aircraft from horizontal to vertical and run it through the gap in the doors. The model, which was four or five feet in length, approached the hangar doors, one of which was a miniature placed a few feet in front of the camera lens while the hangar itself was some 200 feet away. In the background you could see the real doors on the far side of the hangar being closed by a squad of soldiers.

The commander at Northolt had a Hawker Siddeley 127, which was about four times as big as the Bede jet but doubled for it quite effectively in long shots. We used the HS127 for the long approach shots, cut to a close-up of Roger in the cockpit filmed at Pinewood, then cut to the model going into the hangar as the doors began closing. To get the Bede jet 'flying' through the hangar, John stripped an old Jaguar XJ6 down to its chassis and attached a hydraulic rig called a pole arm. By lying on his

stomach on the chassis, he could alter the altitude of the attached aircraft as it made its way through the hangar. The rig gave him terrific control and reached speeds of up to 60 mph. I put scurrying soldiers in the foreground to disguise the vehicle and we camouflaged the pole arm so that it wasn't visible in the finished shot. I shot interior footage at 20 frames per second to speed it up slightly, but I didn't need much help in that department because there was a dizzying impression of speed and chaos anyway. We even put Roger Moore in the cockpit and filmed him going through the hangar for real.

The missile the South Americans launch to destroy Bond's Bede jet was another airborne challenge. I jokingly suggested to John that he used a model for the jet and tied a flaming firework behind it. He laughed at first, then stopped to think about it. 'I'll give it a go,' he announced, then rallied his model-makers at Pinewood to experiment with fireworks until he got it right. It worked perfectly in the end – wherever the plane went, the rocket followed. This was coupled with footage of Corkey flying the Bede jet through ravines in remote desert areas in America. That material was shot for me by Phil Wrestler, who had been the director of *Chemistry for Sixth Forms* over 20 years before.

As the plane sped away from the hangar, we cut to a model shot of the hangar disintegrating in a colossal explosion (I always said John was good at big bangs) and a close-up of Roger in the cockpit, looking over his shoulder. It all added up to one of the best action sequences we ever did.

Phil shot a lot of second-unit aerial work, including the final flight of

Bond's Bede jet eludes a heat-seeking missile by flying into an aircraft hangar and out through a set of rapidly closing doors.

Kamal Khan's plane for the end of the movie. The model had a dummy at the controls and was projected along a stretch of railway track and off a vertical drop of around 1000 feet in the hope it would spiral to its destruction. One day, I received a phone call from a baffled Phil, who told me the entire shoot had been a disaster. 'You won't believe the rushes,' he told me, before explaining that the aircraft had been packed with explosives and sent trundling along the railway track, as planned. With six cameras filming, it went into the dive, as anticipated. Then something incredible happened. Within 100 feet of the valley floor the plane somehow levelled out and flew out of sight with a dummy at the controls. 'That dummy was a brilliant pilot,' said Phil, who told me that the plane's wing tips were missing rocks, boulders and the canyon walls by a fraction of an inch each time. The plane flew for about a mile, crossing a busy freeway before disappearing behind a mountain. The cameras kept turning, and a few moments later a big plume of smoke indicated that the plane had finally crashed. The ultimate irony was that when I came to compile the climactic sequence in the movie, I used the footage of this plane's precarious journey, but the footage of the plane crashing – which was the original point of the whole exercise – was never used. John blew up a model at Pinewood instead.

A large part of the film took place on the train transporting Octopussy's circus across Europe to East Germany. The East Germans still used steam trains at this time and as filming behind the Iron Curtain was out of the question, we had to find a working steam railway in western Europe. In September, we went to the Nene Valley steam railway, a place near Peterborough run by enthusiasts who keep all these lovely old trains going. They had about 20 miles of track and a stretch of tunnel that was in surprisingly good condition. When I saw this, I decided we had to incorporate it in the scene when the atomic weapon is transferred from one train to another.

The story had Bond bypass the guards on the moving train by having him hide underneath it. There's not a lot of room underneath the average railway carriage, so our grip 'Chunky' Huse built a tubular steel rig which was suspended just above the railway line. The rig was large enough to carry a camera and up to three people; Roger was suspended by an extension of the rig further along the carriage. I decided to brief Roger on what I wanted him to do and not add to the weight on the rig by joining him on the journey. Roger, quite understandably, was having none of this. 'If you don't do it, I won't do it,' he told me. This was fair enough, so I added my 13 stone's worth to the rig alongside Roger. There were some alarming creaking sounds as we were going through the tunnel and we bottomed out more than once, but we got some great shots of Roger and emerged in one piece. Roger's game for anything as long as he has faith in the people supervising the shot.

Martin Grace doubled for Roger in the dangerous shots of Bond moving along the outside of the train, hanging on for dear life while Arthur filmed him from a helicopter. Martin is basically responsible for his own safety on shots like these – he inspected the track for safety and chose the particular stretch to work on. Arthur started filming the scene where Bond climbs along the outside of the train in order to gain access to Octopussy's coach.

Bond (Roger Moore) clings to the side of Octopussy's train. Martin Grace was badly injured while doubling for Roger in these scenes.

Unfortunately, the train's designated stopping point was missed and it headed straight for a nasty obstruction – a piece of protruding pipe hit Martin when he was still outside the carriage. He suffered a bad groin injury during the collision, but it's indicative of the man's enormous strength that he managed to hang on until the train stopped. If he had fallen off at the time of impact, he would probably have ended up under the wheels of the train.

Martin's injury was a terrible blow to the unit. Roger and I were among his many visitors in hospital and we were all glad he was so strong – a lesser man would probably not have survived. Martin took several months to recover, but the show has to go on and Paul Weston continued the sequence in his place.

I asked Peter Lamont how we could achieve the shots of Bond clinging to the underside of the train while Kamal's henchman Gobinda (played by Kabir Bedi) thrashes away at him with his sword. The first thing he suggested was transporting two carriages from the Nene Valley to Pinewood. We suspended the two carriages from cranes, put Roger underneath them and put a moving backing beneath him. A moving backing is the oldest trick in the book and consists of a 20 foot-long canvas painting spun at high speed between two rollers. Peter's scenic artist Jacqueline Stears painted railway lines and sleepers on the canvas, so when it revolved you got the impression of the track whizzing past beneath Roger. It was unusual to use this technique horizontally, instead of vertically (on the other side of a car window, for example), but it worked brilliantly.

As Bond tried to avoid Gobinda, the sword struck various metal components on the underside of the carriage. I wanted sparks to fly from the friction of metal hitting metal, so John connected a cable to a 12 volt battery and ran it down Kabir's sword arm to gain the desired effect. John added to the tense atmosphere of the scene by having Kabir's sword rupture one of the steam pipes. Super-heated steam – in reality $CO_2$ – was spraying around and the pipe started thrashing about.

It's exhausting to hold one's body weight up for any length of time and I couldn't expect Roger to do it for too long. I asked John Richardson to rig some very fine wires underneath the train and attached them to a support belt which held Roger in place. Neither the belt nor the wires were visible on screen once I'd obscured them with Roger's body and some clever camera angles.

While we were filming in the Nene Valley, the crew stayed in various pubs and hotels nearby. One night, Alec Mills went to bed and was disturbed by the sound of someone climbing between the sheets next to him. One of the drivers had had one too many and mistaken Alec's hotel room for his own. Wearing only a pair of Y-fronts, Alec jumped out of bed. The driver, who was just as startled, did the same. The two men confronted each other from either side of the bed, each accusing the other of being in the wrong room.

The next morning, Alec was relating the story to the continuity girl Elaine Schreyeck while Roger was in the background, ear-wigging. After Alec explained what had happened, Elaine wondered whether the driver had been drunk. 'Was he tight?' she asked. Quick as a flash, Roger said,

'Only the first time!'

The search for a location took us to Japan and Hong Kong, both of which had featured in previous films in the series, before someone mentioned the possibility of going to India. The country had originally been considered as a location for *Moonraker*, but there had been problems accommodating the locale in the storyline. This time round, however, Dick and Michael felt they could make it work and there were added budgetary incentives. The fragile state of the Indian economy meant the country had very strict currency controls and most American companies that exhibited their films in the country could not repatriate the funds that were generated. The Indian government offered us a deal, however, giving us permission to buy a percentage of frozen rupees at a generous discount. We were able to spend some of those rupees locally, which helped the budget-conscious MGM/UA and enabled me to film certain scenes that would otherwise have been impossible to realise.

After visiting several different locations we decided to film in Udaipur, the 'City of Sunrise' in Rajasthan. On the initial reconnaissance in the area, Alan Hume was asked to bring back samples of water from Lake Pichola, the location of Octopussy's island retreat. He dipped some test tubes into the lake – unfortunately falling in during the process – and also took a sample from the taps in the hotel and the bottled water available in the local shops. When the various samples were analysed in England, it was found that the best water came from the hotel taps. The bottled water was very dangerous and the lake water was infested. I shuddered at the memory of the local kids swimming about in that stuff.

The unit went to India in mid-September and I followed (missing briefcase and passport notwithstanding) a short while later. One problem we immediately encountered was poor transport. All the internal flights were run by the Indian state airline and it was a struggle for the locals to get tickets. As a foreign outfit we had priority, but they sometimes had to throw people off planes in order to get us on them.

Despite the best efforts of our location caterer Phil Hobbs, who supplied us fresh water from his filtration plant, a lot of people still got stomach complaints in India. Phil, who was quite unfairly nicknamed 'Swill' by the crew, was doing his best and it wasn't his fault: we were all Europeans who were unused to the extreme heat and unfamiliar germs. The heat affected us all and Roger couldn't believe I wanted him to wear a tuxedo for the scenes when Bond visited the casino. I assured him he looked very handsome and reminded him that it was one of the rules in Bond film-making that he put his tux on for the casino – regardless of the climate.

Udaipur looked stunning on screen and I think a lot of people decided to go there on holiday after seeing the film. Udaipur offered us every location we needed except the Taj Mahal – in the film you see Bond's helicopter swooping over the Taj Mahal and landing at Udaipur, which is actually some 300 miles away. Udaipur's Lake Palace Hotel, which doubled as Octopussy's retreat, also came in handy to billet a lot of the crew. Another hotel near the lake was being converted to five-star status while we were there, so we used that as the exterior of Kamal's winter palace. Another palace, about 600 feet up a nearby hill, was used as the exterior of Kamal's summer residence.

Kristina Wayborn
(who played
Magda), myself,
Cubby and Dana
Broccoli at the
French premiere of
*Octopussy*. Former
Miss World Mary
Stavin can be seen
wearing a bow tie
on the far left.

The courtyard of the hotel by the lake was the location of the poolside scene where I filmed Bond's arrival. We were blessed with the best crop of girls we ever had on *Octopussy*, and many of them are visible in this scene. I started off with a shot of the lovely Alison Worth or rather the lovely Alison Worth's bottom. By this stage she was getting a little frustrated with the fact her face hadn't been seen on screen. 'John, why do you always film my bottom?' she asked me one day. 'Well, Alison,' I shrugged, 'It *is* very nice…'. Barbara Broccoli would take great delight in parading these girls before me during auditions for non-speaking parts. I would give each one marks out of ten and try to remember which ones I'd liked best. Later on, we used some very athletic girls in the fight sequences filmed at Pinewood, and Kristina Wayborn, who played Magda, acquitted herself especially well.

The lake was artificial and the Maharani of Udaipur had a fantastic garden which had become completely overgrown. It was situated below the lake, so the seeping water made it appear very tropical. I decided it would be an ideal location in which to film Kamal Khan's elephant hunt.

The Maharani was very co-operative and we were able to use some of her wonderful artefacts in his garden. I knew we would have a problem finding some elephants, so I mentioned the problem to our location advisor who said there were some about 300 miles away. My heart sank. 'How are we going to get them here?' I asked him. 'No problem,' he replied. 'We'll walk them!'

Our next challenge was to find a tiger. It looked as though it would be impossible until I attended a cocktail party hosted by the Maharajah. The first thing I noticed when I arrived at his palace was an imposing stuffed tiger, so after being introduced, the first question I asked was, 'Can I borrow your stuffed tiger?' He thought this was most amusing and readily agreed. On location we put the tiger on a wheelbarrow and pushed it along so it appeared to be crashing through the undergrowth. Roger had just returned from America, where the British dog trainer Barbara Woodhouse was all the rage. Her admonishing catchphrase of 'Sit!', generally directed towards some recalcitrant pup, was on every impersonator's lips. Roger suggested Bond should use the instruction on the advancing stuffed tiger. Roger delivered the line, leaving me to find a real tiger to complete the shot. I was surprised to find that it was easier to get tigers in England than it was in India, where they were all wild and unlikely to take any notice of Roger's dog-training instructions. We contacted the circus-owner Jimmy Chipperfield, who bred tigers in captivity in England and exported them to India. Back at Pinewood, we used a tiger that Jimmy supplied in a cage. The crew had been told that if the tiger got out of the cage, everyone was to keep calm and still. From a standing start, this tiger leapt 10 feet out of the open top of the cage and landed in among the crew. Everyone ignored the advice they'd been given and ran for their lives. Everyone, that is, except Barbara Broccoli, the continuity girl and the nurse, who all stood their ground. Fortunately for them, the tiger wasn't very hungry. Or maybe it just didn't like women.

Another animal we used on set was a tame crocodile, which arrived in a big tank on the back of a truck. Unfortunately, the toothsome reptile was in hibernation and even after the water was warmed up, it still didn't become very active. The handler doubling for Bond did his best to appear to wrestle with the beast, then went to put it back in its tank for the journey home. It evaded capture, however, and waddled off underneath the set, where it refused to budge. It stayed there for the next two weeks until we pulled the set down, at which point we discovered it had gone back into hibernation.

Our stunt-driving expert Remy Julienne joined us in India and supervised the sequence with the three-wheeled taxis. He immediately got hold of some of the vehicles and modified them, adding bigger engines and beefing up the brakes. He also put weights on the back, so they could do wheelies more easily. The whole sequence was very carefully storyboarded back in England and Remy knew exactly what he needed to do.

When I came to work out the action scenes for the taxi sequence, I wanted to incorporate the special skills of Davis Cup star Vijay Amitraj, who was playing Bond's Indian liaison. Vijay had been a guest at Cubby and Dana's house in Beverly Hills and he was a friend of the family. He was a tennis champ with a ready smile and a charming personality. In that

Aboard the love
boat with some of
Octopussy's
athletic girls.

sequence, you can see that Vijay uses his tennis racquet to good effect with a few forehand smashes during the fight.

One unintentionally amusing moment occurred when, despite our best efforts to marshal the extras on the busy streets, this guy sailed through the middle of the action on his bicycle without even looking left or right at the chaos going on around him. It was totally unrehearsed, but I thought it looked very funny.

We would ask for two or three thousand extras for a scene, but they would all tell their friends and family about the filming and we'd end up on the day with a crowd of about 10,000 people, all of whom would want paying, regardless of the fact that many of them hadn't been asked to attend. One evening, we found ourselves typically over-staffed with extras and the accountants were in fear for their lives. We decided it would be prudent to pay the crowd anyway.

The final shot of the film was filmed on the lake – our boat advisor Mike Turk reconstructed an authentic vessel that was seen to be powered by 20 of Octopussy's rowing girls, even though it actually had a concealed engine. The girls weren't going to win the boat race, but they made an effort to at least look convincing. The voice of the dominatrix urging them in at the end of the film ('In!...Out!') belongs to Ingrid Pitt, the wife of my occasional golfing partner Tony Rudlin. Ingrid is an actress who made her name starring in Hammer Horror films in the early 1970s.

From October 1982 to January 1983, we rounded off production of the film with shooting at Pinewood. We erected a big top on the lot and spent three days filming the circus show with a crowd of about 5,000 people. It was difficult to maintain their enthusiasm for so long, and we got some acts in specially to entertain the children.

One of the most memorable shots from the Pinewood shoot is the sight of Q's Union-flag hot-air balloon sailing towards the palace. For long shots, John Richardson constructed a remote-controlled model with flames belching forth every now and then. As a background, we used an evening shot of the summer palace – filmed at what we call 'magic hour', when the light has a golden quality – and suspended the model in front of it. We didn't move the model in the end, but slightly swung the arm of the camera crane and it worked perfectly. For close-ups, Roger and Desmond Llewelyn stood in a life-size basket which was lowered by crane into the courtyard set.

One thing that distinguishes *Octopussy* from the other Bond films is the huge numbers of animals that are featured. Octopussy's girls – some tall, some short, some athletes, some models – rode the elephants which were brought in from Germany. The elephants were all very well behaved, but some of the other animals needed treating with kid gloves. One of the second-unit shots supervised by Phil Wrestler in the US was the scene showing Bond (doubled by Bill Burton) jumping from a horse on to the tail of Kamal Kahn's plane. The horse had to be trained for several days before it got used to the noise of the engines and the slipstream. The end result was remarkable, however, and one of the finest stunts I've ever seen.

The first time Vijay is seen in the film, he is undercover as a snake charmer and he didn't like the idea of this one bit. He became even more reluctant when I told him we'd be using a cobra. The snakes were

Tennis champion
Vijay Amitraj
played Bond's ill-
fated ally in India.

delivered to Pinewood by their handler for Vijay's screen test and the colour drained from his face when he clapped eyes on them. The handler assured me that the cobra's venom had been milked that morning, so a bite wouldn't have fatal consequences. I'm not sure Vijay believed him. When we were shooting in India, the inevitable occurred: the snakes didn't like the heat of the studio lamps and slithered off to an early exit. I rushed around with Vijay, picking them up and bringing them back to the handler – I was amused to note how quickly he conquered his phobia in order to succeed in the role. He was a nice man who played a likeable character – when he was killed on-screen by Gobinda's razor-sharp yo-yo, I think the audience were genuinely sad to see him go. The yo-yo itself was an ingenious invention of John Richardson, which he presented to Cubby at the end of filming.

Despite the difficulties, we used real animals wherever we could. This was impossible in the case of Octopussy's pet blue-ringed octopus, so John came to the rescue with one made of rubber. This very convincing creation was attached to an air line, which made it appear to breath and pulsate. When the film came out, I found myself cornered by a friend at my golf club. 'I was cursing you the other night,' he told me. 'I took my 10-year-old son to see your film and when the octopus clung on the that man's face, he was so frightened he had to look away. I had to take him to see it again so he could pluck up the courage to look at the screen. I sat through that thing three times before he finally looked at it!' I apologised that the octopus appeared so realistic, but consoled myself that none of this was hurting the box-office takings.

The other notable mechanical creature was the crocodile-submarine which Bond occupies – we got a big laugh when the jaws opened to reveal the sub's occupant and an even bigger laugh when they snapped shut again. I was never sure if Roger thought we went too far on some occasions, but he played the comedy to the hilt. One morning, he announced, 'I can't say these lines, John, they're awful.' He'd had dinner with a writer friend the night before and between them they'd rewritten the scene, changing all the dialogue. I took a look at what they'd done, and told him 'Roger, this probably sounded great after a couple of drinks, but I'm afraid it just doesn't stand up in the cold light of dawn.' He stared at me for a couple of seconds and then just laughed.

*Octopussy* was a challenging experience that presented many new problems I hadn't encountered on *For Your Eyes Only*. We overcame them all and went on to produce the most commercially successful film of my career. One challenge which I certainly hadn't expected to contend with was a rival Bond picture. Producer Kevin McClory – whom I remembered from my Shepperton days as an outspoken young sound engineer – was producing Sean Connery's Bond comeback movie *Never Say Never Again* at Elstree while we were working at Pinewood. Although based on the same story that had inspired Ian Fleming's novel *Thunderball*, the film stood outside the series of movies produced by Eon. I had great faith in what we were doing and never looked over my shoulder at the 'opposition', but the laboratory got my rushes mixed up one day with the footage director Irvin Kershner had shot on *Never Say Never Again*. We were intrigued to see some of their film arrive at Pinewood, but we resisted

the temptation to watch it and rang Elstree to tell them about the mix-up. We had a laugh about it and quietly swapped the cans over. We even paid for the car over to Elstree.

Meeting Prince Charles at the London premiere of *Octopussy*.

They had Sean Connery, who of course originated the role of James Bond and was fantastic, but we had the established Bond in Roger. I felt our action sequences would be better and after viewing *Never Say Never Again*, I think I was right – they used a completely different technique from the one I used and filmed their action using multiple cameras. As a general rule, I feel that if you film action using too many cameras, you compromise the essential position, but I suppose it's a matter of taste.

I wished Kevin, Irvin and Sean well because I knew that the better their film did at the box-office, the better it would be for us. In the end, they decided not to go head-to-head with *Octopussy* and opened *Never Say Never Again* six months later. We opened in the summer and did very well; they opened at Christmas and did very well, if not quite as well as us. A lot of people probably couldn't differentiate between the 'official' Bond film and the 'unofficial' one, but the commercial success of both movies meant there were no hard feelings from me.

*Never Say Never Again* proved to be a one-off and Sean left Bond behind. The terrific success of *Octopussy*, however, meant that Roger's retirement would have to be delayed a little longer.

# 007

## CHAPTER 10

### VIEW FINDER

The more Bond films I made, the trickier it became to find a title, or at least, a title everyone was happy to accept. When we told MGM/UA that we were making a film called *Octopussy*, their publicity people complained on the grounds that there were certain sexual connotations (goodness knows how they got round 'Pussy Galore' in *Goldfinger*). I rolled my eyes and did my best to maintain my composure, politely explaining that the word 'Octopussy' was from the pen of Ian Fleming – we weren't deliberately trying to be provocative. Two years on, I started getting a sense of *déjà vu*. 'So what exactly does *From A View to a Kill* mean?' came the voice at the other end of the transatlantic phone line. 'It's a hunting term,' I replied, quickly adding: 'It's an Ian Fleming title. And we haven't got many Ian Fleming titles left!' That seemed to do the trick.

The title of Fleming's short story was abbreviated to *A View to a Kill* for our film, but I was glad that we were able to preserve another element of the great man's work in the face of modern marketing pressures.

*A View to a Kill* was a consolidation of the success we had all enjoyed with *For Your Eyes Only* and especially *Octopussy*. During the very early stages of pre-production, there was some discussion about bringing in a new writer, but we decided to go with the now-established writing partnership of Dick Maibaum and Michael Wilson. 'I know we've had our ups and downs,' Cubby said to me once, 'but whatever we've got here seems to work.'

Cubby told me that Fleming had always seen Roger Moore as James Bond and took a while to be won over by Sean Connery. Fleming's Bond was something of an upper crust figure, a former public schoolboy with a taste for the finer things in life. Sean Connery had enjoyed incredible success in the role – partly because he introduced a rough element which co-existed with Fleming's characterisation – but Roger's interpretation was probably a little closer to what Fleming had in mind.

MGM/UA weren't in a gambling mood and they put pressure on Cubby to do another Bond with Roger. I think everyone knew that Roger was nearing the end of his Bond career – Roger and MGM/UA included – but the temptation to safeguard the elements that had made *Octopussy* such a success was too great to resist. Roger had a lot of clout in the negotiations that ensued and I was certainly reluctant to embark on yet another round of screen tests when I strongly suspected that our distributor would lean on Cubby to get their man. Nevertheless, the poker game resumed and Roger got the deal he'd been holding out for.

Cubby had asked me to direct the next picture during post-production on *Octopussy* and I hadn't subjected him to any such lengthy negotiations. This might sound naïve, but money was never foremost in my mind when it came to directing Bond films. My original agent, the late Herb Tobias, and my current agent, Spyros Skouras, always argued the money side of things on my behalf and I tried not to get involved. My fees got higher and higher with each picture, but I never wanted to look a gift horse in the mouth – I've never forgotten that if it wasn't for Cubby Broccoli, I'd probably still be a film editor. I gladly accepted each assignment and my next thought was not 'I wonder how much money I'm going to get?', but more usually 'I wonder how much fun we're going to have?'.

Roger had a similarly light-hearted approach to the Bond films, but was always a consummate professional. He's no fool and he knew that his age would prevent him from playing James Bond again. There was an understanding between us that *A View to a Kill* would be his farewell performance and he entered into it with considerable enthusiasm. Roger's wife, Louisa, accompanied us for much of the shoot and took lots of photographs. She kept an eye on Roger and was always handy to have around if anyone needed bringing back down to earth. While we were shooting at a quarry in San Francisco, she turned to me and said, 'John, why is it you always finish up shooting on rubbish dumps?'

In 1983, Michael Wilson had told me that he wanted to set the next film in California's Silicon Valley, the heart of the world's microchip production. The basic idea of the story was similar to that of *Goldfinger* – Goldfinger planned to irradiate the gold in Fort Knox in order to raise the value of his own stocks; Max Zorin, the villain in our film, planned to wipe out Silicon Valley in order to corner the market in microchip production. The consumer electronics industry was just beginning to boom and this seemed like an excellent idea. As the script began to take shape in early 1984, Dick and Michael refined the idea and decided that the destruction of Silicon Valley could be implemented by initiating a huge flood.

Max Zorin's scheme was a reflection of the fast-changing technological developments in the 1980s, but there were other aspects of the script that showed the influence of contemporary cinema. Action films were changing a lot during this period: Arnold Schwarzenegger and Sylvester Stallone had become huge stars in films that were certainly a lot more violent than anything that had been depicted in the Bond movies. In response to films such as *First Blood*, which starred Stallone as John Rambo, we decided to toughen up our films a bit from here on. In retrospect, this might have been a mistake – Roger certainly had reservations about one or two scenes in *A View to a Kill* – but we always tried to obey the rules of Bond and offset the violence with some throwaway humour afterwards. The world was changing, movies were changing – we had to keep up.

We went on a reconnaissance trip to California and did some research into the local technological industries and the area's geology – Dick and Michael wanted Zorin to submerge Silicon Valley by flooding the San Andreas fault and creating a huge earthquake. We found a research establishment with a

In San Francisco
with my good
friend, Bond
scriptwriter
Richard Maibaum.

beta particle accelerator and we were intrigued to notice that this facility – which featured a two-mile long tunnel in which atoms were bombarded – was built right across an earthquake fault line. We also donned special suits to visit a plant where scientists were trying to create nuclear fission by bombarding particles with laser beams. They had floor after floor of what looked like film projectors, all beaming light which was reflected and gathered into one huge laser that was passed from one building to another. This was eventually concentrated into a huge lens that reduced the ultimate beam to the size of something that could be passed through the eye of a needle. This was awesome technology and with a flick of a switch, the whole thing could be shut down and rendered non-radioactive. One of the scientists there told me that if an earthquake were to have the effect of 'unleashing' this laser before it achieved its ultimate form, it would be powerful enough to illuminate the whole of San Francisco – there would be broad daylight in the middle of the night.

Berkeley University, just outside San Francisco, had a medical facility where patients were treated for brain tumours using lasers. They were put into special cradles, with their heads locked into a rigid position. The cradle was then manoeuvred around a stationary laser beam, so the only part of the body that remained within the focus of the beam was the tumour. The laser burned the tissue only at the pinpoint where it was centred. The success rate was very high and the operation was in such demand that we were able to visit only during the short period when they were changing over from one patient to another.

The Earthquake Centre in Silicon Valley itself was the place that monitored the geological activity in the surrounding areas in an attempt to predict future disasters. After we studied all the instruments, we were taken out for lunch by the absent-minded professor who had showed us around. Over our meal, he told me that although he had all this very sophisticated equipment at his disposal, he still relied on a degree of intuition in his research – he would carefully monitor the classified columns of the local newspapers and when adverts appealing for the return of missing cats reached a peak, he knew there was going to an earthquake. 'Cats have a sense of the impending pressure that causes earthquakes,' he told us matter-of-factly, while we listened slack-jawed. 'They know when there's trouble coming and they run away from it.' It was at that point I noticed he was wearing one red sock and one black sock.

We took all this information back to Dick Maibaum (including the bit about the cats, which he incorporated) along with masses of stills that Michael had taken. I had been gathering ideas for action sequences that had been suggested by, or could exploit, the local scenery.

At Pinewood Studios, we discussed how we could recreate the flooding of the San Andreas fault. Someone suggested using a particular lake in Wales that dried up in the summer. Our schedule didn't allow us the luxury of waiting until winter, however, when it apparently filled up again. Arthur Wooster and I are both yachtsmen, so I asked him about an estuary I'd heard of in the West Country. It filled up and emptied twice a day, and we both agreed it sounded ideal. I sent him down there and he came back with some stills that showed considerable promise. Once we'd had all the boats towed away, it really fit the bill.

Max Zorin was an imposing Bond villain in the traditional mould, and we needed a personality actor to fit the role. I had admired Christopher Walken ever since he first came to prominence in *The Deer Hunter* in 1978 and knew he was a slightly offbeat actor with the rather sinister and unusual appearance we needed for the role. The only problem I had working with Christopher was his habit of wandering off while we were on location. I'd turn my back for a moment, only to discover that he'd gone for a walk somewhere. I ended up giving one of the junior assistant directors the sole responsibility of keeping an eye on Christopher and making sure he was around when I needed him for a shot. This became something of a game for Christopher and as soon as this guy was distracted for a second, he'd nip off in the other direction.

Michael had been very impressed by David Bowie's recent performance in *Merry Christmas Mr Lawrence* and had wanted to cast him as Max Zorin. He came into the office for an interview, but it soon became clear that David's extensive touring schedule would preclude him taking four or five months to make a Bond film. Singers earn an awful lot of money from touring and they have a huge entourage who also rely on those tours for their living. At the end of the day, money speaks and it just wasn't possible for David to take such a lengthy sabbatical.

The search for this movie's 'Bond girl' was a lengthy one and we were without a leading lady almost until we began shooting. We interviewed a lot of actresses for the role of geologist Stacey Sutton, but MGM/UA eventually suggested we take a look at Tanya Roberts, who had just starred in *Sheena, Queen of the Jungle*. *Sheena* had been directed by John Guillermin, and I rang him to ask his opinion of Tanya. He told me that she might not be the best actress in the world, but she was undoubtedly very beautiful. When I met Tanya, I was certainly inclined to agree and was especially struck by her incredible deep blue eyes. I wondered whether she

Max Zorin
(Christopher
Walken), May Day
(Grace Jones),
Stacey Sutton
(Tanya Roberts)
and James Bond
(Roger Moore) in
*A View to a Kill.*

wore contact lenses. 'Are they real?' I asked her. To my surprise, she immediately clutched her breasts. 'Of course they are!' she replied. We had to make a decision quickly and at the end of the day Tanya got the job. Roger knew that Tanya would need a bit of attention off-camera for us to get a good performance out of her, but he was a patient and generous professional who certainly knew the routine by now.

Barbara Broccoli found Grace Jones for the role of semi-villain May Day. Unlike David Bowie, Grace was able to accommodate our lengthy shoot in her schedule and I was very glad to have her along – the chemistry between Tanya as our blonde beauty and Grace as our fearsome Amazon gave us an intriguing combination of female leads. Grace's boyfriend was Mr Universe champion Dolph Lundgren, who later became something of a film star in his own right. I gave him his first screen role, as a Russian gunman, after he impressed me with his gunplay. I was glad to see him do so well afterwards.

Grace was a playful and enthusiastic character and I enjoyed working with her a lot. She was more than a match for Roger and came up with a practical joke even more devastating than one of his traditional stunts. While Bond is working undercover at Zorin's mansion, he inevitably finds his way into bed with May Day. We were filming the scene where Roger slips between the sheets when Grace suddenly produced a huge black dildo from under the covers. She was screaming with laughter for about 10 minutes, although I'm not sure Roger saw the funny side.

Patrick Macnee played Bond's sidekick Sir Godfrey Tibbett and I had fond memories of working with him on *The Sea Wolves*. *A View to a Kill* gave us the opportunity to unite two of the biggest television names of the

1960s – here was the star of *The Avengers* working alongside the star of *The Saint*! Patrick is a wonderful actor and a great friend; I felt rather guilty about devising such a sticky end for his character in a killer car wash. I've always felt slightly uneasy about the loss of control one experiences inside automated car washes – if you were to get mashed, who would hear you screaming above the din of those huge whirling brushes? They have always struck me as potentially ideal places to bump somebody off discreetly. Roger never missed an opportunity to tease Patrick during the scenes where Tibbett was scivvying for Bond. While posing as Bond's chauffeur, Sir Godfrey drove around in Cubby's Rolls-Royce, although we substituted a reconstructed vehicle for the scenes where it was submerged (Cubby was prepared to make any number of sacrifices when it came to making movies, but he drew the line at ditching his beloved Rolls).

Additional glamour was provided by Fiona Fullerton, whose scene in the hot tub with Roger is one of the most talked about moments in any of my Bond films ('The bubbles tickle my…Tchaikovsky!'). I later discovered that the tub had been bought by someone and installed in a penthouse in Dundee. Alison Doody played Jenny Flex and she looked great in jodhpurs. She reminded me a little of Grace Kelly.

*A View to a Kill* was the film where we not only said goodbye to Roger's James Bond, but also to Lois Maxwell's Miss Moneypenny. Lois's departure had been on the cards for a while and although we were sorry to see her go, I think it was somehow fitting that she said goodbye at the same time as Roger. The tragedy for Lois was that there weren't many subsequent avenues of employment open to an actress so closely identified

Between takes with Grace, Walter Gotell and Patrick Macnee.

A spot of impromptu *glasnost* in the hot tub between Roger and Fiona Fullerton.

with one particular role.

During pre-production, disaster struck at Pinewood Studios. At the end of June 1984, a camp fire on the set of Ridley Scott's film *Legend* set light to the plastic jungle set inside the 007 Stage. Although the stage was mainly built of concrete and metal, the plastic was highly flammable and the fire almost completely destroyed the building. The few personnel inside the stage managed to get out, but there were a lot of birds on the set and they sadly perished. The stage was quickly rebuilt to an improved design which incorporated new emergency exits at the upper levels so anyone working above a set could get out quickly if necessary. Peter Lamont and construction company Delta Doric worked very closely on the new 007 Stage (renamed the Albert R Broccoli 007 Stage in honour of our producer) and the result was a remarkable feat of engineering that took only six weeks of construction from beginning to end. The upshot to our schedule, however, was that the sequence in the interior of Zorin's mine was delayed by some three weeks and this cost quite a lot of money. The insurance company was good to us during our three-week hiatus and we managed to make the projected US release date without too much drama.

Arthur Wooster's second-unit began work in June 1984 and the rest of us followed on soon after. Our budget was set at $30 million, approximately the same as my previous two Bond films, and Tom Pevsner ensured it went as far as possible. Tom planned everything meticulously and in as efficient a way as possible, but we were never afraid to spend money on something if we felt it showed its value on screen.

The pre-titles sequence was filmed in Iceland, which was one country we hadn't even considered visiting in the past. The plot was simple – in Siberia, Bond has to recover a microchip from the body of 003, but is intercepted by a squad of skiing Russians. I had pictured Alaska as the ideal location and envisaged shots of glaciers emerging from the sea and great chunks of monolithic ice falling away into the ocean. We tried to find somewhere closer to home and looked at the North Cape, Norway and Greenland before someone suggested Iceland. We made some enquiries and discovered a glacier that ran down to sea level and formed a lake with a bridge on its far side. This sounded ideal, so we jumped on a plane and flew out to take a look. I thought Iceland was a remarkable place. It's a country whose volcanic origins are still all too clear when you look down from the air – the ground is steaming and smouldering and there is a wonderful variety of glaciers, steaming lava fields and raging torrents of water.

We duly arrived at this particular site and stayed at a local lodge. During our first morning, we found the bridge and took in the wonderful view of the glacier. I ventured out in a rubber boat and our guide told us that if a piece of ice fell off the glacier and landed in the lake; the ensuing tidal wave would probably swamp us. He told us we would be lucky to survive more than three minutes in the near-freezing water, but this didn't put us off. I later investigated the inside of one of the nearby ice caverns. It was like a cathedral and the reflected light inside made it one of the most beautiful sights I have ever seen. We boarded one of the floating icebergs outside and as I clambered for a foothold, I turned over possible action sequences in my mind.

Back at Pinewood, we mapped out the structure of the sequence. We decided that, during the chase with the Russians, Bond would improvise a single snowboard using a salvaged component from his destroyed skidoo – a novel innovation that was suggested by my old friend Willy Bogner. Willy came over to London to talk things over before we packed him off to work his magic. I also briefed Arthur about the Iceland shoot and asked John Richardson to devise Bond's getaway vehicle – a motorised ice floe which had to be big enough to house Bond and his beautiful ally Kimberley Jones. Special Agent Jones was played by former Miss World Mary Stavin, who had briefly appeared in *Octopussy* as a photographer. We had earmarked Mary as an actress and we needed a beautiful girl for the pre-titles sequence, so we offered her the role.

Mike Turk, who had worked with us on *Octopussy*, helped construct the ice floe out of fibreglass. We all gathered at his boatyard in Sunbury-on-Thames while he demonstrated the motorised prop on the river. It worked very well and the afternoon was made all the more memorable by the looks on the faces of the astonished local residents. The ice floe was sent to Iceland, where it joined Arthur and stunt arranger Martin Grace, now

There's a fly in my
soup – Monsieur
Aubergine (Jean
Rougerie) is the
victim of a bizarre
assassination.

recovered from his accident and hopping from one ice floe to another for our
benefit. The helicopter used in the sequence was flown from Scotland by
Marc Wolff and he only just made it. We also used a number of small radio-
controlled models. One of the models went out of control and crashed;
another was packed with explosives and flown into a cliff. When I saw the
rushes of the ensuing explosion, I decided it just wasn't big enough for a
Bond movie, so I asked John Richardson to pack a bit more explosive into
the side of a glacier and try again. We then cut from the exploding model to
the even bigger explosion that was triggered a little while later. Bond
snowboards away from the gunmen to the tune of the Beach Boys'
*California Girls*, which I thought was an appropriate tune considering he
looked as though he was surfing across the ice. We couldn't use the original
tune, so I asked John Barry to arrange the recording of a sound-alike version
by a group called Gidea Park. With his mission complete, Roger jumps into
the ice floe to commence the five-day journey to Alaska with only Mary for
company. Nice work if you can get it.

Royal Ascot was an altogether more civilised location for my unit while
Arthur shivered away in Iceland. Dressing Robert Brown, Desmond
Llewelyn and Roger in top hat and tails did give me the impression we were
remaking *My Fair Lady*, but it lent the film a touch of class. The Queen's
racecourse manager was very co-operative and afforded us every opportunity
on the condition we didn't interfere with any of the events. I was able to film
the racing from the grandstand and plant actors in among the crowd. At
Pinewood, we recreated certain parts of the stands for close-up shots.

From there, we went to Paris to film the sequences in and around the Eiffel Tower. The inspiration for May Day's bizarre assassination of the detective Monsieur Aubergine came from a visit I had made to the Café du Paris on the Champs-Elysées some five years previously. We were having dinner right at the back when the show began – a girl started whistling on stage while these butterflies fluttered over the heads of the audience. My son Matthew, who is a keen fisherman, noticed a figure draped in black behind us, manipulating the butterflies on the end of a long fishing rod. He was fascinated by this and the act had stuck in my mind ever since. Barbara tracked the show down to Las Vegas and arranged to meet the butterfly man Dominique Risbourg at the restaurant he owned near Paris. After dinner, he vanished and reappeared wearing a dinner jacket and hairpiece. He then ushered us outside because there wasn't enough room to stage the act inside. Unfortunately it was raining, and the napkins on our heads did little to keep the rain off. The butterflies fared little better: they got so wet that Dominique's performance was ruined. I could see what he was getting at, however, and we decided to recreate his act at Pinewood. In the middle of the first take, when the butterflies were in full flight, I was distracted by the sound of a heated argument going on somewhere off-set. I was slightly amused to notice Dominique engaged in a passionate disagreement with his assistant, but I politely asked them to save the argument for later. The whistling girl was played by Carole Ashby, a model and game-show hostess who had appeared in *Octopussy*. Carole was a beautiful girl, but she couldn't whistle. After a few failed attempts, I taught her to purse her lips and blow and she soon got the point. The sound went in later.

B J Worth dressed as May Day to perform the spectacular stunt where she parachutes from the top of the Eiffel Tower to evade the pursuing Bond. BJ practised the stunt on one of the empty stages at Pinewood and I decided to visit him one day to see how he was doing. I arrived to see him perched on the edge of a diving board, preparing himself to jump off. I asked him where this unusually long diving board was going to go. 'On top of the Eiffel Tower,' he replied. 'We can't attach a diving board to the Eiffel Tower,' I told him. 'It will change the shape of it!' He argued that it was the very shape of the Tower that meant he needed a diving board to clear the superstructure on his descent and I could see his point. BJ did use the diving board in the end, but I got him to reduce it as much as possible.

The French authorities are understandably sensitive about people throwing themselves off the top of the Eiffel Tower and Tom, who speaks fluent French, had to clear it with the Mayor of Paris in advance. The day before our stunt was due to be performed, a couple – one of whom had never jumped before – leapt off the Tower hand in hand, picked themselves up at the bottom and ran away. It rather took the edge off what we were planning to do.

With every safety precaution taken, BJ made a successful jump and parachuted down over the Seine. The day after, BJ's right-hand man Tweet, who looked after his parachute gear and wardrobe, went to the top of the Tower and jumped off BJ's diving board. This annoyed me a great deal as Tweet was supposed to be working for us and his behaviour jeopardised our delicately balanced relationship with the Mayor. In my opinion, it was unprofessional behaviour and I told him in no uncertain terms. The Mayor

Assorted cast and
crew up to no
good in Paris.
Roger is groping
continuity
supervisor June
Randall.

was furious, but fortunately Tom was able to calm him down.

The car chase through Paris was supervised by Remy Julienne and filmed by Arthur. Remy brought a scientific approach to his stunt driving, carefully rehearsing everything on an airfield near Paris by launching cars into huge airbags. He left nothing to chance. I adopted a similarly methodical approach when I contributed an idea to a later sequence where the Rolls-Royce is dumped into the lake with Tibbett's body inside. Bond cannot emerge from the lake for fear he'll be spotted by Zorin, so he's forced to stay underwater. I wondered if he could survive by breathing the air he released from of the car's tyres, and asked an expert if it would be possible. The official verdict was that it was feasible to survive for between five and ten minutes by breathing the tyre's compressed air, assuming of course you could keep the valve closed between breaths.

Max Zorin's château was filmed in an 18th-century estate called Chantilly. During our reconnaissance of the area, I was immediately struck not only by Chantilly but by the equally imposing building opposite. 'What is that building?' I asked. 'That's the stables,' our guide replied. 'The original owner of the château was convinced he would be reincarnated as a horse, so he ensured the stables were as grand as the main house.'

There was a moat surrounding the château and I decided we should fill it with boats and aristocratic young ladies to create the impression that Max was hosting a lavish party. Stacey meets Bond on a bridge over the moat in one of the most romantic and elegant scenes in the whole picture.

At Chantilly, Patrick Macnee examines a racehorse with a bandaged knee. The horse was apparently a better actor than he was a runner because as soon as we put the bandage on his leg he hung his head and started to look very sorry for himself. Racehorses are usually extremely sensitive creatures, but this one had been lifted into an elevated set and made to wear a bandage and he didn't give Patrick any trouble at all.

The location for Patrick's investigation of Zorin's warehouse was actually a Renault spare parts factory somewhere off the M4. This eerie place was completely automated – someone in an office would press a button and the requested part would arrive soon after on a conveyor belt. It was then sent to the loading bay and despatched to its waiting customer. The building itself was supported by exterior beams and rather resembled a huge circus tent. We were limited by the amount of time we could spend in this place and had to recreate some of it later at Pinewood, but we made good use of the conveyor belt to package up two of Zorin's thugs.

After a very pleasant stay at Chantilly, during which time we enjoyed some superb weather, we went back to Pinewood. The next big location was the principal setting for the film: San Francisco.

Every time you go to a famous town, it's almost obligatory to have a riotous car chase through its streets. This time round, we commandeered a fire engine and added a bit of extra tension by having Bond swing from one of its stray ladders. Roger had a lot of fun driving the fire engine and we later complemented the sequence with front projection work filmed at Pinewood. I developed this scene with Michael Wilson and had storyboards prepared at Pinewood. Arthur spent three weeks shooting the sequence, which culminated in the police cars being perched on top of one of the opening halves of a bridge.

Diane Feinstein, the Mayor of San Francisco, gave us permission to stage a fire at the City Hall, which is a beautiful building that film-makers often use to double for the White House. We were told to go ahead, as long as the local Fire Chief approved. I think the city administrators were so co-operative because they realised that a Bond film could bring in as much as $3 to 4 million to the local economy. John Richardson put down big steel sheets to protect the roof during the fire and then set light to butane jets to give the impression of a roaring blaze. Tanya Roberts needed rescuing and I

Zorin (Christopher Walken) and Dr Mortner (Willoughby Gray) greet a new arrival at Chantilly.

Tanya Roberts
showed
considerable
courage during the
filming of the
blazing lift shaft.

remember the local firemen were all too keen to volunteer for the task. The lucky chap who got the job was enthusiastically cheered by his mates as he came down the ladder with Tanya clinging on for dear life. Where his hands went was nobody's business, but Tanya was so terrified that I don't think she noticed. There was no damage done during the shooting of the exterior fire sequences, except one of the firemen discovered the window to the tax office and decided to flood it with his hose. That elicited another enthusiastic cheer.

The interior scenes were filmed at Pinewood and this was where Tanya came into her own. She was extremely brave during the shooting of Bond and Stacey's journey through the blazing lift shaft. We used a lot of flammable petroleum jelly, which can sometimes get out of control. The heat was unbearable and although we used doubles, Tanya appeared in most of the shots herself. I'm not crazy about working with fire, but sometimes you've got no alternative.

When we were filming at Fisherman's Wharf, Maud Adams visited the set. 'Why don't you walk through the background in one of the crowd scenes?' I suggested. 'That way you can say you've been in three Bond films!' Keep an eye out for Maud next time you watch the film.

Across the Bay Bridge, in Oakland, there is a famous old residence called

Dunsmure House. The house was built by a railway baron and is now run as a museum. It was such a perfect location for Stacey's wealthy grandfather's house that we got permission to close it to the public so we could film the inside and the outside. My assistant director Gerry Gavigan had terrible trouble with a pair of identical cats that were supposed to act startled when Bond fires a shotgun loaded with rock salt in order to frighten some villains away. The terrified cats (doubling for a single moggie in the film) were supposed to run up the stairs, but they steadfastly refused, however we tried to coax them. When one of them finally darted up the stairs, it bumped its nose halfway up and skulked off looking very indignant. In the end I had to rewrite the script to have the cat dash *down* the stairs (something neither of them had any objections to) before making a hasty exit. I think those cats were glad to see the end of shooting.

At the climax of the film, Zorin makes his escape in an airship which was supplied to us by Airship Industries Inc. Bond grabs the airship's tow rope and soon finds himself flying over San Francisco, heading for the Golden Gate Bridge. We had a meeting at Airship Industries and one of the pilots told me he was going to go to San Francisco in three weeks time to do some advertising work for Fuji. I said we'd try and make sure we were filming there at that time. I asked him if he could fly as close as possible to the bridge for the benefit of our cameras, but he explained that he was allowed to get no closer than 300 feet.

Arthur arranged for Panavision to fly a camera and several boxes of lenses to the airport for us and we picked them up the next morning (Michael, Barbara and myself joked that we were the film industry's most expensive labourers at that point). As I was lugging these things out of the airport, I grumbled that Arthur, like all cameramen, seemed to order three times as many lenses as he actually needed. We rushed to get into position before the airship approached and as it neared, I noticed that it was backlit by the sun. This worked to our advantage because the shadow obscured the Fuji logo on the side. I'm sure Fuji would have loved some free publicity in our film, but for our purposes the airship had to belong to Zorin Industries and in those days the computer-generated imagery that would enable you to fiddle with things like that just didn't exist.

Zorin and Bond play out their final confrontation high above the bridge, grappling on top of one of the huge supports. After some hazardous second-unit work, which was initially hampered by poor weather, we had to build three sets at Pinewood to complete the sequence. These included a full-size set on the back-lot and another section of the bridge in the studio where we shot the front projection footage.

Charlie Staffell was in charge of front projection at Pinewood and to shoot this sequence he used a machine that must have weighed half a ton. The front projection process uses a beam splitter – a mirror in front of the camera reflects half the image, while the other half of it goes through the mirror so you can still see your characters. In other words, the projector and the camera are linked together and the image of the background is thrown back into the lens. To get the background images we needed, we had to take the heavy VistaVision cameras to the top of the bridge. Most people are unaware that there are lifts that go from the road right to the top of the support towers. These lifts are little bigger than coffins – they can hold only two people at a time – and are generally used only by maintenance workers. I took a trip to the top of the bridge in one of these lifts, and gazed down at the three lanes of tiny traffic below me. We got permission to photograph plates for the front projection and the authorities even let us perform a limited fight sequence up there. The stuntmen wore safety harnesses attached to the tube-like supports which appear spindly from the ground but are actually six feet in diameter.

Of all the front projection shots we did at Pinewood, I think the most successful was the one where Roger is holding Tanya by her fingertips and behind her you can see the traffic and a boat travelling under the bridge. We had to put extra safety lines on all the components of the front projection machine, in case anything fell off it while we were shooting. Most of what is shot on the Bond films is real: there is very little fakery. The 'secret', if there is one, is to cut together footage from numerous different sources in such a way that the audience is given as strong a perception as possible that what they're watching is really happening. In this instance, the combination of studio, location and model shots was very successful, and beautifully photographed by Alan Hume.

The airship meets its demise when it is blown up by the explosives carried by the mad scientist, who was played by the wonderful Willoughby Gray. The props department presented me with a variety of sophisticated-looking explosive devices, but in the end I asked for the most simple: 'Give me taped-together sticks of dynamite with a slow-burning fuse.' I didn't want there to be any doubt over what we were dealing with, and although it might have been a familiar image, I think it worked very well.

The location for the exterior of Zorin's mine was the Amberley Chalk Pits

I knew that the top of the Golden Gate Bridge would be a great setting for the final confrontation between Zorin and Bond.

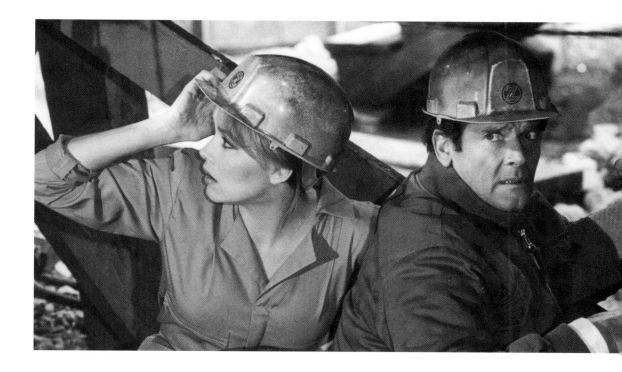

Museum in West Sussex, a little closer to home. Our five days at Amberley got off to a bad start when we came to shoot Tanya's first scene. Our characters were due to enter a working mine and I told the wardrobe supervisor that everyone accordingly had to be issued hard hats. Nobody had a problem with this except Tanya. I went to see her in her trailer and found her sobbing. 'I can't possibly play six pages of script with a hard hat on!' she told me, bleary eyed. I couldn't believe what I was hearing. While the cast and crew kicked their heels outside, I sat next to Tanya and tried to reassure her. 'I think you look very becoming in a hard hat,' I told her. 'Besides, everyone is wearing one so you're not going to get away without one!' I had to work quite hard to convince her before she would leave her trailer to begin work that morning. I later reflected on the irony of the situation – Tanya was game for doing just about any action scene we suggested, no matter how dangerous it seemed, but she reacted with complete horror at the prospect of jamming her beautiful hair under a plastic hard hat. Needless to say, Roger found this all highly amusing.

On another occasion that once again held us up, there was a speedier resolution to the situation. We were about to film a scene where Tanya's character had to descend the ventilation shaft. Tanya arrived at the set, took one look at the ventilation shaft and realised that the camera would be situated at the bottom, shooting up. I turned around and she'd vanished. 'Where has she gone?' I asked the costume lady. 'She's gone to put a pair of knickers on!' came the whispered response.

Time is money and a director never loses sight of his responsibility to achieve a certain amount of work a day and bring a production in on schedule. That said, film-making is obviously never going to be an especially

Six pages of script in a hard hat – Stacey (Tanya Roberts) and Bond (Roger Moore) brave the dangers of Zorin's mine.

efficient business – there are too many personalities and too many opinions involved at every stage of the way. Even when you get on to the floor, there are always grey areas that need sorting out. On one occasion, Danny, who was the prop man on most of my Bonds, was still sweeping the floor when I wanted to start filming a scene. 'Danny,' I called out from behind the camera, 'do you realise that this is costing me $1000 a minute?'. He looked up and started sweeping twice as quickly.

The interior scenes at the mine were filmed on the new 007 Stage and we used its huge tip tanks to supply the water Zorin uses to flood the place. The water went down into the three tanks and could be recirculated or pumped out as we wished. Along with my camera operator Alec Mills, I had gained extensive experience of a real mine during the filming of *Gold* and we were both pleased that our Pinewood version was a convincing recreation of the real thing.

When Grace was being led by Roger through the flooded mine, I asked the special effects technicians to create sparks that would make it seem as if the electricity cables were shorting out in the water. I gave John Richardson the instruction to start the sparks and the cables started arcing on the water. Grace was so terrified I think she practically wet herself. The effect was so authentic that she was convinced something terrible was actually happening and that she and Roger were in real danger. I probably should have warned her, but I was very pleased with the natural reaction that is preserved in the finished film.

For the shots of the airship outside Amberley, we used a combination of a model on a crane and the real thing. The pilot was very clever and managed to navigate his airship around the mine at Amberley, which is full of quarries, hills and trees. During a reconnaissance trip at a nearby airfield, I left my bride-to-be Janine in the car while I went to talk to the pilot. I promised I'd be back in five minutes, but when he offered to take me up in his airship, I couldn't resist. As we flew over the Sussex countryside, the pilot said, 'We see a lot of tonsils from up here!' Sure enough, one motorist spent so long looking up at us that I saw him plough into a hedge by the side of the road. I arrived back at my car an hour-and-a-half later, not very popular at all.

When we finally wrapped *A View to a Kill*, it was time to say an emotional farewell to Roger Moore. It was a sad occasion, but I think the person most upset was Grace. She clung to me and wouldn't leave the studio. 'What is going to happen to me now?' she asked me. 'I can't think of life without you all – you have become my family.' I think she really meant it. She presented me with a lovely book of photographs as a souvenir of our time together. She had recovered in time for the film's première in Paris, where she disturbed the proceedings by making a very grand floodlit entrance in the middle of everything. I didn't think much of it at the time, but I suppose it was typical of Grace to grab the following morning's headlines.

After each Bond movie, there was a period when the Broccoli family rested, although Cubby was never one to take a holiday. He always said to me that he preferred to be in the comfort of his own home and he had a very beautiful home, so I couldn't blame him. The rest of us took a break and generally wound down with our families for about three months. Cubby asked me to direct the next film in the series – my fourth! – during post-production on *A View to a Kill*. I knew that this time we really would

Anne and Arthur Wooster, with myself and Janine at the London premiere of *A View to a Kill*.

have to find a new James Bond.

During the winding down period, I was usually asked to join the publicity tours that travelled the world, promoting the première of the new Bond film in each major territory. On one such tour, I went to Australia with Roger, who had learned a few tricks during his days in rep and taught me the correct way to pack a suitcase. I stood in his hotel room, watching in awe as he demonstrated: you start by taking your trousers and placing them half in and half out of the case. You then alternate the remaining garments in four different directions, placing your shirts, ties and underwear in the centre. Put a cloth over that part of the case and place your shoes on top. Finally you fold your trousers, alternately left and right in rotation, and the whole package should come up square. Close the lid of the case and you're ready to go with a case full of crease-free clothes.

When we publicised *Octopussy*, I visited Kyoto in Japan with Maud, Roger and Rita Coolidge, who sang the theme song *All Time High*. We stayed at an inn that offered hard futon beds and a wooden hot tub in each room. Maud travelled with her boyfriend, who was a well-known plastic surgeon. He came in very useful when a sushi washed down with hot saki left me feeling a little delicate. We were on the bullet train and I was complaining of having a terrible headache. 'Try these,' he suggested, offering me some curious-looking blue pills. 'What are they?' I asked as I swallowed them down. 'They're for period pains,' he told me, as I gulped. Whatever – they did the trick.

I have to be careful when it comes to fish – I'll spare you the gory details – and Japan has always been a problematic place for me to visit as a result. I remember one particularly gruesome press conference at a Japanese film festival when my performance was severely restricted by an outbreak of

Happy times
promoting
*Octopussy* in
Japan. From left to
right: publicity
director Jerry
Juroe, singer Rita
Coolidge, Roger,
Maud Adams and
myself.

rampant hives and a mouth that felt like it was full of rapidly setting glue. I was suffering in the back of the car on the way to this press conference, cursing the trace of mussel that I figured must have found its way into my lunch, when our driver insisted on telling us all about the famous fish market. I did my best to concentrate on the back of the seat in front of me and not look out of the window as he pointed out all the local fishy delicacies on offer. In the end, it all got too much and I asked him to stop the car while I staggered out and threw up on the pavement, which I'm sure went down well with the restaurant owners opposite. Anne Bennett, the publicity co-ordinator from UIP, took me back to the car and we eventually made it to the press conference. The assembled journalists must have thought I was an idiot because after travelling halfway across the world to be there I couldn't say a single word.

The reception for the stars on Bond films has always been incredible in the Far East. Crowds of hysterical fans wait outside your hotel, standing for hours in the hope of catching a glimpse of a cast-member. One particular chap in Japan always presented me with a little gift on each visit and would patiently wait for the opportunity to talk to me outside the hotel. Roger and I were always of the opinion that such people deserved at least a few moments. Roger, in particular, was always careful to make the time to pose for pictures and sign autographs.

I knew I would miss working with Roger and I think we'd built up a good relationship over the years. On my copy of the shooting script he wrote: 'Congratulations, John! You have seen me through my last cowardly performance.' We had enjoyed great success together, but it was time for us all to be brave enough to try something new.

# 007™

# CHAPTER 11

## A CONNOISSEUR'S BOND

Despite what you may have read elsewhere, we really didn't have a clue who to cast as James Bond when Roger hung up his gun holster. After a lot of head-scratching in Los Angeles we drew up rather a long shortlist. Barbara Broccoli had been spending some time in Australia, which was just beginning to reach its potential as an important film-making centre, and she came up with a few suggestions. I took the list back to Pinewood and in summer 1986 started testing the eager hopefuls.

The strongest Australian contenders included a young unknown called Finlay Light. Andrew Clarke was more experienced and was a front runner for quite some time, but after a while he had enough and left. Sam Neill was one of the last actors I tested and I remember thinking he was very good indeed. Among the British names was Trevor Eve, famous for his starring role in the television detective series *Shoestring*. MGM/UA weren't shown any of these tests; we had to satisfy ourselves first and in the end I don't think we submitted any of the footage. It was only when we were some way into the process that I asked Cubby if he'd considered Pierce Brosnan. The young actor we'd met in Corfu six years before was now starring in the successful American television series *Remington Steele*, a tongue-in-cheek drama about a debonair safe cracker. Cubby pondered the suggestion for a while, but he wasn't crazy about the idea.

Cubby eventually came round, and we invited Pierce to Pinewood for a three-day test, no expenses spared. I directed Pierce in my favourite scenes from *Dr No* and *From Russia With Love* and discovered that he could handle himself very well in the punch-ups. If I had one reservation about him, it was that although he was in his mid-thirties, he looked much younger. Cubby, Michael and Barbara were as impressed as I was, so we sent the test footage to MGM/UA, who gave us the thumbs up. As far as we were concerned, Pierce had got the job, and we invited him to a celebratory lunch at the White Elephant.

The party was about to be spoiled by something that was breaking in Hollywood. *Remington Steele* was produced by Mary Tyler Moore Television and, as far as we were concerned, had been cancelled by the network that screened it. Word must have got out about Pierce's casting, however, because we were suddenly hit with the news that that the show was being renewed at the last minute. Cubby told MTM that they could have Pierce for six episodes and no more, but the network wanted the option

Timothy Dalton as
James Bond 007 in
*The Living
Daylights*.

of 22 and it became a deal-breaker. There was no way Cubby was going to
have Pierce play James Bond and be Remington Steele at the same time, so
unfortunately we had to part company. Pierce was extremely upset about it
– he had put a lot of work into securing the role and justifiably felt it was in
the bag. I hoped he'd console himself with the fact that he was still young
and that the role might come his way again.

While scripting continued and the pre-production clock ticked away, we
renewed our search for a leading man. Timothy Dalton had first come to the
attention of Cubby and Harry Saltzman when he appeared in *The Lion in
Winter* in 1968. Timothy had turned Cubby down in the late 1960s but, almost
20 years later, he was more receptive to our overtures. We met Timothy one
evening at Michael Wilson's house in Hampstead and, very soon after, made
up our minds that he was our man. We were so confident that we didn't even
subject him to a screen test. In early August, we were finally able to announce
that we had our new James Bond.

Tim was a serious fan of the Ian Fleming novels and was keen to
incorporate as much of Fleming's original characterisation as possible. He
also felt very strongly that he wanted his portrayal to be different to that of
any of the actors who preceded him in the role. I encouraged this, feeling that
just as there had been no point in Roger imitating Sean, then there would be
no point in Tim imitating Roger. We had to be bold. Tim referred to the
Fleming novels a lot and I could see he was preparing a characterisation for
Bond connoisseurs. Dick Maibaum, needless to say, was delighted.

Tim's input began with the first wardrobe meeting: when Bond wasn't wearing the obligatory tux, he wanted a more casual look, perhaps more in keeping with the times. I remember he told me he felt he should also act in a more casual manner and occasionally put his hands in his pockets. I was very much against this and explained that although we weren't going to see him in uniform in this film, Bond was still a disciplined naval commander. I didn't think he stuck his hands in his pockets in the Fleming novels. Tim didn't agree with me, but he respected what I was saying and went along with it for the most part.

Tim was coming into an established family of film-makers, almost all of whom had worked on previous Bond films. He asked for his own make-up artist, Naomi Dunne, which helped him relax a little. Naomi became very popular with the other members of the crew and, before long, Tim fitted in very well.

Bond movies can be a real mix and match of acting talent: girls picked purely for their looks can play opposite some of the most respected actors in the business. And they don't come much better qualified than Timothy Dalton, who had to learn the same lesson Roger learned before him – certain cast-members needed the benefit of his considerable experience to help them through the schedule.

Dick and Michael Wilson had largely completed the screenplay for the new film, named after Fleming's tense short story *The Living Daylights*, by the time Tim was installed. Although the phrase 'the living daylights' is in relatively common use in England, our transatlantic distributor was left baffled by it and we once again had to explain the origins of our latest title. We fine-tuned the script to suit Tim a little better and introduced a few other innovations. Although I don't like the term political correctness in connection with my Bond films, this was the 1980s and we couldn't close our eyes to the fact that Aids had become rampant. It simply wasn't sensible, or fashionable, to depict Bond as a character who slept around. In *The Living Daylights* he became (pretty much) a one-woman man and I don't think the film suffered for it one bit. In fact, I think it lent the movie a distinctly romantic air and fitted in with the way Tim wanted to play the role.

Dick and Michael were faithful to Fleming's story for the opening part of the plot and developed their own tale from thereon. As usual, a number of reconnaissance discoveries suggested story elements. The story begins when Bond oversees the defection of disillusioned KGB agent General Koskov, smuggling him from Czechoslovakia to Austria inside a natural gas pipeline. We came up with the idea after consulting a professor who worked on the real Trans-Siberian gas pipeline. He told us about the 'cleaning pig', a scouring device which enters the pipeline through an airlock and is then propelled on its way through the vacuum. Dick and Michael seized on the idea and it became a very funny scene in the film. Julie T Wallace, who had made a big impact in the television series *The Life and Loves of a She-Devil*, played the girl who buried the gasworks supervisor in her ample cleavage while Koskov made his getaway. The overwhelmed supervisor was played by Peter Porteous, who was married to our costume designer Emma.

It's harder to pinpoint the origin of other elements in the screenplay. I attended a script conference in Los Angeles after working on some of the action sequences in my office. I came up with the idea that Bond and his ally

Maryam d'Abo as Kara Milovy, a cellist 'who opens her legs for Dvorak rather quicker than for Bond'.

Kara could use a cello case to make good their escape down a snowy hillside – one person could fit in the main body of the case and the other could sit inside the lid. I was convinced it would work beautifully, but the reaction around the table was understandably incredulous. I presented the idea and it was met with something less than enthusiasm from Cubby and Dick. In fact, Cubby stuck a finger in his mouth and made a rude noise with it. Michael knew that my ideas usually worked, but even he wasn't sure about this one. I continued to fight for my cello case, so Cubby picked up the telephone and rang the music stage at MGM studios. He was put through to the musical director and he asked him if they had an orchestra there that day. They did. 'Do you have a cellist there?' he asked. The response was again yes. Cubby then invited us to join him to see if my idea was feasible. In one of the most bizarre script conferences I can remember, Dick, Michael, Cubby and myself scrutinised a cello case. We opened it up and lay it on the ground: Cubby sat in one side and I sat in the other. It was snug, but we both fitted. The more we thought about the idea, the more it made sense – we decided that the spike at the base of Kara's cello could be used as a crude rudder to guide the direction of the case. We then scripted a scene where Bond and Kara reach the border and Bond throws this £100,000 Stradivarius over his head, catching it deftly on the other side of the barrier. When we came to shoot the film, I skied alongside the cello case, directing the scene on the move.

Cellist Kara Milovy was played by Maryam d'Abo, a beautiful half-Dutch, half-Russian actress who was a friend of Barbara. We didn't get off to the best of starts when we met during her interview in Cubby's office. 'What's that dress made of?' I asked her. 'Your grandmother's tablecloth?' As soon as the words came out of my mouth, I was filled with regret, but fortunately she saw the funny side and we got on very well. I was highly amused to learn later that the *Guardian*'s film critic Derek Malcolm described Kara as 'a Czech classical cellist who opens her legs for Dvořák rather quicker than for Bond.' Maryam is a good actress and she certainly made a convincing classical musician; we've gone on to work together a few times since.

The role of General Koskov, the KGB double agent who wasn't all that he seemed, was played by Jeroen Krabbé. Jeroen is a fine actor and a likeable man, who I recall brought his family over from Holland for the duration of the shoot. He was just right for the high-spirited KGB general who embraces Bond and his Harrods hamper of Western luxuries after his defection. It was a terrific characterisation and Jeroen made Koskov a sympathetic villain.

Barbara was once again a big influence on the casting and she came up with Joe Don Baker, who played master villain Brad Whitaker. Joe has switched sides to become Bond's CIA liaison in the most recent movies, but in our film he was a loathsome arms dealer at the heart of a complex drug-smuggling plot. Joe had appeared in Dick Donner's *Lethal Weapon* and the excellent BBC drama *Edge of Darkness*, but he came to Barbara's attention in David Lynch's offbeat series *Twin Peaks*. Brad Whitaker's co-conspirator General Pushkin was played by John Rhys Davies, who had been an Egyptian wide boy in a couple of the *Indiana Jones* films. John was desperate to get away from that kind of role and this was just the type of part he needed. Being Welsh, he has a lovely strong voice, which he used to bring great authority to the role. In the late 1990s, I was shooting a commercial in Vancouver in the same place John was appearing in an episode of the science-fiction series *Sliders*. He greeted me like a long-lost brother. 'Look at me,' he joked. 'Reduced to this!' We're still good friends to this day.

Barbara also found Art Malik for the role of Afghan rebel leader Kamran Shah. Art is a terrific actor, whose notable film appearances include *A Passage to India*. We used the same trick Lewis Gilbert employed on *The Spy Who Loved Me* when Bond met Hosein, the Cambridge-educated Arab played by Edward De Souza. In *The Living Daylights*, Bond is greeted by Kamrahn Shah and soon discovers that that this turban-wearing freedom fighter speaks the Queen's English. I was very pleased that we found Art and I knew he was perfect for the part. I asked him if he could ride a horse. 'I'm not an expert,' he admitted, 'but I'm OK.' When we were shooting in the desert, Art was on horseback leading a charge of some 50 or 60 of his men. I found out only later that he was clinging on for dear life – he told me he knew he'd be trampled to death if he fell off. 'Don't ever ask me to do that again!' he said, ashen faced, when we finished the shot.

After Lois Maxwell's retirement, we cast a new Miss Moneypenny to flirt with the new James Bond. We looked at a number of actresses before we chose Caroline Bliss. The first question I asked her when we met was 'Are you any relation to Sir Arthur Bliss?'. She told me she was indeed the famous composer's grand-daughter. Caroline told me she thought Miss Moneypenny should wear glasses. I think the idea was that when she took her glasses off her hair would shake down and she would go from office secretary to sexy glamourpuss. Personally speaking, I found her very sexy anyway; in retrospect, I think the glasses were a mistake. She looked better without them.

Desmond
Llewelyn as Q. I
told him to leave
the gas mask on!

The glasses weren't the only mistake we made with the new Moneypenny. Lois Maxwell was in the hearts of Bond fans all over the world and you're on a hiding to nothing if you try to take her place. Hindsight is a wonderful thing, but we should have given Caroline a specially written scene that established her in the role and then maybe given her a more important part to play in the story. She needed something a little stronger than we gave her.

Desmond Llewelyn was still on board to give the series some on-screen continuity, although by this stage he was getting on a bit and was finding it harder than ever to remember his lines. There is a scene in Q's new laboratory where he demonstrates a deadly whistle-activated keyring to Bond and they both have to wear gas-masks while this keyring emits dangerous fumes. Timothy took his gas-mask off when the demonstration was over, but after numerous takes I asked Desmond to leave his on. 'Why?' came his muffled voice from behind the rubber. 'Because that way you can add your lines later in the dubbing theatre,' I told him. Tim was bewildered by all this and wore an expression like a stunned mullet when I explained that it didn't matter how often Desmond fluffed his lines – we all loved him, so we would take the time to get it right. Desmond was always quite pleased when there was the prospect of a few extra days post-syncing because it added a few quid to his fee.

The introduction of a new James Bond has always required a great deal of thought. Everybody remembers our first glimpse of Sean Connery through the haze of cigarette smoke in *Dr No*; George Lazenby's first appearance in *On Her Majesty's Secret Service* was given a carefully orchestrated build-up; Guy Hamilton was a little coy about introducing Roger Moore in *Live and Let Die* – Bond didn't appear in the pre-titles sequence at all; but in *The Living Daylights* we threw Timothy into the thick of the action. Dick and Michael came up with the idea of putting three 00 agents, including 007, on a training exercise to test NATO defences; I suggested they should do it in Gibraltar. The exercise is infiltrated by enemy agents, however, and their guns are loaded not with paint pellets but real bullets. It all rounded off with Timothy parachuting on to a beautiful woman's yacht and delivering the line 'Bond…James Bond.'

I had been fascinated by Gibraltar ever since I spent a holiday there with some friends in the early 1980s. The whole rock is honeycombed with tunnels that lead to underground hospitals, ammunition stores and a number of reservoirs. I discovered one reservoir that had been opened by King George VI in 1938. A sandstone colonnade stood in front of the special platform he had used to cut the ribbon during the ceremonial opening of the site. The side of the rock facing North Africa is seasonally blasted by sand from the Sahara Desert, and during our reconnaissance trip I made the perilous journey up a sheer quarry face in a contraption that amounted to little more than a rusty bucket suspended by an even rustier cable. Once I reached the top of the cliff-face and stepped out on to the sandy surface, I realised there were a number of areas where a skilled parachutist could jump. When Bond lands by parachute he is soon disturbed by an alarmed monkey – a variation on my directorial signature that enabled me to incorporate the local wildlife. Legend has it that as long at the monkeys stay on the island, the British will also stay. I hope we didn't do anything to put them off.

We had sadly lost Rande Deluca by this stage, but we nevertheless got a very fine aerial shot of the 00 agents parachuting towards the island at the beginning of their mission. Arthur Wooster's second unit directed most of the subsequent rough and tumble from September onwards and they did a very good job. It was important to me that we quickly established Timothy's Bond as a man who suffered a lot during the course of his work and he certainly got a right kicking in those opening minutes. A lot of the stunt work in that sequence was actually performed by Tim himself and anyone who knows Gibraltar will know that those roads can be very unforgiving – if you get one wheel of your jeep over the edge, then it's goodbye. Pete Davies, one of my editors, was on the spot assembling footage for Arthur. Pete is also a very good driver and happened to know Tim's sister very well, all of which helped things get off to a smooth start. When Tom Pevsner, our insurance-minded associate producer, found out that one of the editors had been doing some of the stunt driving, he had a fit.

At the end of the tussle with the enemy agents, Bond's jeep hurtles off a cliff edge. Bond manages to parachute out of the back of the descending vehicle in the nick of time. John Richardson constructed a model that was roughly a third of the size of a jeep and managed to get a parachute to unfurl out of the back. Bond lands on the canopy of a yacht, just as its bikini-clad owner is bemoaning the fact that she can't seem to find a real man. It was a great introduction.

During the Gibraltar shoot, a problem arose that highlights the dilemma facing any action director – for a technically demanding scene, does one cast a stuntman or an actor? I needed a climber and I made the mistake of hiring a stuntman. Arthur called me and said he was having trouble getting a performance out of the guy. It wasn't his fault, we were just asking too much of someone who wasn't an actor. I saw the rushes the following morning and I knew straightaway that Arthur was right. We had to find someone else. We immediately started scouring the actors' directory *Spotlight*, looking for an actor who would be prepared to do some climbing. We located someone who lived in Wimbledon and I interviewed him at Pinewood. He looked to be in good physical condition and he came highly recommended. He told me he wasn't a climber, but he wasn't afraid of heights and that was good enough for me. 'Are you prepared to leave for Gibraltar right away?' I asked him. 'Just get your car to stop outside my house and take me to the airport,' he replied. When his wife got home that night, she apparently found a note on the kitchen table that read: 'Baby with neighbour, have gone to Gibraltar!' Acting is a crazy business – you can wait for ages for the phone to ring and before you know it, you're halfway up a cliff-face in Gibraltar.

We started shooting in Vienna in October and because things had been so rushed in pre-production, the first thing we had to arrange was a press conference and photocall to show the world the new Bond. On our first weekend in Austria, the day before we were due to begin filming, Timothy answered journalists' questions and posed with Maryam and Bond's new Aston Martin V8.

Memories of *The Third Man* were strong in my mind as we shot the romantic scene with Bond and Kara at the Reisenaad big wheel in Prater Park. I remembered Anton Karas and Carol Reed as we filmed the beautiful city, but I stopped short at tilting the camera in the same oblique angles Reed had used. Reed's style was partly born of necessity – because so many men wore trilby hats in the 1940s, their close-ups fitted the frame better from end-to end than they did from side-to-side. You can't force such a style on to a modern film – the scene must dictate how you photograph it.

My new wife Janine made a brief appearance in the background at Prater Park, in one of the rare occasions when one of her cameos actually stayed off the cutting room floor. She jokes that the last thing I usually tell her before I leave the house in the morning is, 'Goodbye – oh, I'm going to cut you out of the film today.' It isn't deliberate. I've never had the great desire to appear in any of my films – I find it difficult enough to watch my work as it is – but many Bond fans are aware that Michael Wilson has made a number of cameos over the years. *The Living Daylights* featured another unaccredited appearance: together with his wife Jane, Michael can be spotted among the audience members in the opera house.

At the Summer Palace opera house, I arranged for the local director to stage an excerpt from an opera for our benefit. I explained that we'd probably want to use no more than two or three minutes' worth in the film. After I finished shooting the scene, I cut the cameras but he just kept going. There

Just one of the on-board gadgets that didn't come supplied by Aston Martin.

had obviously been some kind of misunderstanding and we all stood around rather bemused as he just went on and on. In the end, I had to walk up to him and have a word, and he got quite upset. He just didn't quite understand how it works when you're making a film.

It was great to have the gadget-laden Aston Martin back in the Bond films – I was very pleased that we got to show off all its gadgets in the scene where it literally skis across a frozen lake. We originally went to Weissensee because we wanted to find a way of incorporating the unusual local sport of ice sailing. I developed a big action sequence with boats on skis, whizzing around the lake. We adapted the idea and gave the Aston Martin skis instead, although we almost regretted it when, during take one, the weight of the car broke the surface ice and it began to sink. We rescued it and filmed the scene at the other end of the lake, where the ice was a little sturdier. The Aston Martin gets written off and Bond and Kara make their escape back to the West by tobogganing in her cello case. This part of the filming was mainly a second-unit job for Arthur, but I spent three days with Tim and Maryam shooting close-ups.

Up until *The Living Daylights*, I always had a very open attitude to film-making; anyone from the crew was allowed to view the daily rushes. Tim would watch the rushes with the rest of us, but some evenings he would then ask the other crew-members what their opinions were. I don't know if he was insecure, but it was almost as if he was inviting criticism. One day, Tim approached me and said that one of the secretaries had criticised the way he had kissed Maryam in one particular scene. I don't need that kind of input when I'm in the middle of making a film – I feel that any discussion of that type should be between the actor and the director; any comments made outside that relationship undermine the director's authority. You simply can't tell how a film is going to work out by looking at rushes of one scene in isolation – you need an overall view of the whole film before you can understand what the director is trying to achieve. I changed the rules there and then and restricted crew access to screenings. I should have done it sooner.

Tangier was a new location for us to visit. Morocco is a very interesting country and had been used in several previous films, notably *Lawrence of Arabia*. While we were there, a terrific storm left a ring of snow-capped mountains in the background, which helped promote the impression that we were in Afghanistan. The King of Morocco ensured that we received the full co-operation of the military and we used a lot of Army vehicles and one of the Air Force's C130s. It came in useful not just as a means of ferrying our supplies and equipment, but also as a prop in the film. Alec Mills had been promoted from camera operator to director of photography, but he came dangerously close to having an accident that would have cut his career short there and then. We were filming quite near to a taxiing C130 when I noticed a panicked expression on the pilot's face. I looked down to see that the huge propellers were spinning dangerously close to Alec's head. Alec was blissfully unaware of their proximity, so I quickly dragged him to the ground as the plane rumbled on.

Our desert location was a place called Ouorzazate, which the unit quickly nicknamed 'Whereizat', and we were all fortunate that some quite comfortable hotels had recently been constructed. The crew's favourite restaurant was a little bistro run by a French lady who had followed her lover when the Foreign Legion had stationed him there. After a while, he was posted somewhere else and she was marooned. She had stayed in Ouorzazate ever since. Janine and I celebrated our first wedding anniversary in the desert and our Spanish caterers were good enough to prepare us a special dinner which they said they'd serve to us in our hotel room. I had to attend a very long rushes session with Tim, who was always interested in looking at rushes whether he was in them or not. On this occasion, we were looking at material shot by several units, including footage shot by the model unit. Model units shoot at high speed, so their material always takes a long time to get through. The viewing session took about two-and-a-half hours and as we left the theatre, we were joined by Tim's friend Vanessa Redgrave. As we walked back to the hotel, the food was being taken in for our anniversary dinner, so I spontaneously asked Tim and Vanessa if they'd like to join us. There was plenty to go round and we opened a bottle of champagne to celebrate. Vanessa was a very sweet lady and had already been touring the local schools, spending time with the children.

In Tangier, we discovered an impressive house belonging to Malcolm Forbes, the owner of *Fortune* magazine. The house contained his large collection of motorcycles and toy soldiers, which gave us the idea for the war games Brad Whitaker plays when he hunts Bond down. We had some effigies of history's greatest military tacticians built for those scenes; if you look carefully at their faces, you can see that they're all a likeness of the egotistical Whitaker.

Another pre-existing location was the boat that Felix Leiter (played by John Terry) used as his base. We found the luxurious catamaran when it was being advertised for sale for $3 million. The first thing I noticed when I went aboard was a grand piano, which I figured was a fairly impressive decorative statement in any boat. I thought this vessel was the most uncomfortable thing

afloat and I wouldn't have liked to have been anywhere near that piano in choppy water. An unusual actress called Katie Rabett played CIA agent Liz and I thought she was very good. For the scene in which Bond is abducted and taken to the boat, I prostrated myself on the bonnet of a convertible car in order to direct the action. Getting my hands dirty again reminded me a little of my second-unit days.

A hands-on approach to directing Timothy Dalton and Katie Rabett in *The Living Daylights.*

We returned to Pinewood to continue studio shooting towards the end of November. In December, the Prince and Princess of Wales visited the set. They were both real Bond fans and had attended all the premières during the 1980s. Diana cracked a prop wine bottle made of sugar glass over Charles's head and we made the front pages of the newspapers the following day. We had a great time and it was good publicity.

Another rare visitor to the set was composer John Barry. John had made an immeasurable contribution to the James Bond films from *Dr No* onwards and sadly it seems that *The Living Daylights* will prove to be his final score for the series. It was lovely to see him again, but I think he must have known this would be his farewell because he asked me if he could make an appearance in the film. I was happy to oblige, so I arranged for him to play the conductor of the orchestra in Kara's closing concert. He was eminently qualified for the job.

Peter Lamont constructed a set that doubled for the interior of a C130. It was built on top of a hydraulic rig, which pitched and yawed just like a real plane in flight. Cyril Howard, the Pinewood studio manager, was very impressed by this and asked if I would allow a delegation of Chinese visitors on board during a rehearsal. I'll never forget the astonished looks on their faces when the hydraulics activated, the fans started blowing and the cargo hold opened to reveal Jacqueline Stears' painted mountainscape beneath us. It was such a realistic experience that it felt more like a flight simulator than a film set.

When General Koskov arrives in Britain, he is taken to a rather grand safe house, the exteriors for which were filmed at Stonor House near Henley in the

The picture of the year – Princess Diana smashes a prop wine bottle over her husband's head during a visit to our set at Pinewood Studios.

second half of December. Krone the parrot, who was last seen squawking at Margaret Thatcher in *For Your Eyes Only*, made a second appearance here. Koskov is snatched back from the British by the terrorist Necros (played by Andreas Wisniewski) who enters the house disguised as a milkman and gives the butler (Bill Weston) a particularly savage beating in the kitchen. I've always considered the kitchen to be the most dangerous place in any house, packed with devices that could be potentially lethal in the wrong hands. Together with the stunt arranger Paul Weston, we set about designing a sequence that could feature a number of these instruments, including a particularly nasty electric carver. John Richardson used $CO_2$ to create the impression of boiling water which could be safely thrown over someone. I was very pleased with the results. The house was owned by Lord and Lady Camoys and I don't know what their reaction was when they saw the result of Necros's exploding milk bottles – the windows were blown clean out of their frames. Or at least, that's what it looked like on screen. Peter Lamont obviously had a great deal of respect for this 12th-century property and temporarily removed some of the original windows beforehand, replacing them with dummies which were blown out by the blast. When we finished, he put the original windows back. John Richardson is very good at controlled explosions and the house suffered very little damage. I think the oil paintings needed cleaning afterwards, but they probably needed a wash and brush-up anyway.

Stonor House is quite close to where I now live, although I had only recently moved to the area when we filmed *The Living Daylights*. I was a little unfamiliar with the area, which Arthur discovered to his cost when I offered to show him my new house. 'It's just a short distance through those woods,' I indicated. It took me over two hours to find it by road and he hasn't forgiven me to this day. We often go sailing, and he never lets me navigate.

I think *The Living Daylights* features the best protracted action sequence of any of my films. It starts with Bond escaping Afghanistan in the C130, aided by Kamran Shah's brigands. Arthur Wooster and John Richardson excelled themselves with the pitched battle that ensues on the airfield, distracting Koskov. There is a close shot of a jeep driving up the lowered ramp of the plane just before it takes off. This was a difficult shot to achieve because, aside from being extremely dangerous, such ramps are at least a foot above ground level even when fully lowered. Peter Lamont cleverly substituted a furniture van for the close shot and Remy Julienne drove into the back, skilfully slamming on the brakes before he collided with the camera at the other end. This and many other scenes combined to make a magnificent battle sequence and everyone involved in it should be very proud.

The script called for a bridge spanning a gorge, which the horses flee across to escape from the Russian tanks. We searched high and low, but couldn't find anything suitable. The closest thing I found was a bridge that was just 10-feet high and crossed a dried-up wadi. It wasn't terribly impressive. Peter Lamont and his brother Michael suggested using a foreground miniature. I initially had reservations because I'd never tried the process with anything this elaborate. We made a model riverbed, using silicone to represent water and a five-foot high bridge made from miniature trestles. It was constructed at Pinewood and shipped out to us in sections. When it was placed 10 feet in front of the camera, it merged with the existing bridge, which was some 200 feet away.

To film our bridge, we attached a nodal head to the camera tripod. This meant that the crossover point of the lens was sitting directly above the pivoting point of the camera, so moving the camera would have no effect on the perspective of the shot. The combination of the foreground miniature and the nodal head had an incredible effect – a 10-foot high bridge was transformed into a 300-foot structure and I could pan the camera and even zoom in on explosions without spoiling the tricked perspective. We had tanks bombarding the bridge, horsemen racing across and the C130 flying overhead with shell bursts all around it. This was incredible film action achieved with wonderful technology – but not new technology.

Michael Lamont is an expert in foreground miniatures and some of the results he and his colleagues achieved were not only breathtaking but sometimes economical too. Nowadays, a similar shot would probably be achieved by digitally recreating the bridge and the surrounding action in a computer, but it would cost many times more and not look half as good. The only people that don't use the old-fashioned techniques are the new generation of young special effects technicians and that's simply because they don't know what those techniques are.

In January 1987, we arrived at the last major scene on the schedule and the final element of this long action sequence – the climactic struggle between Bond and Necros as both men cling to the netted cargo of narcotics trailing in mid-air behind a huge transport plane. Our first problem was the Red Cross, whose distinctive symbol we had used on the sacks that were being used to smuggle the dope. Perhaps understandably, the Red Cross objected and Cubby had to make a financial contribution in an attempt to appease them. B J Worth and the usual team filmed the precarious stunt in the US and used a twin-engined plane. The C130 has four engines, so I knew we risked highlighting the discrepancy from shot-to-shot. It was a calculated gamble: the C130 is a gas-guzzler and using it for two or three weeks in the Mojave desert would have broken our budget. So we got hold of a cheaper aircraft and

Necros (Andreas
Wisniewski) and
Bond (Timothy
Dalton) fight to the
death in mid-air.

hoped that no one would notice the lack of engines.

Bond has to deploy a jeep with a special landing parachute, which I understand is something the military do all the time (albeit not with a girl sitting in the driving seat).

In the first instance, we dropped a real jeep and we were dismayed to see that it got absolutely flattened when it hit the ground. John Richardson constructed two radio-controlled model C130s, each with a nine or 10-foot wingspan. The model jeeps were deployed at a pre-determined point and it worked like magic.

B J Worth and Jake Lombard doubled for Bond and Necros on the oscillating cargo net and there was an additional parachutist inside the plane, instructed to skydive after them if either was knocked off. The third member of the team would deploy his colleague's parachute in case he'd fallen off after being knocked unconscious. There are several shots where you can see B J being buffeted up and down and he could easily have hit his head on the fuselage. The safety parachutist made a few jumps, every time someone fell off the net. The close-ups of Tim and Andreas were filmed at Pinewood. We took a Vickers' rostrum and covered it with a mountain landscape made of plaster. The mountains were carefully painted to match those seen in the distance in the American aerial shoot. Scaffolding was used to suspend the cargo netting over the rostrum and we swung the arm of a camera crane to create the impression of movement. We were a little restricted by the small background area, but we changed the angles as much as we could and in the end it looked as though Tim and Andreas were 10,000 feet above the ground, not six.

*The Living Daylights* was a very satisfying film and I was especially pleased that Tim had hit the ground running with a radical new characterisation of Bond. The movie was successful on its release and we all felt Tim was firmly established in the role. At this point, I felt my career with 007 must surely have come to end – nobody had directed more than four James Bond films. Would I be asked back for a fifth?

# 007™

## CHAPTER 12

## A FAREWELL TO ARMS

There was a collective sigh of relief at Eon when we discovered that *The Living Daylights* had been a hit. Cubby had been around longer than most of us and he in particular remembered the problems caused by the relatively poor critical and commercial performance of *On Her Majesty's Secret Service* back in 1970. Those problems were solved by picking up the phone and calling Sean Connery, who made his first comeback in *Diamonds Are Forever*. This time round, we didn't feel we needed to call Roger Moore, who I'm sure wouldn't have wanted to come back anyway. Timothy Dalton had been a success and we started planning his second picture as James Bond.

Cubby asked me if I was interested in staying on and, although it was getting progressively harder to find new locations and dream up new action sequences, I said yes without hesitation. The new film was to be called *Licence Revoked* and would be my fifth consecutive James Bond as director. It was made clear to me from the outset that this was going to be a harder-edged Bond film than any that had gone before. Bond's old friend Felix Leiter would be maimed by a ruthless drug baron and Bond would have to resign from the secret service and enter the field on his own to take revenge. We were about to go further than we had ever gone before – maybe too far.

The screenplay was prepared by Dick Maibaum and Michael Wilson, but before long, Michael found himself working on his own. Dick was a loyal and pioneering member of the Writers' Guild of America and during 1988 their members voted to go on strike for a better deal. Dick hated causing us problems, but he was loyal to the Guild and honourable enough not to ghost the script under another name. He worked with Michael on the initial outline and then stepped back while Michael wrote the actual script. Dick wasn't very happy with the film when it came out, although there was possibly an element of sour grapes in his criticisms. I know we certainly missed his guidance and I was personally sorry we never got the chance to work together again; I was very sad to hear of his death in 1991.

Michael embarked on some meticulous research into the way drug barons command respect and loyalty and he uncovered some frightening stories of coercion, intimidation and violence. These ruthless patterns of behaviour can spread from the heart of such organisations like a disease, harming everyone who comes into contact with them. We all agreed that

Bond's discovery
of the mutilated
Leiter (David
Hedison) was a
scene straight from
the pages of Ian
Fleming's *Live and
Let Die*.

there was no point in making a film about the drug trade if we were not prepared to show this side of the business. Michael is, of course, not a violent person, but he did his best to get under the skin of some very violent characters. It was rather ironic, perhaps, that in scripting the scene in which Felix Leiter was mutilated, we looked not to contemporary headlines for inspiration but to Ian Fleming's 1954 novel *Live and Let Die*. In the book, Leiter is savaged by a shark and Bond discovers his bloody and mutilated body. A scrap of paper jammed into Leiter's mouth read: 'He disagreed with something that ate him.' Like the keelhauling scene that we appropriated in *For Your Eyes Only*, this was another element that hadn't been used in the film of *Live and Let Die* (censorship fears had possibly made its inclusion problematic in previous films), so we used it as the fulcrum of the plot in *Licence Revoked*.

There was humour in *Licence Revoked* as well. Like Sean Connery and George Lazenby before him, Timothy decided his Bond should be true to the books and be seen smoking cigarettes. The script featured an exploding cigarette packet, so I felt we were doubly justified in warning that 'Smoking Can Be Dangerous To Your Health' on the end credits and the packet itself.

We were always looking for exciting new locations in the Bond movies and one of the places we considered when we were setting up *Licence Revoked* was China. Cubby, Michael, Barbara and myself went there on a reconnaissance and speculated over the possibility of having a motorcycle chase on the Great Wall. Then we went to see the vast army of 600–700 terracotta soldiers that had recently been dug up at Xian. Each soldier was life-size and had unique facial features. Michael and I discussed a sequence where Bond could have got into a scrap inside the museum housing these soldiers, but we reluctantly concluded that it would have stretched our resources too far. The Chinese government would have allowed us only to shoot long shots and exteriors, and we would have had to recreate the museum interiors and the soldiers in the studio – a considerable headache. Another problem was that, even in the mid-1980s, quite a few tourists had begun visiting Beijing and Shanghai and I think we would have experienced the same crowd problems we had encountered while filming *Moonraker* in Venice.

The conditions in China left a little to be desired. On an internal flight, Dana Broccoli was less than amused to be served up a cockroach as part of her meal and Janine and I had a close encounter with some similarly unwelcome wildlife in our hotel room. Before we went to bed, we heard a knock on the door and discovered that boy scout Michael had been busy with his water filter. He handed me two pints of purified water to get us through the night and then retired. I was lying in bed when I heard a scratching noise from the other end of the room. I put my ear next to the skirting board and heard a munching noise from the other side – a rat was literally trying to eat his way into our room. I grabbed one of my shoes and gave the skirting board a sharp whack. The noise stopped. I waited a while and then the munching started again. After a couple more whacks, the rat seemed to get the message and I went back to bed.

After being entertained by representatives of the Chinese film industry in Beijing, the local technicians showed us a short James Bond film they had made in our honour. I don't speak any Chinese at all and I assumed this thing was a comedy. When it finished I laughed out loud, comparing it to the wanker reel we compiled after each film at Pinewood. The Chinese film had been completely serious, however, and the withering looks from my colleagues encouraged me to shut up. Luckily, the Chinese hadn't understood a word I'd said, much to the relief of Barbara, who didn't know whether to laugh or cry.

All these concerns were rendered academic when the Chinese government, who had been very co-operative during our trip, insisted on the right to veto our script and remove anything they weren't happy about. Cubby told them this was unacceptable. In the end, I wasn't that concerned because *The Last Emperor* opened before us and would have stolen our thunder.

MGM/UA were giving us a bit of a hard time about budget control since *Licence Revoked* was budgeted at approximately the same level as every Bond film since *Moonraker*. This hadn't posed too much of a problem with *For Your Eyes Only*, but by the end of the 1980s it was becoming a bit of a struggle to make ends meet without compromising the quality expected of a Bond film. We remained economically minded and extremely efficient, but we were making first-division action films on a fraction of the budget available to our principal competitors in the US.

Our problems were compounded by the Thatcher government's unfriendly attitude towards film-makers in England and for a while it was looking impossible to balance the books. Our financial controller Douglas Noakes found a solution: he went to Mexico and came back with a report that claimed we could find everything we needed out there. Together with Michael, Barbara, Peter Lamont and Tom Pevsner, I followed in his footsteps, surveying studio facilities and nearby locations. It felt painful

Lupe Lamora
(Talisa Soto) and
her ruthless lover
Franz Sanchez
(Robert Davi).

breaking with tradition and not using Pinewood, but we had done it before during the production of *Moonraker* and it wouldn't hurt us to do it again. I don't think I knew what we were letting ourselves in for when we decided to go Mexico, but we had to stay within the budget and that was that.

We based the production of *Licence Revoked* at the Churubusco Studios in Mexico City. The place was built in the 1940s by Howard Hughes and was in a fairly dilapidated state by the time we got there: at one point, Tom reckoned he had found 177 leaks in the roof. Churubusco was basically a good facility that had had been starved of investment. There were four main stages and a handful of smaller ones, but everything was smaller than we had been used to and not all the stages were available to us. The workmen were brilliant technicians, carpenters, painters and sculptors – very artistic people with a genuinely happy attitude. It was a pleasure to work with them and the quality of the sets they constructed was like nothing I'd ever seen before.

The fact that we were based in Mexico meant that much of the casting was done from local or American agencies. Robert Davi was perfect for the role of callous drug baron Franz Sanchez. Robert was a friend of Cubby's daughter Tina and since we made this film together, he's been a good friend of mine as well. I was looking for a villain who could be the physical equal of Tim's Bond, in much the same way Robert Shaw had been the equal of Sean Connery in *From Russia With Love*. The balance between hero and villain fascinates me and Robert Davi played the villainous side of the equation perfectly. The point was proved when I was conducting the screen tests for the leading ladies. We dressed Robert up in the tuxedo and asked him to play Bond opposite the girls. He was very good indeed and told me afterwards that he slightly regretted that he got cast more as villains than as romantic leads. Robert trained as an opera singer and is very versatile, but I think he gets cast as heavies because of his rugged, Humphrey Bogart-style features.

When I was looking for an actress to play freelance agent Pam Bouvier, one of the first people I talked to was Sharon Stone. I had seen her in *Allan Quartermain and the Lost City of Gold* the year before and thought she was very good, but I think she was unlucky enough to have seen us early in the casting process. Timing is everything when it comes to these things! Cubby still took an active interest in casting: he would look at all the tapes and attend the interviews.

A little later on, a girl called Carey Lowell came to see us and when she walked through the door, I was amazed. She had a gorgeous, full figure; what you might call an old-fashioned kind of beauty. I decided quite quickly that she should get the job and she remains one of my favourite actresses. She is a stunning-looking girl with a lovely disposition and I think every fella on the unit fell in love with her. Alec Mills was the director of photography and we gave his son Simon a job as the clapperboy – the poor lad practically fell to pieces every time he looked at her. He thought she was delicious. We all did.

Sanchez's unfortunate girlfriend Lupe Lamora was played by another beautiful girl, Talisa Soto. Talisa was a very successful model with a slight Latin-American look to her. She hadn't done very much in the way of acting, but she was willing to learn. It was hard work and I think it always pays to go to acting school to learn how to be as natural as possible, but she was pretty good support to Carey and we had two very beautiful girls in the picture without any doubt. The name Lupe Lamora was dreamed up by Dick, who told me it was inspired by a Latin–American beauty of yesteryear. Dick always put a great deal of effort into naming the characters in his scripts.

Anthony Zerbe played the villainous Milton Krest, who was a character from the Fleming short story *The Hildebrand Rarity*. Krest's cover was the marine biology laboratory investigated by Bond. Krest's cover story was that he was breeding fish for Third World consumption. The background to Krest's dubious activities was partly inspired by a reconnaissance trip we made to the Caribbean: we landed on a small island which was devoted to creating a species of fish that could live in either fresh or saltwater. Through crossbreeding, they had succeeded in creating a fish rather like salmon, but unfortunately it was black. Apparently, people don't like eating black fish, so something had to be done about this. They had turned this species' colour from black to red, but there had been a number of interesting permutations along the way, including a striped specimen. This was a legitimate research laboratory, partly funded by the US government, but I left thinking that it all seemed a little mysterious and I hope we captured some of that unease in the film.

Krest came to an especially gruesome end when Sanchez threw him into a decompression chamber and he literally exploded in a shower of blood. We rehearsed the scene with Anthony and Robert, but when we came to shoot it, Robert was about to throw Anthony into this chamber when Anthony held up his hand. 'Er, where's the stunt man?' he asked. 'I thought you were going to do it yourself,' I replied, slightly surprised.

Anthony was an actor of the old Hollywood school and there was no way he was being thrown head first anywhere. We had to find a stuntman and a wig at very short notice. The guy we substituted got a hefty kick up the backside from Robert when he was shoved inside, so maybe Anthony knew something I didn't.

The character of Felix Leiter hadn't been as important to the James Bond films as he had been to the books. Although Leiter had appeared in a lot of the movies, he'd always been played by someone different and had rarely made much of an impact. Leiter was a crucial character in *Licence Revoked* and the film would mark the first – and, to date, only – occasion where we asked an actor back to play the role for a second time. David Hedison had first played Leiter in *Live and Let Die* back in 1973. In 1988, he attended a party at Cubby and Dana's house and they told me he was in great shape, even though he was nearing 60. I agreed that he looked much younger than his years, but harboured doubts about how a man that age would cope with some of the more demanding action sequences. During the shooting of the pre-titles sequence, during which Bond and Leiter deliver Sanchez to the police before parachuting in to attend Leiter's wedding, there was a slight accident. For the close-ups of David touching the ground, his parachute harness was attached to a crane and gently lowered before the harness was released some two feet from the ground. On take three or four, David was dropped the last few feet, but he landed badly and his leg gave way. He wasn't seriously hurt, but the accident left him with a bit of a limp for the rest of the film. The schedule wasn't interrupted, but I learned an important lesson about the treatment of actors of a certain age.

Heller, Sanchez's head of security, was played by Don Stroud, who was cast from Hollywood. He was an interesting guy with a nice sense of humour and when I directed *Aces: Iron Eagle III* a few years later, I thought of him again. I was going to cast without interviewing him, but I'm very glad I did ask to see him because I was astonished to discover that he'd been in a terrible fight and someone had hit him over the head with a bar stool. He was quite badly scarred and unfortunately I wasn't able to use him. It was a great shock to see a friend with such a bad injury. I'm sure Don's fully recovered now, but it reminded me never to consider casting blind again.

Desmond Llewelyn was delighted when he found out that we'd given Q a much bigger role than in any of the previous films. He was excited at the prospect of earning some real money for once, although I was concerned about the old boy's advancing years. Desmond was determined to go to Mexico with us, but Tom didn't want him to go. Desmond was 74 years old and Tom told me that his age had made it impossible for him to get insurance for the shoot. I had heard horrendous stories about the air and water quality in Mexico and Tom reminded me that we would be exposed for a huge sum of money if Desmond got sick. But I knew Desmond wouldn't get sick – he was too professional for that. He might get sick when he got home, but he wouldn't succumb while he was working. Tom was not convinced and I fought hard to get Desmond to join us. I won the fight and Desmond paid me back, plus some, with the performance of his career.

With Desmond's plane ticket booked, I asked him about his wardrobe. 'What are you going to wear in Mexico?' I said. 'Oh,' he replied, 'I shall be wearing my usual check suit.' I feigned surprise. 'Don't you think you

should wear a nice pair of colonial shorts?' I asked, knowing full well that Roger Moore had spent years ribbing Desmond about the baggy shorts he had worn in *You Only Live Twice*. 'Absolutely not!' Desmond replied, doubtless fearing that his foreign jaunt was about to be spoiled.

Q takes some leave and unofficially joins the ostracised Bond in the field, bringing a suitcase full of useful gadgets with him. He poses as Bond's uncle, keeping a watchful eye over his old friend. Q's presence in Bond's hotel room initially comes as a surprise and when Bond sees a figure sitting with his back to him, he attacks him. A rather crumpled Q emerges from a heap on the floor, much to Bond's astonishment. I told Desmond that of course we didn't expect him to be the person sitting in the chair when Bond launched his attack. 'I'll get a stunt double in for you,' I said, but Desmond was having none of it. 'No, no, no, no,' he replied. 'I'll be perfectly all right doing it myself.' I didn't want him to get hurt, however, so we put a grey wig on Paul Weston and asked him to do it. Desmond got about three weeks' work in Mexico and I think it must have made a real difference to his bank balance.

Desmond had reached a grand old age when he died in a car crash at the end of 1999. He had been through a lot as a prisoner of war in the 1940s and had earned the right to die in his bed, but fate had other plans. I was sad that I didn't get the chance to ask him for a signed copy of his biography before he died, but some months later a friend of mine presented me with a copy. She had been to one of Desmond's book-signing sessions and mentioned that she knew me. Desmond immediately dedicated a book to me and some time later my friend finally got round to giving it to me. I was

Pam Bouvier (Carey Lowell) and James Bond (Timothy Dalton) receive an unexpected visit from an off-duty Q (Desmond Llewelyn) in *Licence To Kill*.

enormously grateful and the book is something I treasure. Desmond was a very special part of the Bond family and we all miss him.

Things were difficult in Mexico from day one. The bureaucracy was a nightmare and everyone was so poorly paid that bribery and corruption were rife – if you wanted anything done, a backhander was obligatory. Getting the guns we needed was one such problem. We were stopped on the border and although we had all the proper licences, they still wouldn't let us proceed into Mexico. When Tom tried to do things by the book, the Mexicans demanded money from us. Tom refused to pay and two days later the amount doubled. This was just one of the problems that made Tom's life a misery while we were out there; the whole shoot brought him to the verge of a nervous breakdown. Tom was doing all the deals, but even if we got permission from one government department, this was no guarantee that another one wouldn't block us when we finally arrived at our destination. Everything could have been done much quicker if we'd have been based in Pinewood. The story obviously demanded that we visited a Latin-American country as a location, but I think we could have found one that was easier to work in.

Cubby joined us for the beginning of shooting in July 1988 and soon got very ill. We were working 7000 feet above sea level in some of the most polluted air in the world and he suffered with breathing difficulties. The atmosphere was so bad that the local sparrows apparently fell out of the air and the authorities swept them up, sweeping the story under the carpet in the process. Barbara and Michael got Cubby on to a special plane with a respirator and flew him back to LA just in time to save his life. Janine and I rented a house for the seven months we were there and were lucky enough to stay healthy. We had a housekeeper called Carlotta and a valet called Miguel looking after us. I got ill only after taking a dip in the pool at the beach club in Acapulco. During our seven-month stay in Mexico, Janine tried to learn Spanish so she could talk to Carlotta. Whenever she attempted a conversation, however, it was usually left to me to explain what we actually wanted – in English.

*Licence Revoked* offered Tim quite a lot to get his teeth into and he threw himself into every aspect of the filming. One day at Churubusco, I was shooting a scene between Tim and Benicio Del Toro, who underplayed Sanchez's vicious accomplice Dario to magnificent effect. Benicio is something of a Method actor and likes to do things as realistically as possible. We were filming a fight scene and were using a real knife because we needed to get the reflections glinting off the blade. Benicio got a little carried away and Tim received a very nasty cut on his hand. We got Tim to a doctor, who stitched the wound, and while we were waiting for the ambulance to arrive to take him to hospital, I was lumbered with the unfortunate task of going to see Tim in his dressing room so we could ask him for his watch and rings. Tim gave me a wry grin; he knew I would have to give all this to a double so we could carry on filming the scene in his absence. Tim knew the show had to go on and we continued with his double for the rest of the day until Tim came back. I know some actors who would have taken the week off after such an injury, but Tim was very good about things like that and was back at work as soon as possible.

One of the bonuses of shooting in Mexico was the buildings. The Central

Post Office in Mexico City was an absolute work of art that doubled very nicely as the Banco de Isthmus, where Sanchez laundered his money. The post office was constructed of wrought iron, with some of the most ornate staircases I had ever seen. As soon as I saw it on the reconnaissance, I knew it was a must. We filmed the interior on a Sunday and we received the best co-operation. The biggest problem was finding the group of Japanese investors who visit Sanchez at the bank. We practically emptied all the Japanese restaurants in Mexico City in order to find the people we needed. After we finished shooting at the post office, I couldn't resist having my shoes polished at one of the old-fashioned shoe-shining booths on the street outside. I don't think my shoes have ever looked better.

Tim was injured during the filming of this confrontation between Bond and Dario (Benicio Del Toro).

The obligatory casino sequence proved even harder to shoot because gambling is outlawed in Mexico. Peter Lamont found the palatial Casino Espagnol, a beautiful marble building that had once been used for such purposes, but we had to specially import all the gaming machines, tables, shoes and cards from the US. The casino lift was actually filmed inside the Ciudad de Mexico, or Grand Hotel, and Tim was able to use it to climb on to the roof and gain access to the building's upper stories. It was a potentially dangerous situation – not to mention extremely dirty and greasy – and I initially hesitated to put our leading man into that environment. Peter Lamont checked out the lift and the lift shaft thoroughly to make sure Tim wouldn't find himself trapped in any way. We had been a bit spoiled at Pinewood because anything we needed we simply constructed. It's quicker and usually safer doing things that way, but I knew that Tim was very precise with his action, so once we'd satisfied ourselves that it was safe, we shot it for real.

In Sanchez's office inside the casino, we see his pet iguana sitting on his shoulder. I'm always keen to use animals in my films whenever possible and after having a discussion with Robert Davi about it, we found a local trainer who kept a couple of reasonably tame lizards. Robert improvised freely with the iguanas – I remember one time he turned to one of them and said 'give us a kiss' and it did!

One of the extras in the casino was Dr James D'Orta – known to one and all as 'Dr Jim'. Dr Jim was related to the Broccoli family, and his company, Lifestar International, was there to look after us in case we needed any medical assistance. It was very reassuring to have a good doctor like Jim about, and as a way of saying thank you, we dressed him up in a tux and gave him a small part in the film. I think he quite enjoyed himself. For other small parts in the film, we used a lot of local actors. The puppet president Hector Lopez was played by Pedro Armendariz, whose father had so memorably played Kerim Bey in *From Russia With Love* back in 1963. I didn't think Pedro Jr was quite the actor his father had been, but it was nice to have him in the film.

The close-ups of Bond and Pam's romantic interlude on a boat were originally going to be shot at sea, but we eventually staged it at Churubusco. With the help of Jacqueline Stears, who painted a realistic backdrop, Peter Lamont strung some little pieces of silver paper over the 'sea' to give the impression of twinkling moonlight reflecting off the waves. Together with Tim and Carey, I looked at the rushes the next day and decided to re-shoot certain bits again, but overall I felt that we had once again used old-fashioned techniques quite effectively. My mind went back to the filming of *Murphy's War* and the day I had to break some bad news to director Peter Yates: unfortunately, we had lost some of our rushes in the developing bath in the laboratory. I thought Peter would be furious, but all he said was 'Oh good! That means I can do those scenes again!' I've always had much the same attitude towards disappointing rushes – as long as there is the time and money, I welcome the opportunity to have a second crack at filming a scene.

The pre-titles sequence takes place on the day of Felix Leiter's wedding to his fiancée Della (played by Priscilla Barnes, who had been a regular cast-member in the American sit-com *Three's Company*). Before they tie the knot, however, Felix and his best man James Bond capture the errant drug baron Franz Sanchez in a daring mid-air interception high above the church. The whole idea of capturing an aircraft in mid-air was made possible by using a very fast helicopter and a very slow Cessna, which was travelling at a mere 50–60 mph. Bond comes down on a wire and lassoes the tail of the aircraft before the helicopter tips it up and away it goes. The sequence was filmed by the aerial unit during the month we spent at Key West in Florida and starred my old friends B J Worth and Jake Lombard. The first test we conducted with the rig taught us that we would have to weight the nose of the plane a bit. As soon as the aircraft was winched to the helicopter, it started to fly – it went from being nose down to horizontal and then, rather alarmingly, began to climb towards the helicopter.

We asked the local electricity authority to move their lines in anticipation of Bond and Leiter parachuting into the church. Nothing like this was ever a problem in the USA – it just cost money. Of course, Sanchez escapes custody with the help of some corrupt members of the Drug Enforcement Agency, who steer the van off a causeway. John Richardson arranged the plunge on a disused part of the causeway and received all the help he needed from the local coastguards. The coastguards even gave me a thrilling lift home in one of their state-of-the-art Dolphin helicopters, which was flown by a pilot on loan from the Royal Navy. Sanchez is met by his accomplices underwater and makes his getaway from there. Ramon Bravo shot the excellent underwater footage in Cancun and the close-ups were shot in the antiquated tank at Churubusco. The tank hadn't been used for many years, but we cleaned it out and constructed a tent over the top so we could control the light.

One of the most memorable underwater shots was also one of the simplest to achieve. Bond has to infiltrate Milton Krest's ship, the *Wavekrest*, without being spotted by the underwater surveillance cameras. He does this by swimming beneath a huge manta ray, which effectively cloaks him for his journey. I got this idea during a reconnaissance trip – as our plane was taking off from Acapulco, I looked out of the window and below us I saw a manta ray gliding through the water as though it was flying. I mentioned the idea to Cubby and Michael and was greeted with incredulous stares that reminded me a little of the reception I had received when I said 'What about a cello?' during pre-production of *The Living Daylights*. Once again, they needed to be convinced with a demonstration, so I got Ramon Bravo to oblige. He fashioned a tarpaulin to vaguely resemble a manta ray and it looked convincing.

Like all the other important action sequences in my films, the success of these underwater scenes was partly dependent on the preparation of evocative storyboards. My storyboard artist on *Licence Revoked* was Roger Deer, a brilliant artist I had worked with on a number of previous occasions. People would gaze at the storyboards pinned to my office wall and I could see they were inspired by them. Roger still had a certain amount of work to do, translating a backlog of my rough sketches to his dynamic illustrations, and I was keen to take him to Mexico with us. Roger is a paraplegic and requires a wheelchair and specially adapted car, so Tom Pevsner was initially a little concerned about the problems this might cause both us and Roger. In the end, Roger did indeed accompany us to Mexico City and worked in the art department at Churubusco for many weeks. His colleagues in the art department made every allowance they could for his disability. By the time we moved to Key West, Roger's work was nearing its end, but I suggested he stayed in my house in Mexico City. He worked in the garden for three or four weeks with the visiting humming birds for company while Carlotta and Miguel made him comfortable.

Sharks started to gather off Key West at around 6pm, which was about the time that we would begin shooting our 'magic hour' night scenes. We were filming around the outlying islands, which have been uninhabited for centuries, and it was quite disconcerting to see fins circling in the water nearby. Those of us wading around in the shallow water also had to keep an eye out for stone fish, which could give you a very nasty sting if you trod on them. The channel back to Key West is not lit at all and one evening we finished after dark and got lost. The unit comprised eight boats in total and the other seven made it back OK, while ours ran aground on some coral sand. We all jumped out and tried to push our boat back into deeper water. Then someone reminded us that these shallows were among the sharks' favourite breeding grounds and they could get aggressive if disturbed. We all hopped back into the boat fairly sharpish and tried to think of another strategy.

Things were looking pretty hopeless and I was starting to feel a little hungry. During the day, one of the divers had caught me a lobster which I had put in a cold box, hoping to eat it for my dinner. I was busy feeling sorry for myself when one of the special effects boats appeared out of the gloom, towing a punt. We called out to them and they ferried us home. I finally got back to my hotel room at three o'clock in the morning and after a quick call to room service, Janine and I ate our lobster at 3.30am. We lost a bit of time over the incident and didn't start work until noon the following day.

The people at the local golf course, which I was amused to note was built on an old rubbish dump, loaned Janine and I some clubs so we could play a round or two during our time off. Janine was playing off the ladies' tee and was at the top of her backswing when an alligator leapt out of the water behind her. 'What do I do?' she whispered, sheer terror forcing the words out between clenched teeth. 'Hit the ball!' she was urged, so she did – right into a nearby mango swamp. Janine escaped in one piece, although there were no volunteers to go searching the swamp for her ball. We later read in the paper that a woman had rung the police after she struck an alligator with her car. When the policeman approached what he thought was an injured alligator, it grabbed him and wouldn't let go. His fellow patrolman shot the beast four times, but it escaped and the poor policeman was left with four bullet wounds. Luckily, he survived.

One of the most popular tourist attractions in Key West is the house where novelist Ernest Hemingway lived for 30 years until his death in 1961. It is on the veranda that Bond reluctantly resigns and M revokes his licence to kill. Hemingway had a huge collection of cats and some of their inbred descendants can be seen when M confronts Bond. Some of the cats were so inbred they had six toes on each paw.

The interior of Milton Krest's research laboratory was one of the most intricate sets constructed at Churubusco. John Richardson came up with bucket-loads of rubber maggots – feed for the fish – which we put into a huge drawer and vibrated to make it look as though they were writhing around. I knew that when Bond put his hand into the drawer, this would get a reaction from the more squeamish members of the audience and I wasn't wrong. One of the villains got a nasty shock when he was thrown into a tank containing an electric eel and another gets eaten alive when Bond throws him a suitcase full of money – he clutches the suitcase and falls into a tank full of sharks. At this point in the film, we cut to some footage Ramon Bravo filmed in Cancun – Ramon used a one-legged diver, who somehow induced a shark to attack and tear off his false leg. The result looked so horrific that I was forced to cut most of the scene for the censor, but what remained was still very effective.

The current market value of Sanchez's cocaine is broadcast to his clients in coded signals. These signals are cleverly incorporated into the televised fund-raising appeals made by Joe Butcher, the charismatic but corrupt front man for the Olimpatec Meditation Institute, a dodgy cult promoting something called 'cone power'. Joe Butcher was played by Wayne Newton, a Las Vegas singer and a well-known personality in the US. Wayne had been a multi-millionaire, lost everything and earned it all

Wayne Newton
played Joe
Butcher, a corrupt
TV evangelist
implicated in
Sanchez's cocaine
operation.

back again. I could see how he'd lost everything – his touching generosity seemed to know no bounds and he gave us all lovely gifts. He was very keen to appear in the film and did a great job of playing this slimeball character that was something of a comment on the less reputable TV evangelists cropping up in the States.

Joe Butcher made his broadcasts from the Olimpatec Meditation Institute, which was an imposing and abstract structure that one could have been forgiven for thinking had been constructed by Ken Adam were it not in fact real. The OMI buildings seen in the film were in fact a huge concrete structure near Toluca, which had been constructed as a ceremonial site for the Otomi people in 1980. Michael Wilson and myself had been tipped off about this place during one of our reconnaissance visits. We spent three or four hours searching for this remote temple-like building and were on the verge of giving up when I saw what seemed to be a monument at the top of a mountain. As we got closer, I could see that this place must have been some past president's excuse to offload thousands of tons of cement – it was full of little beehive structures, dominated by a huge quadrangle. It was starting to crumble a little, but that didn't matter too much to us – this magnificent place was the answer to our prayers.

Although the buildings looked tailor-made for our purposes, they had their limitations. When the script called for a flap to open in the roof and a helicopter to land inside, I knew we'd have to get our thinking caps on. Peter and Michael Lamont once again came to the rescue with another ingenious foreground miniature. In the film, you see a giant hinged flap open and the helicopter descends behind it. Although the flap looked as though it must have weighed many tons, it was actually no more than six feet wide, and placed right in front of the lens while the roof of the building was in the distance. For the scene showing the cavernous depot supposedly beneath the hatch, we cut to a night shot of the helicopter landing between the soundstages at Churubusco. It worked a treat.

We always tried to get an action first in each Bond film I made, and I was very proud of the scene in *Licence Revoked* when Bond is underwater and spears what he thinks is a boat passing overhead. As he is towed by this object, he surfaces and it becomes apparent the object was not a boat but a seaplane. As it gathers speed, Bond water-skis barefoot behind the plane and is whisked away from danger. He gets closer and closer to the plane until he is able to get into the cockpit, throw the pilot out and fly it away. I developed this scene with Michael and B J Worth and it was the best kind of action scene a director could have – it solved a narrative problem and gave the audience something they'd never seen before. The shots behind the boat were a combination of Tim and an expert water-skier who could actually ski in bare feet, sharks permitting.

The final confrontation between Bond and Sanchez took place after a climactic truck chase which we spent seven weeks shooting on the Rumarosa Pass in Mexicali. This film-within-a-film was a huge sequence and Barbara was in charge of the organisation. Arthur Wooster's unit had completed most of the filming by the time I arrived on the scene. I went straight to the editing van, where a Mexican editor was assembling footage on the spot. I opened the door of the van expecting to find this editor and his female assistant hard at it. I gazed downwards and instead discovered them both on the floor, hard at something else. 'I'll come back in five minutes,' I rather uncharitably barked, before closing the door. They had regained their composure by the time I went back in and they played me some footage. I wasn't terribly surprised to discover that it was rather disappointingly cut, but it proved illustrative enough to help Tim match his close-ups the next day.

The Kenworth Truck Company of Seattle refurbished 10 giant rigs for the sequence and Remy Julienne masterminded the breathtaking stunt driving as usual. Kenworth modified their trucks to Remy's instructions, which meant putting huge weights on the prime movers so he could do wheelies. In another scene, one of Remy's drivers was doubling for Bond, who has to tip his truck and drive it on one side in order to avoid an incoming bazooka missile. I don't think this had ever been attempted before with such a big truck. Remy's vehicles had to be in excellent shape, so we beefed up the engines and the brakes, and strengthened their chassis. All the engineering work made a big dent in the budget – each truck cost about $100,000 new, so I'm sure you can work out a ballpark figure yourself.

Corkey Fornof, who had done such a good job with the Bede jet in *Octopussy*, flew the plane that deposits Bond on top of one of the tankers. We had to bulldoze an airstrip especially in the Rumarosa mountains so he would have somewhere to take off and land. The plane was supposedly being flown by Pam Bouvier and Carey managed to look convincing behind the controls after only the most rudimentary briefing. The plane was

Remy Julienne's
stunt team in
action at the
Rumarosa Pass.

hanging from a crane during the close-ups showing her in the cockpit. At one point she forgot her training and opened the throttle – to everyone's alarm, the plane started pulling away, even though it was still attached to the crane. A quick word on the cockpit radio quickly remedied the situation. When Carey was seen driving the truck that picks up the battered and bruised Bond right at the end, Remy constructed a dual control device that enabled him to drive the truck from the sleeping compartment behind her.

There are plenty of films that show planes driving over cars, but we took great pleasure in showing a blazing jeep full of Sanchez's henchman shoot off a mountain road and fly over the aeroplane flown by Pam. Corkey had great reservations about flying a plane with a blazing vehicle shooting through the air above him, so John Richardson built a three-quarter scale model jeep and fired it out of an air cannon. There's an interesting sound editing trick in that sequence – if you listen carefully when Bond is crawling around the speeding rig while Sanchez is shooting at him from his car, you'll be able to hear the James Bond theme played out in the sound of the ricocheting bullets.

The disused stretch of road where we were filming was four or five miles long; I later discovered that it was disused for a reason. Years before, a coach carrying some nuns had an accident. The coach went off the road, plunging down the mountainside and bursting into flames. Everyone on board, including the nuns' pet dog, was killed. Ever since then, a number of accidents had occurred on this stretch of road and the locals swore it was haunted. A bypass had been built, leaving the road unused and therefore ideal for our purposes, or so we thought.

We were plagued by bad luck for the duration of the shoot in Mexicali. One day, Timothy was accompanying one of Remy's drivers in one of the trucks when an ambulance came straight out of nowhere in the other direction. There was very nearly a head-on collision and I thought we were going to lose our leading man there and then. During the night, our trucks were all parked in the same area, away from the road. One night one of the trucks' handbrakes must have slipped by itself – the truck slipped off the road and plunged off the mountainside. It was a complete write-off. We hired a security guard to keep an eye on the trucks, just in case anybody was interfering with them. In the early hours of one morning, the guard saw someone, but as he approached the figure, it simply melted away in front of him.

On another occasion, one of the drivers was driving a truck down the road when another truck came right at him, driving on the wrong side of the road. He had just enough time to swerve his rig off the road and jump into the sleeping compartment behind him, which basically saved his life in the crash that ensued. So that was two trucks we had to write off.

The bazooka rockets fired in an attempt to stop Bond's truck were launched by John Richardson, who felt safe in the knowledge that we had the area to ourselves. In another instance of incredible bad luck, one of the rockets hit an engineer who was working at the top of a telegraph pole two miles away. This poor chap was fixing a telephone line when this rocket suddenly came out of nowhere and hit him on the elbow. He had to be taken to hospital.

There was definitely a strange atmosphere on that stretch of road and the weather could behave in some extremely unpredictable ways. Arthur was convinced the place was spooky and I soon came round to his point of view. If there was any doubt left in my mind, it was dispelled by a bizarre photograph taken by one of the special effects boys. One of the trucks explodes in a huge fireball and the still showing the explosion shows something that isn't at all visible in the movie – the flames seem to form the face of a dog, and a column of fire extending from the explosion appears to make the shape of a forearm and five fingers, reaching out from the fire. The more I looked at this spine-chilling photograph, the more I was reminded of that terrible accident.

I was very pleased with the footage of the truck chase in Mexicali, but we were all extremely glad to get out of that place. We went to the altogether more hospitable climes of Acapulco for the final week's shooting on the schedule. Sanchez's house was, in fact, the private residence of Baron de Portinova, a friend of Cubby and Dana's. The house was made of gleaming marble and had a swimming pool filled level with the marble surrounding it. When the light hit it in a certain way, the water and marble appeared to merge with Acapulco Bay in the background. The glare from all that white marble made the house very difficult to light and photograph effectively, but it was worth the effort. The first time I saw the place was during a reconnaissance with Cubby. The Baron was in London, but he left his 60 staff behind to look after us. We were each given a guest suite with our own swimming pool. I remember taking my clothes off to have a shower, and coming out of the bathroom to discover that everything had been washed and pressed in my absence. These staff moved around the house quietly and efficiently, and you never saw any of them. I think it would have been cheaper for Cubby to have booked us into a hotel: when we left, he gave each staff-member a handsome tip.

Look carefully at
this chilling
picture – is that a
hand emerging
from the flames?

Shooting rounded off in November with some night filming of a party at the Baron's house. Bond jumped from the balcony to join Pam in a romantic clinch in the swimming pool. Paul Weston doubled for Tim during the jump, which he explained to me had the potential to be quite dangerous – the water was relatively shallow, so he had to do a kind of back flop on to some cushions placed at the bottom of the pool. Paul jumped into the pool, flattening out at the last minute and Tim emerged from the water to pull Carey in with him.

Things ended in a bit of a sour atmosphere, unfortunately – I was feeling a little unwell and Tim wasn't in the best of moods either. The whole thing was a bit of an ordeal and Tim and I had a bit of a slanging match across the pool. I don't know whether to put it down to tiredness at the end of the schedule or the accumulated tension of what had had been an unusually arduous shoot.

Post-production was done at the cosy and familiar confines of Pinewood Studios and I was glad to get home. We came across an unusual problem during the scene which showed Lupe watching an old movie aboard the *Wavekrest*. I needed to know that we could run a movie we could get copyright clearance on, so we contacted MGM/UA and they said we could use the old John Wayne Western *Red River*. We had used the movie in the background when filming the scene at Churubusco, but back at Pinewood we got a last-minute message saying that we could show *Red River*, but we couldn't use its soundtrack. We had to finish dubbing the very next day and I started to get a little anxious. 'Don't worry,' said my son Andrew, who was the music editor. 'I'll fix it tonight.' Andrew had his own studio at home and that night he got together with some of his mates and recreated a short section of the soundtrack of *Red River*, complete with music, horses' hooves and gun shots. He arrived the following morning with a tape ready for mixing. Tom Pevsner was so delighted with this quick-fix solution that he gave Andy a bonus of £600 for being enterprising. Andy still gets royalties from the music he wrote.

The marketing men struck again and asked us to change the title of the film. For the first time, we didn't have the fallback position of arguing that *Licence Revoked* was a Fleming title, and we had to give in to their protestations that American audiences wouldn't know what the word 'revoked' meant. As a result, the film we had all known as *Licence Revoked* became known as *Licence To Kill* on its release. I found it hard to believe that anyone would be baffled by the word 'revoked'. I was also slightly concerned that our new title was a little close to *A View to a Kill*, a film that had been in release only four years previously. Quite aside from anything else, I thought it was a little peculiar that *Licence To Kill* was the only James Bond film in the entire series in which our hero *didn't* have a licence to kill. But hey, that's showbusiness.

With the title fixed at *Licence To Kill*, we could put the last piece of the jigsaw into place – the titles. Maurice Binder always sailed pretty close to the wind when it came to deadlines and I knew his after-the-last-minute delivery of titles had caused a few headaches over the years. Before the release of *Licence To Kill*, I was called to a meeting to discuss Maurice's future. Barbara felt that times were changing and we should commission someone else to design our main titles for us. Cubby chaired the meeting and I think he noticed the look of amazement on my face as I listened to the suggestion that Maurice should be retired. I recalled the boys' club première of *For Your Eyes Only* in New York – although Maurice had delivered his titles right at the last minute, the appearance of his name on the credits had elicited a huge cheer from the audience. This man was a star and an integral part of the team. I was asked for my opinion over whether Maurice should stay and receive the commission for *Licence To Kill*. 'I think he's a great asset to us, for all his faults,' I said. 'I think he should stay.' I looked around the table. I was outvoted three-to-one. 'Fortunately for Maurice, this isn't a democracy,' said Cubby after a long pause. 'He stays.' Cubby made the right decision and *Licence To Kill* proved to be Maurice's final Bond film anyway. Unbeknown to us, he had been ill for some time and he died early in 1991. We were old friends, although he never did get round to taking me and Janine out for dinner, as he'd often promised he would.

I was working in the cutting room on *Aces: Iron Eagle III* on Sunset Boulevard when I heard that Maurice had passed away. The *Independent* newspaper in London called and asked if I'd be prepared to write an obituary. I stopped work and put pen to paper right away, trying to emphasise his enormous contribution to the Bond series and recount some of the more light-hearted incidents involving naked girls and Vaseline-smeared lenses. The obituary appeared in the newspaper and two weeks later a cheque for $100 and 65 cents appeared as payment, completely out of the blue. That night, I took Janine out to dinner at the Cheesecake Factory in Beverly Hills. We drank to Maurice and laughed about how he never did get round to taking us out for dinner. At the end of the evening, the waiter presented me with the bill and my blood ran cold. In stunned silence, I showed Janine the amount due: $100 and 65 cents.

With Maurice's titles in place, *Licence To Kill* still had another hurdle

to jump before it made it on to cinema screens. The censors balked at the violence in the film and made us jump through hoops to get a '15' certificate – still the highest certificate a Bond film had ever been granted. James Ferman, the secretary of the British Board of Film Classification, was unrelenting and virtually stood over me in the cutting room as I made the necessary cuts myself. The scene that particularly aggravated him was the showdown between Bond and Sanchez, when Bond uses Felix's cigarette lighter to ignite the drug baron's petrol-soaked suit, turning him into a ball of flame. Maybe we were to blame all along for choosing a subject that was unsuitable for children, but I still feel the censors were unnecessarily hard on that scene in particular. To make things worse, the version screened in

Bond (Timothy Dalton) exacts a terrible revenge on Sanchez (stunt man Paul Weston) – and gets us into trouble with the censors.

America wasn't as cleanly cut as the version that played in England and that upset me. In trying to be true to the violent nature of the Fleming stories, we had clearly overstepped the mark.

The certification prevented any youngsters from seeing the film, but other things conspired against us. MGM/UA had supposedly spent a fortune on marketing the film in the States, but I personally saw little more than a television commercial and some posters in bus stops. The competition in cinemas was stiff – we were going up against *Lethal Weapon 2*, *Indiana Jones and the Last Crusade* and the ultra-hyped *Batman*. I was heartened to learn that *Licence To Kill* received the highest test-screening results of any Bond film, but I knew that despite this the odds were stacked against us.

I could see it coming, but I was nevertheless disappointed when *Licence To Kill* failed to find the audience it deserved. I can blame the subject choice or the marketing, but what really frustrated me more than anything else was that even though *Licence To Kill* was the finest film I had ever made, it was ultimately seen by fewer people than had watched my previous Bond films.

Another boardroom shuffle at MGM/UA initiated a period of uncertainty at Eon and the ensuing deadlock between production company and distributor meant that production of the James Bond series was put on hold. During that hiatus period, shortly after the release of *Licence To Kill*, Cubby phoned me with some bad news. He told me that MGM/UA had decided that when the new Bond film went into production, it should have a new director at the helm. I had been hired only on a picture-by-picture basis, so I didn't take the news personally. 'I think it would be a very good idea to get someone new in,' I responded. 'It will give the series some fresh blood.' My admiration for Cubby was undimmed and I closed the conversation by sincerely thanking him for the wonderful years we'd had together.

Tim Dalton was certainly under the impression that he was going to stay on and make a third Bond picture, but as the years of production inactivity went on, the situation changed. It wasn't until 1994 that Tim formally gave way to Pierce Brosnan, who got his second chance to play Bond in *GoldenEye* the following year. *GoldenEye* presented the public with a new director, new writers and a new star, and after such a long period away it was probably no bad thing.

I was fortunate to carry the baton for eight films – five as director – of a series that has gone from strength to strength. I'm extremely proud of my work on the Bond films and especially glad that the two Timothy Dalton movies have enjoyed a growing reputation among those who recognise their authentic quality. Those two films have, I think, aged particularly well and were probably ahead of their time because they certainly seem fresh and up-to-date when viewed today. In 1990, however, I knew I faced an important new challenge. Feelings of anxiety I hadn't experienced for many years crept on me – would there be life after Bond?

# 007™

# CHAPTER 13

## BOND AND BEYOND

I soon discovered that there was a certain stigma attached to the James Bond films. Many people in the business looked down their noses at the movies, labelling them as cynical money-making exercises. Others thought that, having directed five Bond films, I must be a good director on only technical grounds. I also encountered a number of particularly snobby actors who considered the Bond films to be demeaning exercises in mere 'entertainment'. I'm sure that much of this condescension was veiled jealousy, but it's nevertheless harmed a number of very talented people. I feel particularly sorry for many of the leading ladies who have found themselves pigeon-holed, their careers stymied by the label 'Bond girl'. If you want to move on to something else, it can be difficult when your 15 minutes of fame are endlessly repeated on television all over the world. *Dr No* must be the only 40-year-old picture that still receives prime time screenings, and I'm sure the others will all stick around on the small screen for many years to come.

I have encountered a very particular Bond-related problem over and over again in recent years: when my name comes up for consideration as a potential director, producers often dismiss me on the grounds that they won't be able to come up with enough money to match the budgets I've supposedly been used to. Although I'm used to managing four or five units simultaneously and ran an 18-month schedule on each Bond, I hope that one thing has become apparent from reading this book – the Bonds are not extravagant films. They don't operate anywhere near the cost of today's top bracket action movies, although every penny spent is up there on screen. The dedicated and loyal crews that do so much to give the films their distinctive gloss all consider that their reputations are enhanced by their involvement with the Bonds. Although they may not earn big money on the Bond films, they will almost certainly earn big money elsewhere as a result of their association with Bond. But all of this takes a bit of explaining and more often than not you simply don't get that far.

In 1990, I directed a pilot for an American television series called *Checkered Flag* and I confounded some of the crew with my practical 'sealing wax and string' approach to what they considered to be some extremely technical challenges. The series was about motor racing and filmed in Phoenix, Arizona, where we had some very good facilities. We

With Janine and
my agent Spyros
Skouras on
location for *Aces:
Iron Eagle III* in
Arizona.

had a lot of fast-moving shots to do and I was told that there wasn't enough money in the budget for things like big crowds and complex blue screen photography. 'Why don't we use a moving backing?' I said, thinking back to our adventures with the railway carriage in *Octopussy*. The blank stares that greeted me made me realise how little the American crew knew about old-fashioned techniques. I remembered we had used a moving backing on *Licence To Kill* and we tried to have it sent to us from Churubusco. It proved impossible, apparently because we didn't have the necessary import licence. I refused to be beaten, so instead suggested we made a drum, which was an even more primitive technique. More blank stares. I got the art department to make a drum of about 20 feet in diameter, with a pivot in the middle. Blurred images of grandstands were painted on the surface, and when it was revolved at speed it just about passed muster on the small screen. When the actors saw the results the next day, they thought it was magic. I thought it was a last resort, but we got away with it.

Racing cars are difficult to shoot in an exciting way because whatever you do with the camera they never appear to be going very fast. The Tom Cruise film *Days of Thunder* had cost a lot of money but hadn't been a great success and I think it was partly due to the fact that the vehicles themselves often resembled toys. We got the co-operation of the best-known car companies and all the famous drivers at Phoenix enjoyed the extra practice our filming allowed them. We set out in a very fast camera car and filmed three laps of a staged race with a head-to-head finish at around 120 mph. The drivers were very bright and knew exactly what to do. In fact, I think our race was probably more exciting than the real thing later that afternoon.

I think there are a number of reasons why *Checkered Flag* failed to become a series, not the least of which was the amount of capital you would have needed to raise to buy your own cars. I moved on and someone else directed enough extra footage to bring the episode up to feature-film length so it could receive theatrical distribution. If a pilot is picked up by a network in the US, the director often gets a percentage of the subsequent episodes whether he's responsible for them or not. So if you launch a successful series that lasts for a number of episodes, you can make an awful lot of money. The part you play in creating a formula can earn you subsequent rewards, which is something I bet Terence Young wished had been in practice when he directed *Dr No*.

My next project was the feature film *Aces: Iron Eagle III*, starring Louis Gossett Jr and Christopher Cazenove. I would have liked to have directed a comedy or a love story, but Hollywood had me down as an action director, so they were the only films I was offered. I looked at the first two films in the *Iron Eagle* series, both of which were directed by Sidney Furie. I enjoyed the first one, but was less than impressed with the second. I decided to do the third partly because I felt I could inject a bit of humour to proceedings.

The distributor, Carolco, were under the impression that this ambitious aerial adventure could be made for $10 million and I did my best to oblige them. I had an encouraging meeting with the producer, Ron Samuels, who told me that we would be getting the co-operation of the Air Force. He gave me a copy of the script to read and when I discovered that the plot was about drug running using American Air Force planes, I predicted that no such co-operation would be forthcoming. Our leading lady was Ron's wife Rachel McLish, whom I remembered meeting at a body-building contest in Las Vegas when we were interviewing actresses for the role of May Day in *A View to a Kill*. The script was written with her in mind and there were moments when she was able to use her strength to impressive effect. She was a great mover and could run like a hare.

We shot *Aces* in Arizona and it cost a little more than we anticipated because we had to use gas-guzzling Confederate planes when the American Air Force unsurprisingly refused to play ball. Much of the film was set in Peru and we were lucky that Arizona offered us convincing-looking scenery in the shape of distant snow-capped mountains. John Richardson supervised the special effects for me and did what I consider to be some of the most outstanding work of his career. We used a modern airfield on the Mexican border and there was a good runway which we used to drive a truck and trailer along for the moving model shots. I thought that some of the model work in the second *Iron Eagle* film had been below par – it was obvious that some of the models weren't moving because when they were blown up the ensuing flames went up, instead of trailing behind. We mounted our models on the back of a speeding truck and I think this gave our sequences some added realism. Alec Mills, another reliable and hard-working colleague from the Bond films, was my cameraman.

Most of our work was done in Tucson and it was proved to me yet again that America is the easiest place on earth to shoot a film. The dollar is king and if you're going to spend money, you'll always be welcome. The first question the local mayor usually asks you is, 'How much money are you going to be spending here?' The amount of co-operation you get depends on your answer.

I brought *Aces* in a week ahead of schedule, but by this time I had long been aware that things weren't at all well at Carolco. As far back as pre-production, I noticed that the preparations were going on for rather too long and that they seemed to be reluctant for us to actually begin shooting. At one point, I confronted the executive in charge of production with my suspicions. 'If I wasn't pregnant with you and Lou Gossett, I would cancel this project!' he exploded. He knew that we were on 'pay or play' deals and if he cancelled the film, he would still have had to pay us and presumably Ron Samuels as well. I think Carolco were in all sorts of trouble that I didn't know about and they seemed to be keen to get rid of me and my film. We had some unpleasant behind-the-scenes moments, but I have only happy memories of shooting the film and working with the American technicians. The *Iron Eagle* films are the sort of movies you rent to watch on video during a rainy Sunday afternoon, but *Aces* has done quite well over the years and Ron has since made a fourth instalment of the saga.

The political machinations at Carolco were nothing compared to the seemingly endless spiral of despair that was *Christopher Columbus: The Discovery*. I'm sure one day someone will write a book about this film alone – even now, it's painful to dredge the memory banks for my experiences on this movie. I was contacted by Ilya Salkind in 1991, and asked if I would be interested in directing a lavish costume drama commemorating the 500th anniversary of Columbus's discovery of America. I knew Ilya from my enjoyable stint on *Superman* over 10 years before and I had a lot of respect for him. In retrospect, maybe the early difficulties should have warned me off the project, but I persevered to the bitter end.

Ilya was honest with me from the outset: he told me he was hiring me because he had fallen out with his first choice, Ridley Scott. Ridley had left the production and was in the process of setting up his own version of the Columbus story, *1492: Conquest of Paradise*, at Paramount. As if this wasn't improbable enough, Alan Hume was at Pinewood, preparing to photograph the first new *Carry On* film for 14 years. The title? *Carry On Columbus*. So I was going up against two other Columbus movies, at least one of which posed a serious international box-office threat.

It got worse: I discovered that Ilya's father Alexander had blown some $5 million launching the movie at the Cannes Film Festival. By the time I arrived, more than a third of the budget had been spent on helicopters, boats and various stunts which had attracted huge media attention to the film and its star, Timothy Dalton. While waiting for his third Bond assignment, Tim had agreed to play Columbus. My arrival, however, seemed to initiate a change of heart and Tim soon decided he didn't want to appear in the film after all. I don't know whether Tim thought that appearing in another John Glen film would typecast him, but I hope that his departure wasn't entirely due to me. Whatever his reasons, the official story was that Tim had decided not to play Christopher Columbus because of 'creative differences' – whatever that means.

Before long, what had the potential to be the biggest film of my career was falling to bits around my ears. Alexander urged us to press on with pre-production, I suspect partly because he had ploughed a lot of his own money into the project and was keen to recoup as much as possible. As time went on, yet another cloud loomed on our horizon – politically correct rumblings in the US had created a lot of adverse publicity about Columbus

himself. There was a lot of talk about the fact that Columbus had introduced slavery to America and human rights groups were becoming very active in their condemnation of the way Columbus had persecuted the Native Indians. Virtually overnight, our hero become a villain.

I met the Salkinds in Paris to discuss the script. Alexander and Ilya were as generous as usual and treated me like royalty in a luxurious suite at the Royal Monceau Hotel. Alexander's ex-wife, who apparently had an interest in the film, was also present. Screenwriters John Briley and Mario Puzo had already left the project, so not only was I without a leading man, but I also had no scriptwriter. It was a lonely feeling. When I say I was without a scriptwriter, that wasn't strictly true: I was introduced to Ilya's mother, who told me she had written a scene that she would like me to consider including. I listened patiently as she read out this scene, which described how the Native Indians foretold the arrival of Columbus by looking into the flames of their fires. When she'd finished, I walked across the room to get a glass of water and when I returned every eye was on me: my verdict was eagerly awaited. 'I think that's one of the most beautiful stories I've ever heard,' I said, 'but I don't think it's quite right for this film.' I think everyone was quite pleased to get that over with. Later on, I was very glad when Carey Bates joined us and worked continuously to rewrite the script.

As our unusual script conference was breaking up, I mentioned to Alexander that I had been giving our leading man some thought and had decided that Georges Corraface, a young actor who lived in Paris, would be worth interviewing. I told Alexander that Georges had come highly recommended and he said it sounded like a good idea. 'I'm glad you think so,' I said, 'because I've taken the liberty of inviting him along.' Georges was waiting outside, so I invited him in to meet the producers there and then. Georges got the part of Christopher Columbus as soon as Alexander and Ilya realised that the project's bad reputation would preclude them

At work on the troubled *Christopher Columbus: The Discovery.* From left to right: Georges Corraface, Robert Davi, camera operator Mike Frift, focus puller Frank Elliot, myself and continuity supervisor June Randall.

finding an A-list actor for the role. The wheels were then set in motion to find a famous supporting actor in an attempt to beef up the cast.

The budget for *Christopher Columbus: The Discovery* was supposedly $40 million, but I reckon I made that film for somewhere between $12 and $14 million excluding Marlon Brando's fee. He was paid something in the region of a whopping $5 million. This was an awful lot of money, but the Salkinds needed to get Marlon on board in order to give the film some star value and sell the package to foreign distributors. Over the following months, we assembled a good cast, mainly comprising British actors. The American faces included Robert Davi and Benicio Del Toro, both of whom had given excellent performances in *Licence To Kill* and I knew could be relied upon to do just as well here. Another old friend was Oliver Cotton, an actor that Barbara Broccoli had once suggested could be a good James Bond. One of the supporting artists was up-and-coming Welsh actress Catherine Zeta Jones, a girl I had spotted in a television show called *The Darling Buds of May*. The show had been a huge success in Britain, but few people in the US had seen it. As soon as we met, I was immediately struck by her beauty and felt she would easily make the transition from television to the big screen. I'm glad to say I was right and *Christopher Columbus: The Discovery* proved to be an early stepping stone on the path to international fame. One late addition to the cast was Tom Selleck, whom we cast as the King of Spain. Ilya told me that Tom wanted to be involved because he wanted the opportunity to work with Marlon Brando. I was happy to have him along.

We made a reconnaissance trip to the Virgin Islands, a place I had visited with Michael Wilson, Barbara Broccoli, Tom Pevsner and Peter Lamont while we were setting up *Licence To Kill*. That visit hadn't exactly been a resounding success. We were travelling around in a taxi and the driver seemed to take exception to the way Michael was asking him to show us different places. In the end, he started getting quite rude, so Michael asked him to take us back straightaway and we got out of the car. The driver then demanded payment for a whole day's driving, even though our trip had been cut short and Michael refused to pay. There was an argument and this guy suddenly grabbed Barbara's bag, which contained all out travellers' cheques and cash. He threw the bag inside his car and we offered him half his fee in attempt to get the bag back. He wouldn't take it, so Michael went into the car and retrieved the bag. At this point our driver went ballistic and there was a tug of war with Barbara's bag in the middle. The strap broke and she somehow managed to get hold of the bag, at which point the man lunged for her with a tyre iron. Reacting quickly I jumped on his back to stop him hurting her, despite the fact that he must have been twice as big as me and his eyes were turning a rather disturbing shade of red. We struggled for a while and when the chance came, I jumped off and put a couple of cars between me and him. I made up my mind that if things got really rough, I would make a run for it and jump into the sea, but in the meantime I just dodged around him. He wasn't terribly fit and started slowing down quite a lot. By the time the police arrived, he had calmed down a bit and eventually accepted half the dough, as we'd originally offered. On the way home, I pondered whether all that hassle was worth a $30 taxi fare.

The irate taxi driver was a minor contributory factor in our decision not to shoot in the Virgin Islands. Co-operation from the locals is a crucial element in any location shoot and the director almost being murdered by one of them isn't a terribly good start. The head of the local film commission was very embarrassed by the whole incident, so when I came back on a reconnaissance for *Christopher Columbus* a few years later, he went out of his way to be as helpful as possible. I put aside my reservations about the local transport and we decided to film there after all.

We started shooting in the Virgin Islands during Christmas 1991 and I was grateful that my old friend Brian Cook was on board as assistant director. I had first worked with Brian during my days editing television shows at Elstree in the 1960s and I remember he once hospitalised me during an impromptu football match, but I'd long since forgiven him for that. Brian kept us all cheerful during adversity and soon gained a good reputation among the crew. Alec Mills was once again my cameraman and one day I suggested I could give him a lift to the set so we could discuss the morning's schedule. 'Thanks for the offer, John,' he told me, 'but I couldn't miss Brian's performance on the crew bus – it's priceless!'

On the first day, I discovered that Brian had lost none of his old charm. The film was obviously set in 1492 and I was confronted by scores of extras with gleaming white teeth. 'Brian, these guys are supposed to be living in medieval squalor – look at them.' Brian saw my point straightaway. 'Make-up!' he called out over his megaphone. 'Put a bit more shit on their teeth!'

There were cash-flow problems almost straightaway and rumours soon spread among the cast and crew that they weren't going to be paid. One morning, Brian told me that we were about to have a strike on our hands because the actors were convinced they weren't going to get their wages. In the end, Brian organised a whip-round among the British technicians so at least the extras got some money. Needless to say, I think everyone did get paid – eventually.

Later on in the shoot, there were further rumblings that the producers' coffers were dry. Robert Davi rang me from his hotel room and I could

Directing Catherine Zeta Jones, who played Beatriz, and Georges Corraface, who played Columbus.

hear the trepidation in his voice. 'I rang my agent last night,' he began. 'He says we haven't been paid for two weeks and I shouldn't do any more work until we see some money. I feel terrible about this, John, but I think he's right. Unless I make a stand, I don't think I'm ever going to get my wages.' I sympathised with him and said I could appreciate the way he felt. I told him to stay in his hotel room until the situation was sorted out, but I wanted him to understand that I had to carry on working in his absence. I arrived on the set and did a quick headcount among the cast – Robert wasn't the only actor missing. We couldn't afford to waste any time, so I spread the missing actors' lines around, giving them to the actors who were present. The film had a cast of thousands, so there wasn't much of a problem finding someone. Within minutes, word got round that I was taking lines away from absent actors and giving them to the ones that were actually there. Before long Robert and the other missing faces had all reappeared – they wanted their lines back, pay or no pay. I think the Salkinds and their fellow producer Jane Chaplin eventually put their hands in their pockets to ensure that everyone got the wages they were promised and I admired them for doing it. The golden rule of film producing is 'Never use your own money' and they broke that rule to ensure their promises were kept.

We were staying at the Stouffers Hotel and even the staff there got wind that maybe their bills weren't going to get paid. We were getting so short of cash that at one point they impounded the negatives of all the film we had shot – in total about 10 reels of film were kept inside a padlocked refrigerator and held to ransom. Brian suggested we give them a credit at the end of the film – 'Processing by Stouffers'.

Three replica ships were making a commemorative voyage from Spain to the US, so we arranged for them to stop at the Virgin Islands for three days so we could get some footage. Ilya had done a deal to allow the ships to be used in a television commercial and I and the rest of the crew donned period costumes one Sunday so we could help out. Ilya approached me beforehand and explained that although this was our day off, would we mind shooting some footage while we were on board? We had a great day out on board these ships being filmed by an overhead helicopter. When we got back in the evening we had some nice material of our own, showing the ships' workings. I soon had a glum Ilya on the phone, however, complaining that the advertising agency had refused to pay him anything – we had been so busy filming that our cameras and modern equipment had ruined all their shots!

Arthur Wooster and his second unit were on board one of the ships, filming the voyage across the Atlantic. They had a fairly tough time of things – they had to take their own food and conditions were so austere that they had to sleep on deck. To make things worse, they didn't receive a tremendous amount of co-operation from the captain of the ship. When they reached El Salvador, the local Indians came out in protest and threatened to board the ships and take them over. Luckily, the Spanish Navy had given them a destroyer escort for the voyage, but it was unfortunate that they came to the verge of an all-out battle. The intention was to sail the ships into New York harbour, where they would be fêted with firework displays and big celebrations. By the time the voyage came to its end, however, the whole Columbus anniversary had

turned so sour that this was all quietly forgotten.

After we finished filming in the Virgin Islands, we flew to Spain to commence shooting in Madrid. We were based at an old studio complex just outside the city and our principal location was a two-hour drive away. Marlon Brando was available to us for 10 days, which included him arriving and departing, so I basically had him for about a week. His fearsome reputation preceded him a little and I was more than a little edgy as I approached his hotel room. I was soon stopped by his squad of bodyguards, none of whom spoke English. Marlon always surrounded himself with tight security because wherever he went he was absolutely hounded by hordes of paparazzi photographers. I tried to explain to the bodyguards that I was the director of the film and I wanted to meet Mr Brando. They wouldn't let me in. I consoled myself with the fact that I'd get to meet him soon enough on the set.

On Marlon's first day, he didn't turn up, so I gave his lines to my old friend Michael Gothard, who had played Locque in *For Your Eyes Only*. Tom Selleck was particularly upset and that night he came to see me in my hotel room. 'John, I have always wanted to make a film with you and I have a great deal of respect for you and your work, but the only reason I took this role was because it gave me the chance to work with Marlon Brando. Now I find out that he refuses to play the scene with me.' I let out a deep sigh, exhausted at this latest trauma on a film that seemed to present me with an one problem after another. 'I hear what you're saying, Tom, and if you want to quit, then I'll just have to recast.' The following morning, Marlon decided to join us. I introduced myself to him in his trailer and he was very charming, offering me a coffee and asking me to sit down as though we had all the time in the world. We got on extremely well and my fears over his reportedly confrontational attitude towards directors proved to be unfounded. As far as I could tell, he seemed to have a problem with producers, which is something common to many actors I've worked with. Marlon told me he was doing the film purely for the money – his son and

Marlon Brando as Tomas de Torquemada in *Christopher Columbus: The Discovery*.

217

The beautiful
Indian girl (Tailinh
Forest Flower) is
amongst those who
learn they are to be
left behind in
*Christopher
Columbus: The
Discovery.*

daughter were having some problems and he apparently needed the cash to pay some legal fees. I walked into his trailer expecting to be confronted by a monster – I left feeling that Marlon Brando was in fact a considerate and rather humble man. Marlon had obviously had a word with Tom because he turned up for duty as well.

Among Marlon's entourage was a very pleasant lady who disappeared into an adjoining room while we rehearsed his first scene. This used to happen whenever we rehearsed or filmed; I later found out that Marlon was wearing a small device in his ear and receiving his lines through it from this lady, who was reading the script to him off-set. Before I realised what was going on, I had naïvely asked Marlon if we could pick the pace up a little bit, as it was taking six minutes to play scenes that should only have taken three. I decided in the end to fix it in the editing – Marlon obviously had his own reasons for adopting this system and I wasn't about to spoil it for him.

We went out of our way to protect Marlon from the paparazzi, who continued to hound him while we were shooting. During one exterior scene, I looked up and saw some photographers perched on the roof of a building opposite. I got the gaffer to erect a big black screen on the pretence that it was to shield Marlon from the sun. It was really there to give him some privacy, away from the snooping zoom lenses.

I suffered from a persistent dry cough when I was in Madrid; I'm not sure if it was due to the atmosphere or my nervousness at being around Marlon. He soon noticed that I was suffering and told me that the climate was making him cough as well. When I got back to my suite at the Palace Hotel, there was a gift waiting for me – Marlon had sent me a humidifier to help me breathe during the night. I plugged the device in and it promptly exploded – it ran on an incompatible voltage – but I was touched by his thoughtfulness. Our hair stylist Vera Mitchell had worked with Marlon before on *A Dry White Season* and recounted a similar tale of generosity. She had a small cottage on the Pacific Coast highway and she had been subjected to a series of natural disasters. A fire, torrential rain and a huge mud slide had all threatened the house she jokingly referred to as her 'dog kennel'. During this rain storm, the roof started leaking and as she looked up at the hole above her, the phone rang. It was Marlon, making a social call to see if she was OK. She explained about all the problems she was having and told him the roof was leaking. The next thing she knew, he was outside with a huge tarpaulin, strapping it over the hole in her roof so she could keep dry.

People react differently in different situations and differently with different people. Marlon was nothing but kind and considerate to me and my crew. Brian had got hold of Kitty Kelly's unauthorised biography of Marlon and for a joke asked him to autograph it for his son. I couldn't believe his nerve. Marlon took a long look at the book, paused, looked up at Brian and broke into a broad grin. He took Brian's pen, signed the book and handed it back to him. That signed edition is probably unique.

Some last-minute script changes addressed the political activists' concerns over Columbus's links with slavery, specifically in the scene where Columbus brings some Indians to show the King of Spain and then tries to teach them a Christian hymn. Columbus did some very unfair things and we didn't whitewash the issue.

We filmed the storm sequences in Malta and poor Robert Davi had to deliver his lines while John Richardson was showering him with tip-tanks of water and high-pressure hoses. It was hardly necessary because we had some pretty awful weather out there anyway. We were shooting in a tin shed doubling as a makeshift studio. When Catherine Zeta Jones and Georges Corraface were doing their love scene, the gale outside was so fierce I though the earth really was about to move, but they were game and carried on.

The shed was built next to a big tank that had been constructed for model photography. The art department constructed the three huge ships that made up Columbus's fleet – the *Santa Maria*, the *Pinta* and the *Nina* – and an additional ship that carried the Jews the Spanish exiled to North Africa as Columbus's voyage began. When the ships set sail for the Indies, John Richardson fixed ropes to the replicas and towed them across the tank. Just like the actual boats used by Columbus, our replicas didn't have keels, so if the wind blew, they would sway in the opposite direction. They relied on a ballast of sandstone in the hold to keep them upright but were nevertheless quite unstable. When we experienced gales, we would have to anchor the boats to the bottom of the tank with steel cables and if we were shooting on one side of a ship we would have to move the crowd to the other side to counterbalance our weight. At least the wind filled the sails. I couldn't move the camera too far left, or too far right, because the edge of the tank would creep into shot. This narrow angle of shooting meant we had to manhandle the boats in order to change the angles and bring in some extra sails to obscure the land behind. We got quite expert at it in the end and it looked very realistic.

The craftsmen in Malta were excellent and I was especially pleased with the scene showing Columbus's arrival in the New World. We shot part of

The *Santa Maria* embarks on a voyage of discovery.

this in the tank and I wanted to see rats coming down the ropes and swimming ashore – a symbolic point illustrating the spread of new European diseases into paradise. The ratcatcher we used had his animals very well trained and he offered them food through the portholes as an incentive to scurry on cue.

I had always wanted a lot of music in the film and I became friendly with one of the local priests, who had a choir. I went to see him with my sound recordist and we taped some beautiful Christmas carols to use on the voyage. Robert Davi, who was trained as an opera singer, led the singing. The composer Cliff Idelman wasn't hired until we'd virtually finished shooting and he told me it was a shame he hadn't been around earlier as he could have supervised the recording of the hymns and helped synchronise them.

In 1992, the 500th anniversary of Columbus's landing in America was never really celebrated. All three Columbus movies – mine included – got a bit of a roasting from the critics. We benefited by beating Ridley Scott's film into cinemas, although this may have meant that we also bore the brunt of the political backlash against the whole anniversary. I remain very proud of *Christopher Columbus: The Discovery*, although at the time I was just enormously relieved it was over and that I'd been able to complete the film in the face of some terrible adversity. I honestly doubt that many other directors could, or would, have stayed the distance. The film was made for very little money and was completed through the sheer determination of a very talented and efficient team.

I needed some time to recover after all that, but once I recharged my batteries I decided to take up an offer I couldn't resist. In the 1950s Gerry Anderson was a sound editor working on low-budget British films, much like myself. While I went on to become a film editor and eventually a director, Gerry literally transformed the business with such ground-breaking puppet shows as *Stingray*, *Thunderbirds* and *Captain Scarlet*. In the 1960s, children's television belonged to him and he created countless episodes of top-quality entertainment that are still regularly screened all over the world. Our paths rarely crossed when we both left sound editing behind, although I was aware that Derek Meddings had done some of the finest work of his career on Gerry's shows. In fact, I recommended Derek to Lewis Gilbert for *The Spy Who Loved Me* partly on the strength of his contribution to *Thunderbirds*.

In 1993, Gerry called me up and told me he was producing a new series called *Space Precinct*. He had already produced a pilot episode, but he wasn't entirely happy with it and wanted a new opening episode to take its place. Could I recommend anyone to direct it? I wasn't doing anything at the time so I said, 'What about me?'. There was a silence at the other end of the phone. 'Would you really do it?' asked Gerry. Before I knew it, I was back at Pinewood directing *Protect and Survive*, the first episode of *Space Precinct*, a show that mixed actors such as Ted Shackleford, Rob Youngblood and Simone Bendix with all manner of animatronic creatures from alien planets. The technology involved and the heavy prosthetics worn by some of the actors playing the creatures made it a challenging programme to shoot, but we had a lot of fun and Gerry was very pleased with the result. Gerry gave me complete autonomy and a great deal of support; to cut a long story short, I enjoyed working with him so much I ended up directing seven episodes in total.

Gerry is basically a very shy man and it can take a while to get to know him properly. Like many shy people, he can sometimes be mistaken for being brusque, but he really isn't like that at all. One of his greatest qualities is that he is prepared to take a chance on new talent and will give people every encouragement. If you have done good work for him and are loyal to him, he won't ever forget it. In that respect, he reminds me very much of Cubby Broccoli. Gerry's career has seen its ups and downs over the years and I know he was very hurt when Derek Meddings told him he could no longer afford his services. He similarly didn't reap the full rewards of *Thunderbirds*' phenomenal success because he sold his rights in the show to Lew Grade in the 1960s. Nevertheless, Gerry's imagination has served him well over the years and he's continued to come up with innovative and entertaining programmes. *Thunderbirds* was being repeated by the BBC while we were making *Space Precinct* and there was some talk that a new feature film was in the offing. Gerry didn't know if the chance to produce the film would come his way, but he told me that if it did, he'd like me to direct it for him. The film ultimately proved too expensive to make, but I was flattered that Gerry considered me for something so important.

*Space Precinct* gave me an excuse to work with lots of old friends again

-- I cast some very talented and well-known actors such as Oliver Cotton and Steven Berkoff. I think Gerry was pleasantly surprised by the calibre of the names we were getting: Burt Kwouk was another old friend of mine, whom I always used for re-voicing work. Maryam d'Abo and Jack Hedley both did episodes and it was good to see them again. Lots of old friends appeared in the series simply because I asked them to – they certainly didn't do it for the money.

Although my life moved on after *Licence To Kill*, Janine and I kept in touch with the Broccoli family during their long legal struggle to bring Bond back to the screen. We had travelled the world together – Janine had been Cubby's secretary and I had grown as a director as Michael had grown as a writer. Dana had always been very supportive, as well as making a number of valuable scripting contributions. We had all watched Barbara follow in her father's footsteps to become a talented producer in her own right. I felt like part of the extended family. Cubby had supported and championed me when the chips were down and I hope I repaid his loyalty. I had seen Cubby's health progressively deteriorate during the late 1980s and early 1990s and he was quite ill the last time I saw him. I visited Cubby and Dana's home in Beverly Hills and Cubby was in a wheelchair. I was quite alarmed when he tried to stand up and I remember grabbing one of the wheels of the chair to prevent it flying away from him. He was proud that he was strong enough to stand, however, and he was clearly a fighter to the very end. The strain on Dana during those years was enormous and caring for Cubby was starting to take quite a lot out of her. Cubby achieved an enormous amount and when he died, I think he knew he had been blessed with a fine family, and that his legacy to the world of entertainment was in safe hands.

Cubby died in 1996. When I heard the news, I reflected on the times we'd spent together – from that first meeting on location for *On Her Majesty's Secret Service*, through to the ski-parachute jump in *The Spy Who Loved Me*, the day he placed his trust in me to direct *For Your Eyes Only* and the laughs we'd enjoyed on that and the subsequent four Bond movies. During the evenings we'd share a drink and sometime discuss the nature of the Bond films themselves – just what was the secret ingredient in the Cubby's world-beating formula? I don't think Cubby had a definitive answer. One thing that I know about Cubby, however, was that he was a father figure who recognised the enormous value of keeping a loyal family of skilled creative people together for as long as possible. Ken Adam, John Barry, Dick Maibaum and countless others all contributed something unique under Cubby's guidance; the combined talents of all these people made Bond what it is. Cubby never really understood what that winning formula was – I don't think anyone does – but he was reluctant to change it. This philosophy saw a hit film become a hit series and a hit series become a phenomenon which is now ingrained into the consciousness of people all over the world.

# 007

## CHAPTER 14

### SCENE ONE, TAKE ONE

'You don't leave the film business – the film business leaves you.' Peter Hunt told me that many years ago and I've never forgotten it.

Today is 1 June 2000 and I'm glad to say the film business hasn't left me yet. The location is Luxembourg and the film is *The Point Men*, a political thriller starring Christopher Lambert. I have wanted to work with Christopher ever since we met in 1984 to discuss the possibility of him playing James Bond. At that time his French accent ruled him out, but he tells me he is still fascinated by the Bond films and would like the opportunity to play a villain.

Shortly before shooting began, I had a happy reunion with Roger Moore, who was filming a TV movie in Luxembourg while I was in pre-production. We had dinner together and got a little nostalgic for the days when it felt like the world was at our feet. We both love the camaraderie of the film set and agree that it's good to be working.

There are old friends both behind and in front of the camera on *The Point Men* – Alec Mills is my director of photography and Maryam d'Abo is playing one of the female leads. We last worked together on *Space Precinct* and she still looks as gorgeous as she did in *The Living Daylights*. There are plenty of new faces too – Vincent Regan plays the Palestinian terrorist pitted against the Israeli point man played by Christopher and Kerry Fox is our leading lady. Both are extremely talented and I'm sure they'll both be a pleasure to work with.

What the young Luxembourg crew lack in experience, they make up for in enthusiasm. They seem to hold both me and Alec in the highest regard, which is just as well because I'm going to rely on them to help me perform miracles over the next few months. The budget is modest, the facilities crude and the schedule punishing – we have Christopher's services for exactly 30 days. I have already scheduled a number of split days, starting at 2pm and finishing at 2am, so we can film both day and night scenes. When principal photography is over, I'll be directing the second unit myself. Among the challenges facing me is the problem of how to make Luxembourg, which is green and wet, look like Israel, which is dusty and dry.

There are a hundred things for me to do, but for now I'm focused on *Scene One, Take One*. Our hero is on a stake-out, unaware that he is about to be set on by three vicious heavies. Everyone is in place, Christopher is waiting for his cue and the cameras are turning over. All eyes are on me.

'Action!'

# 007 CREDITS

## JAMES BOND CREDITS

### ON HER MAJESTY'S SECRET SERVICE
### (Editor & Second-unit Director)

George Lazenby *James Bond*, Diana Rigg *Tracy*, Telly Savalas *Blofeld*, Gabriele Ferzetti *Draco*, Ilse Steppat *Irma Bunt*, Lois Maxwell *Moneypenny*, George Baker *Sir Hilary Bray*, Bernard Lee *M*, Bernard Horsfall *Campbell*, Desmond Llewelyn *Q*.

*Stock Car Sequence Director* Anthony Squire. *Assistant Director* Frank Ernst. *Camera Operator* Alec Mills. *Special Effects* John Stears. *Main title designed by* Maurice Binder. *Stunt Arranger* George Leech. *Costume Designer* Marjory Cornelius. *Music composed, conducted and arranged by* John Barry. *Director of Photography* Michael Reed BSC. *Production designed by* Syd Cain GFAD. *Art Director* Bob Laing. *Production Supervisor* David Middlemas. *Associate Producer* Stanley Sopel. *Screenplay by* Richard Maibaum. *Additional dialogue* Simon Raven. *Produced by* Harry Saltzman, Albert R Broccoli. *Directed by* Peter Hunt. Released 18 December 1969

### THE SPY WHO LOVED ME (Editor & Co-Second-unit Director)

Roger Moore *James Bond*, Barbara Bach *Major Anya Amasova*, Curt Jurgens *Stromberg*, Richard Kiel *Jaws*, Caroline Munro *Naomi*, Walter Gotell *General Gogol*, Geoffrey Keen *Minister of Defence*, Bernard Lee *M*, George Baker *Captain Benson*, Michael Billington *Sergei*, Olga Bisera *Felicca*, Desmond Llewelyn *Q*, Edward De Souza *Sheikh Hosein*, Vernon Dobtcheff *Max Kalba*, Valerie Leon *Hotel Receptionist*, Lois Maxwell *Miss Moneypenny*.

*Assistant Director* Ariel Levy. *Camera Operator* Alec Mills. *Second-unit Director* Ernest Day. *Special visual effects* Derek Meddings. *Special optical effects* Alan Maley. *Special effects (studio)* John Evans. *Action Arranger* Bob Simmons. *Main title designed by* Maurice Binder. *Ski jump performed by* Rick Sylvester. *Ski sequence photographed and supervised by* Willy Bogner. *Music by* Marvin Hamlisch. *Director of Photography* Claude Renoir. *Production designed by* Ken Adam. *Art Director* Peter Lamont. *Assistant Art Director* Ernie Archer. *Production Manager* David Middlemas. *Production Co-ordinator (Canada)* René Dupont. *Associate Producer* William P Cartlidge. *Screenplay by* Christopher Wood, Richard

Maibaum. *Produced by* Albert R Broccoli. *Directed by* Lewis Gilbert. Released 13 July 1977

**MOONRAKER (Editor & Co-Second-unit Director)**
Roger Moore *James Bond*, Lois Chiles *Holly Goodhead*, Michael Lonsdale *Drax*, Richard Kiel *Jaws*, Corinne Clery *Corinne Dufour*, Bernard Lee *M*, Geoffrey Keen *Frederick Gray*, Desmond Llewelyn *Q*, Lois Maxwell *Moneypenny*, Toshiro Suga *Chang*, Emily Bolton *Manuela*, Blanche Ravalec *Dolly*.
*Assistant Director* Michel Chekyd. *Camera Operators* Alec Mills, Michel Deloire, Guy Delattre, John Morgan, James Devis. *Second-unit Director* Ernest Day. *Visual Effects Supervisor* Derek Meddings. *Visual Effects Art Director* Peter Lamont. *Special Effects* John Evans, John Richardson, Rene Albouze, Serge Ponvianne, Charles Asscla. *Main title designed by* Maurice Binder. *Action sequences arranged by* Bob Simmons. *Costume Designer* Jacques Fonteray. *Music by* John Barry. *Director of Photography* Jean Tournier. *Production designed by* Ken Adam. *Associate Producer* William P Cartlidge. *Executive Producer* Michael G Wilson. *Screenplay by* Christopher Wood. *Produced by* Albert R Broccoli. *Directed by* Lewis Gilbert.
Released 26 June 1979

**FOR YOUR EYES ONLY (Director)**
Roger Moore *James Bond*, Carole Bouquet *Melina*, Topol *Columbo*, Lynn-Holly Johnson *Bibi*, Julian Glover *Kristatos*, Cassandra Harris *Lisl*, Jill Bennett *Brink*, Michael Gothard *Locque*, John Wyman *Kriegler*, Jack Hedley *Havelock*, Lois Maxwell *Moneypenny*, Desmond Llewelyn *Q*, Geoffrey Keen *Minister of Defence*, Walter Gotell *General Gogol*, James Villiers *Tanner*, John Moreno *Ferrara*, Charles Dance *Claus*, Paul Angelis *Karageorge*, Toby Robins *Iona Havelock*, Jack Klaff *Apostis*, Alkis Kritikos *Santos*, Stag Theodore *Nikos*, Stefan Kalipha *Gonzales*, Graham Crowden *First Sea Lord*, Noel Johnson *Vice Admiral*, William Hoyland *McGregor*, Paul Brooke *Bunky*, Eva Reuber-Staier *Rublevich*, Fred Bryant *Vicar*, Robbin Young *Girl in Flower Shop*, Graham Hawks *Mantis Man*, Janet Brown as *The Prime Minister*, John Wells as *Denis*.
*Make-up* George Frost, Eric Allwright. *Hairdressers* Stephanie Kaye, Marsha Lewis. *Wardrobe Master* Tiny Nicholls. *Wardrobe for Miss Bouquet and Miss Harris by* Raemonde Rahvis, London. *Ski Suits by* Bogner. *Second-unit directed and photographed by* Arthur Wooster. *Assistant Director* Anthony Waye. *Camera Operator* Alec Mills. *Visual Effects Supervisor* Derek Meddings. *Special Effects* John Evans. *Stills photographer* Keith Hamshere. *Continuity* Elaine Schreyeck. *Main title designed by* Maurice Binder. *Action sequences arranged by* Bob Simmons. *Driving Stunts arranged by* Remy Julienne. *Skating scenes staged by* Brian Foley. *Costume Designer* Elizabeth Waller. *Music by* Bill Conti. *Title song performed by* Sheena Easton, *music by* Bill Conti, *lyrics by* Michael Leeson. *Editor* John Grover. *Additional Editor* Eric Boyd-Perkins. *Dubbing Editors* Colin Miller, Bill Trent, Vernon Messenger. *Director of Photography* Alan Hume. *Production designed by* Peter Lamont. *Art Director* John Fenner. *Additional Art Directors* Michael Lamont, Mikes

Karapiperis, Franco Fumagelli. *Assistant Art Director* Ernie Archer. *Unit & Location Managers* Vincent Winter, Peter Bennett, Michalis Lambrinos, Redmond Morris, Umberto Sambuco. *Production Supervisor* Bob Simmonds. *Associate Producer* Tom Pevsner. *Executive Producer* Michael G Wilson. *Screenplay by* Richard Maibaum, Michael G Wilson. *Produced by* Albert R Broccoli.
Released 24 June 1981

## OCTOPUSSY (Director)

Roger Moore *James Bond*, Maud Adams *Octopussy*, Louis Jourdan *Kamal Khan*, Kristina Wayborn *Magda*, Kabir Bedi *Gobinda*, Steven Berkoff *Orlov*, David Meyer *Twin One*, Anthony Meyer *Twin Two*, Desmond Llewelyn *Q*, Robert Brown *M*, Lois Maxwell *Miss Moneypenny*, Michaela Clavell *Penelope Smallbone*, Walter Gotell *Gogol*, Vijay Amitraj *Vijay*, Albert Moses *Sadruddin*, Geoffrey Keen *Minister of Defence*, Douglas Wilmer *Fanning*, Andy Bradford *009*, Philip Voss *Auctioneer*, Bruce Boa *US General*, Richard Parmentier *US Aide*, Paul Hardwick *Soviet Chairman*, Suzanne Jerome *Gwendoline*, Cherry Gillespie *Midge*, Dermot Crowley *Kamp*, Peter Porteous *Lenkin*, Eva Reuber-Staier *Rublevitch*, Jeremy Bullock *Smithers*, Tina Hudson *Bianca*, William Derrick *Thug with Yo-yo*, Stuart Saunders *Major Clive*, Patrick Barr *British Ambassador*, Gabor Vernon *Borchoi*, Hugo Bower *Karl*, Ken Norris *Colonel Toro*, Tony Arjuna *Mufti*, Gertan Klauber *Bubi*, Brenda Cowling *Schatzl*, David Grahame *Petrol Pump Attendant*, Brian Coburn *South American VIP*, Michael Halphie *South American Officer*, Roberto Germains *Ringmaster*, Richard Graydon *Francisco the Fearless*.
*Make-up Supervisor* George Frost. *Hairdressing Supervisor* Christopher Taylor. *Costume Supervisor* Tiny Nicholls. *Second-unit directed and photographed by* Arthur Wooster. *Assistant Director* Anthony Waye. *Camera Operator* Alec Mills. *Special Effects Supervisor* John Richardson. *Stills photographers* Frank Connor, George Whitear. *Continuity* Elaine Schreyeck. *Main title designed by* Maurice Binder. *Action sequences arranged by* Bob Simmons. *Driving stunts arranged by* Remy Julienne. *Costumes designed by* Emma Porteous. *Music composed and conducted by* John Barry. *'All Time High' performed by* Rita Coolidge, *music by* John Barry, *lyrics by* Tim Rice. *Supervising Editor* John Grover. *Editors* Peter Davies, Henry Richardson. *Sound Editor* Colin Miller. *Director of Photography* Alan Hume. *Production designed by* Peter Lamont. *Art Director* John Fenner. *Additional Art Directors* Michael Lamont, Ken Court, Ram Yedekar, Jan Schlubach. *Assistant Art Directors* Ernie Archer, Jim Morahan, Fred Hole. *Location Managers* Peter Bennett, Rashid Abassi. *Associate Producer* Tom Pevsner. *Executive Producer* Michael G Wilson. *Screen story and screenplay by* George MacDonald Fraser, Richard Maibaum, Michael G Wilson. *Produced by* Albert R Broccoli.
Released 6 June 1983

## A VIEW TO A KILL (Director)

Roger Moore *James Bond*, Christopher Walken *Max Zorin*, Tanya Roberts *Stacey Sutton*, Grace Jones *May Day*, Patrick Macnee *Tibbett*, Patrick Bauchau *Scarpine*, David Yip *Chuck Lee*, Fiona Fullerton *Pola Ivanova*,

Manning Redwood *Bob Conley*, Alison Doody *Jenny Flex*, Willoughby Gray *Dr Carl Mortner*, Desmond Llewelyn *Q*, Robert Brown *M*, Lois Maxwell *Miss Moneypenny*, Walter Gotell *General Gogol*, Geoffrey Keen *Minister of Defence*, Jean Rougerie *Aubergine*, Daniel Benzali *Howe*, Bogdan Kominowski *Klotkoff*, Papillon Soo Soo *Pan Ho*, Mary Stavin *Kimberley Jones*, Dominique Risbourg *Butterfly Act Compere*, Carole Ashby *Whistling Girl*, Anthony Chin *Taiwanese Tycoon*, Lucien Jerome *Paris Taxi Driver*, Joe Flood *US Police Captain*, Gerard Buhr *Auctioneer*, Dolph Lundgren *Venz*, Tony Sibbald *Mine Foreman*, Bill Ackridge *O'Rourke*, Ron Tarr *Guard I*, Taylor McAuley *Guard II*, Peter Ensor *Tycoon*, Seva Novgoredtsev *Helicopter Pilot*.
*Make-up Supervisor* George Frost. *Hairdressing Supervisor* Ramon Gow. *Costume Supervisor* Tiny Nicholls. *Additional Wardrobe for Grace Jones* Azzedine Alaia. *Second-unit directed and photographed by* Arthur Wooster. *Assistant Director* Gerry Gavigan. *Camera Operator* Michael Frift. *Special Effects Supervisor* John Richardson. *Stills photographers* Keith Hamshere, George Whitear. *Continuity* June Randall. *Main title designed by* Maurice Binder. *Action Sequence Arranger* Martin Grace. *Driving Stunts Arranger* Remy Julienne. *Ski sequence directed and photographed by* Willy Bogner. *Costumes designed by* Emma Porteous. *Music composed and conducted by* John Barry. *Title song performed by* Duran Duran, *composed by* Duran Duran, John Barry. *Editor* Peter Davies. *Sound Editor* Colin Miller. *Director of Photography* Alan Hume. *Production designed by* Peter Lamont. *Art Director* John Fenner. *Additional Art Directors* Michael Lamont, Ken Court, Alan Tomkins, Serge Douy, Armin Ganz, Katharina Brunner. *Assistant Art Directors* James Morahan, Ted Ambrose, Michael Boone. *Location Managers* Nick Daubeny, Agust Baldersson, Stefan Zurcher, Jean-Marc Deschamps, Steph Benseman, Rory Enke. *Production Supervisor* Anthony Waye. *Associate Producer* Tom Pevsner. *Screenplay by* Richard Maibaum, Michael G Wilson. *Produced by* Albert R Broccoli, Michael G Wilson.
Released 12 June 1985

## THE LIVING DAYLIGHTS (Director)
Timothy Dalton *James Bond*, Maryam d'Abo *Kara Milovy*, Jeroen Krabbé *General Georgi Koskov*, Joe Don Baker *Brad Whitaker*, John Rhys-Davies *General Leonid Pushkin*, Art Malik *Kamran Shah*, Andreas Wisniewski *Necros*, Thomas Wheatley *Saunders*, Desmond Llewelyn *Q*, Robert Brown *M*, Geoffrey Keen *Minister of Defence*, Walter Gotell *General Anatol Gogol*, Caroline Bliss *Miss Moneypenny*, John Terry *Felix Leiter*, Virginia Hey *Rubavitch*, John Bowe *Col Feyador*, Julie T Wallace *Rosika Miklos*, Kell Tyler *Linda*, Catherine Rabett *Liz*, Dulice Liecier *Ava*, Nadim Sawalha *Chief of Security, Tangier*, Alan Talbot *Koskov's KGB Minder*, Carl Rigg *Imposter*, Tony Cyrus *Chief of Snow Leopard Brotherhood*, Atik Mohamed *Achmed*, Michael Moor, Sumar Khan *Kamran's Men*, Ken Sharrock *Jailer*, Peter Porteous *Gasworks Supervisor*, Anthony Carrick *Male Secretary, Blayden*, Frederick Warder *004*, Glyn Baker *002*, Derek Hoxby *Sergeant Stagg*, Bill Weston *Butler, Blayden*, Richard Cubison *Trade Centre Toastmaster*, Heinz Winter *Concierge, Vienna Hotel*, Leslie French *Lavatory Attendant*.

*Make-up Supervisor* George Frost. *Hairdressing Supervisor* Ramon Gow. *Costume Supervisor* Tiny Nicholls. *Second-unit directed and photographed by* Arthur Wooster. *Assistant Director* Gerry Gavigan. *Camera Operator* Michael Frift. *Special Visual Effects* John Richardson. *Stunt Supervisor* Paul Weston. *Driving Stunts Arranger* Remy Julienne. *Aerial Stunts Arranger* B J Worth. *Stills photographers* Keith Hamshere, George Whitear. *Continuity* June Randall. *Main title designed by* Maurice Binder. *Costumes designed by* Emma Porteous. *Music composed and conducted by* John Barry. *'The Living Daylights' performed by* a-ha, *written by* Pal Waaktaar, John Barry. *'Where Has Every Body Gone?' and 'If There Was a Man' performed by* The Pretenders, *music by* John Barry, *lyrics by* Chrissie Hynde. *Editors* John Grover, Peter Davies. *Sound Editor* Colin Miller. *Director of Photography* Alec Mills. *Production designed by* Peter Lamont. *Art Director* Terry Ackland-Snow. *Additional Art Directors* Michael Lamont, Peter Manhard, Ken Court, Thomas Riccabona, Fred Hole, Bert Davey. *Assistant Art Directors* James Morahan, Dennis Bosher, Ted Ambrose. *Military dioramas* Little Lead Soldiers. *Production Supervisor* Anthony Waye. *Associate Producers* Tom Pevsner, Barbara Broccoli. *Screenplay by* Richard Maibaum, Michael G Wilson. *Produced by* Albert R Broccoli, Michael G Wilson.
Released 29 June 1987

## LICENCE TO KILL (Director)

Timothy Dalton *James Bond*, Carey Lowell *Pam Bouvier*, Robert Davi *Franz Sanchez*, Talisa Soto *Lupe Lamora*, Anthony Zerbe *Milton Krest*, Frank McRae *Sharkey*, Everett McGill *Killifer*, Wayne Newton *Professor Joe Butcher*, Benicio Del Toro *Dario*, Anthony Starke *Truman-Lodge*, Pedro Armendariz *President Hector Lopez*, Desmond Llewelyn *Q*, David Hedison *Felix Leiter*, Priscilla Barnes *Della Churchill*, Robert Brown *M*, Caroline Bliss *Miss Moneypenny*, Don Stroud *Heller*, Grand L Bush *Hawkins*, Cary-Hiroyuki Tagawa *Kwang*, Alejandro Bracho *Perez*, Guy De Saint Cyr *Braun*, Rafer Johnson *Mullens*, Diana Lee-Hsu *Loti*, Christopher Neame *Fallon*, Jeannine Bisignano *Stripper*, Claudio Brook *Montelongo*, Cynthia Fallon *Consuela*, Enrique Novi *Rasmussen*, Osami Kawawo *Oriental*, George Belanger *Doctor*, Roger Kudney *Wavekrest Captain*, Honorato Magaloni *Chief Chemist*, Jorge Russek *Pit Boss*, Sergio Corona *Bellboy*, Stuart Kwan *Ninja*, Jose Abdala *Tanker Driver*, Teresa Blake *Ticket Agent*, Samuel Benjamin Lancaster *Della's Uncle*, Juan Peleaz *Casino Manager*, Mark Kelty *Coast Guard Radio Operator*, Umberto Elizondo *Hotel Assistant Manager*, Fidel Carriga *Sanchez's Driver*, Edna Bolkan *Barrelhead Waitress*, Edie Enderfield *Clive*, Jeff Moldervan, Carl Ciarfalio *Warehouse Guards*.
*Make-up Supervisors* George Frost, Naomi Dunne. *Hairdressing Supervisor* Tricia Cameron. *Second-unit directed and photographed by* Arthur Wooster. *Assistant Directors* Miguel Gil, Miguel Lima. *Camera Operator* Michael Frift. *Special visual effects* John Richardson. *Stills photographers* Keith Hamshere, George Whitear. *Continuity* June Randall. *Main title designed by* Maurice Binder. *Stunt Co-ordinator* Paul Weston. *Driving Stunts Arranger* Remy Julienne. *Aerial Stunt Arranger* 'Corkey' Fornof. *Costume Designer* Jodie Tillen. *Original score composed and*

*conducted by* Michael Kamen. *'Licence To Kill' performed by* Gladys Knight, *written by* Jeffrey Cohen, Walter Afanasieff, Narada Michael Walden. *Editor* John Glover. *Sound Editor* Vernon Messenger. *Director of Photography* Alec Mills. *Production designed by* Peter Lamont. *Art Director* Michael Lamont. *Additional Art Directors* Dennis Bosher, Ken Court. *Assistant Art Directors* Neil Lamont, Richard Holland, Andrew Ackland-Snow, Hector Romero. *Associate Producers* Tom Pevsner, Barbara Broccoli. *Written by* Michael G Wilson, Richard Maibaum. *Produced by* Albert R Broccoli, Michael G Wilson.
Released 13 June 1989

# SELECTED OTHER CREDITS

d: director
p: producer
dp: director of photography
sc: screenplay
lp: leading players
gc: guest cast
dates given are year of first transmission/release

## Commercials

Commercials include Airwalk shoes (Canada and USA), Drambuie (Italy) and Ford Navigator (Mexico and USA).

## Television

### THE FOUR JUST MEN (Sound Editor)
**US: 1957, UK: 1959–60**
directors included: Basil Dearden, Don Chaffey, Anthony Bushell, William Fairchild, Harry Watt
p: Sidney Cole, Judson Kinberg sc: Louis Marks, Leon Griffiths, Marc Brandel, Jan Read, Lindsay Galloway
lp: Dan Dailey, Jack Hawkins, Richard Conte, Vittorio De Sica, Honor Blackman, Lisa Gastoni, June Thorburn

### CHEMISTRY FOR SIXTH FORMS (Editor)
**1960**
d/p: Philip Wrestler

### MAN OF THE WORLD (Editor)
**1962–63**
directors included: Harry Booth, Anthony Bushell, Charles Crichton, John Moxey, Jeremy Summers
p: Harry Fine
lp: Craig Stevens, Tracey Reed, Graham Stark

### THE SENTIMENTAL AGENT (Editor)
**US: 1962, UK: 1963**
directors included: Harry Booth, Charles Frend, Harry French, John Paddy Carstairs
p: Harry Fine
lp: Carlos Thompson, Burt Kwouk, John Turner

### DANGER MAN (Editor, Seasons 2–4)
**1964–6**
directors included: Don Chaffey, Charles Crichton, Robert Day, Pat Jackson, Quentin Lawrence, Patrick McGoohan, Jeremy Summers, Michael Truman, Peter Yates
p: Sidney Cole, Aida Young (season two only)
lp: Patrick McGoohan, Richard Wattis, Lionel Murton

**MAN IN A SUITCASE (Supervising Editor/Director)**
**1967**
**'Somebody Loses, Somebody…Wins?'**
d: John Glen
p: Sidney Cole
sc: Jan Read
lp: Richard Bradford
gc: Jacqueline Pearce, Philip Madoc, Carl Duering

**CHECKERED FLAG (Director)**
**1990**
p: James Margellos
lp: Rob Estes, William Campbell, Amanda Wyss, Robert Forster

**SPACE PRECINCT (Director)**
**US: 1994, UK: 1995**
p: Gerry Anderson
lp: Ted Shackleford, Rob Youngblood, Simone Bendix
**'Protect and Survive'**
sc: Paul Mayhew-Archer
gc: Oliver Cotton, Burt Kwouk, Tom Waft
**'The Snake'**
sc: J Larry Carroll, David Bennett Carren
gc: David Baxt, Joseph Mydell, Ken Drury
**'Deadline'**
sc: David Bennett Carren, J Larry Carroll
gc: Steven Berkoff, Truan Munro, Ken Whitfield
**'Illegal'**
sc: Marc Scott Zicree
gc: Tony Haygarth, Tim Matthews, Pat Roach
**'Takeover'**
sc: J Larry Carroll, David Bennett Carren
gc: Maryam d'Abo, Clive Merrison, Rob Thirtle
**'The Fire Within'**
sc: Steve Brown, Burt Prelutsky
gc: Jack Hedley, Lisa Orgolini, David Quilter

# FILM

**THE THIRD MAN (Assistant Sound Editor)**
**1949**
d/p: Carol Reed dp: Robert Krasker sc: Graham Greene
lp: Joseph Cotten, Trevor Howard, Alida Valli, Orson Welles, Wilfrid Hyde White

**THE WOODEN HORSE (Second Assistant Editor)**
**1950**
d: Jack Lee p: Ian Dalrymple dp: C Pennington-Richards sc: Eric Williams
lp: Leo Genn, David Tomlinson, Anthony Steele, David Greene, Michael Goodliffe, Bryan Forbes

**THE LONG DARK HALL (Second Assistant Editor)**
**1951**
d: Anthony Bushell, Reginald Beck p: Anthony Bushell dp: Wilkie Cooper sc: Nunnally Johnson, W E C Fairchild
lp: Rex Harrison, Lilli Palmer, Raymond Huntley, Denis O'Dea, Anthony Bushell, Henry Longhurst

**THERE WAS A YOUNG LADY (Second Assistant Editor)**
**1953**
d/sc: Lawrence Huntington p: A R Rawlinson dp: Gerald Gibbs story: Vernon Harris, John Jowett
lp: Michael Dension, Dulcie Gray, Sidney Tafler, Geraldine McEwan, Marcel Poncin, Robert Adair, Kenneth Connor, Bill Owen

**MAKE ME AN OFFER (Assistant Editor)**
**1954**
d: Cyril Frankel p/sc: W P Lipscomb dp: Denny Densham
lp: Peter Finch, Adrienne Corri, Meier Tzelniker, Rosalie Crutchley, Finlay Currie, Ernest Thesiger, Wilfrid Lawson, Alfie Bass

**JOHN AND JULIE (Assistant Editor)**
**1955**
d/sc: William Fairchild p: Herbert Wilcox dp: Arthur Grant
lp: Colin Gibson, Leslie Dudley, Peter Sellers, Moira Lister, Wilfrid Hyde White, Sidney James, Andrew Cruikshank

**THE EXTRA DAY (Assistant Editor)**
**1956**
d/sc: William Fairchild p: E M Smedley Aston dp: Arthur Grant
lp: Richard Basehart, Simone Simon, Sidney James, Josephine Griffin, George Baker, Colin Gordon, Laurence Naismith, Charles Victor, Olga Lindo, Beryl Reid, Dennis Lotis

**THE GREEN MAN (Sound Editor)**
**1956**
d: Robert Day p: Frank Launder, Sidney Gilliat dp: Gerald Gibbs sc: Sidney Gilliat, Frank Launder
lp: Alastair Sim, George Cole, Jill Adams, Terry-Thomas

**THREE MEN IN A BOAT (Assembly Editor/Sound Editor)**
**1956**

d: Ken Annakin p: Jack Clayton dp: Eric Cross sp: Hubert Gregg, Vernon Harris
lp: David Tomlinson, Jimmy Edwards, Laurence Harvey, Shirley Eaton, Robertson Hare, Jill Ireland, Lisa Gastoni, Martita Hunt, AE Matthews, Ernest Thesiger

### THE ADMIRABLE CRICHTON (Sound Editor)
**1957**
d: Lewis Gilbert p: Ian Dalrymple dp: Wilkie Cooper sc: Vernon Harris
lp: Kenneth More, Cecil Parker, Sally Ann Howes, Diane Cilento, Martita Hunt, Jack Watling, Peter Graves, Gerald Harper, Miles Malleson

### THE SCAMP (Sound Editor)
**1957**
d/sc: Wolf Rilla p: James H Lawrie dp: Freddie Francis
lp: Richard Attenborough, Dorothy Alison, Colin Petersen, Terence Morgan, Jill Adams

### A CRY FROM THE STREETS (Sound Editor)
**1958**
d: Lewis Gilbert p: Ian Dalrymple dp: Harry Gillan sc: Vernon Harris
lp: Max Bygraves, Barbara Murray, Colin Peterson, Dana Wilson, Kathleen Harrison

### LIFE IS A CIRCUS (Sound Editor)
**1958**
d: Val Guest p: E M Smedley Aston dp: Arthur Graham sc: Val Guest, Len Heath, John Warren
lp: Bud Flanagan, Jimmy Nervo, Teddy Knox, Charlie Naughton, Jimmy Gold, Eddie Gray, Shirley Eaton, Lionel Jeffries

### DENTIST IN THE CHAIR (Sound Editor)
**1960**
d: Don Chaffey p: Bertram Ostrer dp: Reginald Wyer sc: Val Guest (additional scenes: Bob Monkhouse, George Wadmore)
lp: Bob Monkhouse, Peggy Cummins, Kenneth Connor, Eric Barker, Ronnie Stevens, Vincent Ball, Eleanor Summerfield, Reginald Beckwith

### FOXHOLE IN CAIRO (Sound Editor)
**1960**
d: John Moxey p: Steven Pallos, Donald Taylor dp: Desmond Dickinson sc: Leonard Mosley
lp: James Robertson Justice, Adrian Hoven, Albert Lieven, Niall MacGinnis, Peter Van Eyck, Robert Urquhart, Fenella Fielding

### BUENO SERA, MRS CAMPBELL (Additional Sound Editor)
**1968**
d/p: Melvin Frank dp: Gabor Pogany sc: Melvin Frank, Denis Norden, Sheldon Keller
lp: Gina Lollobrigida, Shelley Winters, Phil Silvers, Peter Lawford, Telly Savalas, Lee Grant, Janet Margolin, Marian Moses

### BABY LOVE (Editor)
**1968**
d: Alastair Reid p: Guido Coen, Michael Klinger dp: Desmond Dickinson, Michael Ballhaus sc: John Sayles, Alastair Reid, Guido Coen
lp: Linda Hayden, Ann Lynn, Keith Barron, Derek Lamden, Diana Dors,

Patience Collier, Dick Emery

## THE ITALIAN JOB (Additional Sound Editor)
**1969**
d: Peter Collinson p: Michael Deeley dp: Douglas Slocombe, Norman
Warwick sc: Troy Kennedy Martin
lp: Michael Caine, Noel Coward, Benny Hill, Raf Vallone, Tony Beckley,
Rosanno Brazzi, Maggie Blye, Irene Handl

## MURPHY'S WAR (Co-Editor/Second-unit Director)
**1971**
d: Peter Yates p: Michael Deeley dp: Douglas Slocombe sc: Sterling
Silliphant
lp: Peter O'Toole, Sian Phillips, Philippe Noiret, Horst Janson

## CATLOW (Supervising Editor/Second Unit Director)
**1971**
d: Sam Wanamaker p: Euan Lloyd dp: Ted Scaife sc: Scot Finch, J J Griffith
lp: Yul Brynner, Leonard Nimoy, Richard Crenna, Daliah Lavi, Jo Ann Pflug,
Jeff Corey

## PULP (Editor)
**1972**
d/sc: Mike Hodges p: Michael Klinger dp: Ousama Rawi
lp: Michael Caine, Mickey Rooney, Lizabeth Scott, Lionel Stander

## SITTING TARGET (Editor)
**1972**
d: Douglas Hickox p: Barry Kulick dp: Ted Scaife sc: Alexander Jacobs
lp: Oliver Reed, Jill St John, Edward Woodward, Frank Finlay, Ian
McShane, Freddie Jones, Robert Beatty

## A DOLL'S HOUSE (Editor)
**1973**
d: Patrick Garland p: Hillard Elkins dp: Arthur Ibbetson sc: Christopher
Hampton
lp: Claire Bloom, Anthony Hopkins, Ralph Richardson, Denholm Elliott,
Anna Massey, Edith Evans

## GOLD (Editor/Second Unit Director)
**1974**
d: Peter Hunt p: Michael Klinger dp: Ousama Rawi sc: Wilbur Smith,
Stanley Price
lp: Roger Moore, Susannah York, Ray Milland, Bradford Dillman, John
Gielgud

## DEAD CERT (Editor)
**1974**
d: Tony Richardson p: Neil Hartley dp: Freddie Cooper sc: Tony Richardson,
John Oaksey
lp: Scott Antony, Judi Dench, Michael Williams, Nina Thomas, Mark
Dignam, Julian Glover

## CONDUCT UNBECOMING (Editor)
**1975**
d: Michael Anderson p: Michael Deeley, Barry Spikings dp: Bob Huke
sc: Robert Enders
lp: Michael York, Stacy Keach, Trevor Howard, Christopher Plummer,

Richard Attenborough, Susannah York, James Faulkner, James Donald

## SHOUT AT THE DEVIL (Second Unit Director)
**1976**
d: Peter Hunt p: Michael Klinger dp: Michael Reed sc: Wilbur Smith, Stanley Price, Alastair Reid
lp: Lee Marvin, Roger Moore, Barbara Parkins, Ian Holm, Maurice Denham, Jean Kent, Robert Lang, George Colouris

## SEVEN NIGHTS IN JAPAN (Editor)
**1976**
d/p: Lewis Gilbert dp: Henri Decaë sc: Christopher Wood
lp: Michael York, Hidemi Aomi, Peter Jones, Charles Gray, Yolande Donlan, James Villiers

## THE WILD GEESE (Editor/Second Unit Director)
**1978**
d: Andrew V McLaglen p: Euan Lloyd dp: Jack Hildyard sc: Reginald Rose
lp: Roger Moore, Richard Burton, Richard Harris, Hardy Kruger, Stewart Granger, Jack Watson, Frank Finlay, Kenneth Griffith, Barry Foster

## SUPERMAN (Second Unit Director)
**1978**
d: Richard Donner p: Pierre Spengler dp: Geoffrey Unsworth sc: Mario Puzo, David Newman, Robert Benton, Leslie Newman
lp: Christopher Reeve, Marlon Brando, Margot Kidder, Jackie Cooper, Glenn Ford, Phyllis Thaxter, Trevor Howard, Gene Hackman, Ned Beatty, Susannah York

## THE SEA WOLVES (Editor)
**1980**
d: Andrew V McLaglen p: Euan Lloyd dp: Tony Imi sc: Reginald Rose
lp: Gregory Peck, Roger Moore, Trevor Howard, David Niven, Barbara Kellerman, Patrick Macnee, Patrick Allen, Bernard Archard

## ACES: IRON EAGLE III (Director)
**1992**
p: Ron Samuels dp: Alec Mills sc: Kevin Elders
lp: Louis Gossett Jnr, Rachel McLish, Paul Freeman, Horst Buchholz, Christopher Cazenove, Sonny Chiba

## CHRISTOPHER COLUMBUS: THE DISCOVERY (Director)
**1992**
p: Alexander Salkind, Ilya Salkind dp: Alec Mills sc: John Briley, Carey Bates, Mario Puzo
lp: Marlon Brando, Tom Selleck, Georges Corraface, Rachel Ward, Robert Davi, Catherine Zeta Jones

## THE POINT MEN (Director)
**2001**
p: Sylvio Muraglia dp: Alec Mills sc/p: Avi Nesher
lp: Christopher Lambert, Kerry Fox, Vincent Regan, Cal Macaninch, Donald Sumpter, Maryam d'Abo, William Armstrong, Oliver Haden

# INDEX

Page numbers in *italic* refer to pictures.